24699

LANDMARKS
IN THE STRUGGLE BETWEEN
SCIENCE AND RELIGION

BY

JAMES Y. SIMPSON, M.A., D.Sc., F.R.S.E.

PROFESSOR OF NATURAL SCIENCE
NEW COLLEGE, EDINBURGH

NEW YORK
GEORGE H. DORAN COMPANY

LANDMARKS IN THE STRUGGLE BETWEEN SCIENCE AND RELIGION
— HC —
PRINTED IN THE UNITED STATES OF AMERICA

TO

THE MEMORY OF

ALL FORWARD-LOOKING MEN

THROUGHOUT THE AGES

PREFACE

DURING recent years many have been visiting the battle-fields of the Great War, reconstructing in imagination, and in some instances living once again through, crises in the long struggle associated with this particular salient or that prominent supporting position, around which, with varying fortune, the tide of battle had swung from one side to the other. Similarly, throughout the centuries, another struggle has been engaged in by two opposing, though not necessarily opposed, forces, very differently equipped, and campaigning, as it seemed, on fundamentally different principles. And here, likewise, from the vast area of conflict stand out positions of the nature of landmarks round which the struggle has been especially intense. The following chapters are in a sense guides to these old battlefields. In part historical, they deal with some of the most vital phases in this struggle, attempting to restate and discuss the issues, with perhaps a new ray of light illuminating the field at this point or at that.

Of previous works dealing with this particular subject, two in particular have held a deserved pre-eminence—J. W. Draper's *The Conflict between Religion and Science,* and the monumental study by A. D. White, entitled

A History of the Warfare of Science with Theology in Christendom. The fact that both these works are issued in new editions to this day indicates the strong hold that they have secured on the minds of those who are interested in what has proved to be one of the most living questions that stirred the thoughts of previous generations. This is all the more remarkable seeing that the first of these books was published in 1874, and the second, in that particular form, in 1896. Both works are of a strongly polemical character, having been written in a particular historical situation by men who were impatient of the influence of dogma or anything that seemed to hinder scientific investigation. The lapse of time has not merely added to our knowledge but changed our perspective somewhat, and further acquaintance with the facts seems to call for some softening of the strictures occasionally passed upon the earlier representatives of Christianity. To this point attention is drawn in Chapter V. The separation of the different topics has necessitated at points a minimum of repetition.

Certain of the chapters were originally delivered as lecture courses of varying length under the Carew Foundation at Hartford Theological Seminary, Conn., and under the Lyman Coleman Foundation at Lafayette College, Easton, Pa., both in the United States, as also under the Thomson Foundation at the United Free Church College, Aberdeen, in 1924—institutions whose Presidents and Faculties have shown the writer the greatest kindness. Chapter X. represents substantially the Drew Lecture on Immortality delivered at Hackney and New College,

London, under the title 'Beyond the White Poplar.' It
has been possible, however, in every case to expand and, it
is hoped, add to the serviceability of the form in which
these lectures were originally delivered. So far as they
deal with the re-presentation of Christian truth in relation
to the science and philosophy of the day, they may be
considered as supplementary to two previous works,
The Spiritual Interpretation of Nature and *Man and the
Attainment of Immortality.*

Where many have given generous assistance it is not
easy to discriminate, but the writer would in particular
express his appreciation of the sympathetic co-operation
of Miss Katharine Cameron, Mr. John Duncan, R.S.A.,
Prof. Donald Tovey, and Mr. Alfred Noyes in connection
with the topic dealt with in Chapter IV. He is also
greatly beholden to Prof. H. A. A. Kennedy for aid in
connection with translation from Greek, as also to Dr.
Adam Mitchell Hunter who kindly read the proofs and
offered helpful suggestions at various points.

J. Y. SIMPSON.

NEW COLLEGE, EDINBURGH.

CONTENTS

CHAPTER I

CHAPTER II

CHAPTER III

CHAPTER IV

CHAPTER IX

CHAPTER X

CHAPTER XI

CHAPTER XII

LIST OF ABBREVIATIONS

H.D.B. . . Hastings' Dictionary of the Bible.

E.B. . . Encyclopaedia Biblica.

E.G.T. . . Expositor's Greek Testament.

E.R.E. . . Encyclopaedia of Religion and Ethics.

H.J. . . Hibbert Journal.

I.C.C. . . International Critical Commentary.

Scriptural quotations are from the Revised Version, unless where otherwise stated.

CHAPTER I

THE story of the human race is in a peculiar degree the history of religion. While this is pre-eminently true of some countries, as for example Scotland and Italy, there have been, as a matter of fact, few periods or lands where the determining factor in civilisation—*i.e.* in the development of relationships within the tribe or between the tribe and other tribes—has not been the influence exerted by religion. For in this instinctive sense of a relationship to a mysterious, yet in some degree responsive, superhuman, environmental Power or Powers in the Universe which were felt to secure the place of the tribe or individual in the world, and with which, therefore, the mere instinct of self-preservation dictated the desirability of coming into harmony, has lain the secret of that fundamental attitude towards existence which is known as religion. As such, therefore, it could not help inspiring, colouring, and shaping the historical development both of the tribe and of its individual members.

The origin of religion lies very far back in the history of the race. As yet the data are scant, and the interpretation of them is rarely free from ambiguity and uncertainty. We cannot judge of the end by the beginnings, but we cannot help being growingly interested in the beginnings just because of what the end has come to mean. If the positive process of actually re-thinking or re-feeling in terms of the capacities of the mind of primitive man is for ever denied us, it may be none the less possible by the aid of child psychology to form a vague impression of the mental outlook of Palaeolithic

I

man on the basis of the Recapitulation Theory :[1] to this are often added data drawn from the study of present-day savage life. In face, however, of the ever-growing accumulation of material bearing upon the beliefs and outlook of contemporary savage tribes, it can never be too strongly asserted that, while useful and helpful in forming an estimate of the gamut of human culture to-day, present-day savage life, apart from affording a basis for speculation, is of comparatively little value in making a trustworthy reconstruction of the conceptions of primitive man. There is no modern savage tribe of which it can be said in any definite sense that it is a contemporary ancestor,[2] so to speak, and in few cases can we have certainty that their ideas have been correctly set down and interpreted. Continually the investigator is in danger of reading his own ideas and introducing his own problems into the savage mind that he is trying to understand, while the subject of investigation some-times tries to please and even occasionally to mislead or mystify. One of the most remarkable, doubtful assump-tions of modern scientific work is that it is possible for any trained anthropologist *qua* anthropologist to arrive at as sound a knowledge of the religious beliefs and practices of a tribe after, let us say, some five or six months' sojourn in an island, as he has reached in his purely anthropometric investigations. This implicit assumption, which becomes explicit in many misleading ways, simply serves to show how far the nature of the problem is from being even understood. It can only be an error in judgment that supposes it possible for an irreligious man to make any satisfactory investigation of religion in a people ; he does not *know* what he is investi-gating. Only by long residence amongst a tribe and by a life of sympathetic service, that will in turn elicit a

---

[1] Briefly, the theory that the individual organism passes through stages in its developmental history corresponding to stages in its ancestral history.

[2] The native Australian perhaps comes closest to this designation.

corresponding response in which the secrets and mysteries of the tribal and individual experience are laid bare, can any investigator hope to approximate to a satisfactory understanding of the matter which he is pursuing. And if all this is true in any degree of modern tribes, it must hold *a fortiori* with regard to our knowledge of the religious outlook of primitive man. For he was ancestral both to civilised man and the savage races of to-day. In him, therefore, there must have lain that capacity for development which led to the higher types of modern man, and which seems to have atrophied to a considerable degree in the savage of to-day.

If in the slow ascent of organic life, we find it difficult to set our finger upon the precise point when the man-like ape passed over into the ape-like man; if we become increasingly convinced that the point in question is more correctly represented by a long period during which the sub-personal *Homosimius* took on, haltingly and doubtless with intermittent lapses, incipient personality; if we are certain that that period was more remote even than was supposed in the beginning of this century,—none the less the fact of it becomes, every decade, more assuredly one of the corner-stones of the scientific construction of the world. The tentative daylight life of primitive man— of man, that is to say, with a brain even less developed than that of Neanderthal man, which, Professor Anthony assures us,[1] if of normal volume and with the areas of association connected with vision and hearing well developed, yet in its convolutions suggests a mentality of low development—was already a life illumined by the idea of a possible continuity of individual existence after death, at any rate in the case of the great ones of the tribe. We have spoken of the ' tentative daylight ' life, for even in the Mid-Palaeolithic the evening, and still more the darkness of the night, must have heightened the sense of awe till perhaps it had a completely numbing effect upon all activity that involved journeying through

[1] Reference in *Nature*, cxiii. 207.

the forest or down the river after dusk—in short, absence from home and the fellow-man.

Long previous to this stage, however, there is posited a phase characterised by R. R. Marett as ' pre-animistic,' in which ' there must have been numberless dimly-lighted impressions of the awful that owned no master in the shape of some one systematising thought.' [1] By this is not meant a period in which animism was necessarily absolutely unknown, but rather one when the penumbra was still relatively much greater than the area within which sharply-defined animistic conceptions—*i.e.* the belief in spirits or visionary forms—were current. Further, that penumbra is definitely magico-religious from the earliest moment that we become aware of it, although with the course of the ages a gradual differentiation of religion and magic takes place. Here, as in all else, man's relationship was developmental. Revelation and his growing appreciation of the character of the world-process in which he found himself, and of which he was a part, as also of the Power manifesting itself in it, are correlative terms.

The endeavour to reproduce this veritable morning Götterdämmerung in which the dim fragmentariness of the external world is matched by the vagueness of man's internal perception of it, can perhaps only in any measure be made imaginable to us, as we have noted, by investigation of the mind of the young child. Of the point of commencement of its mental functioning we have no knowledge. The movements of the new-born infant are probably almost wholly automatic in character. Consciousness, at any rate in that degree of intensity which later characterises normal human life, can hardly be said to be an essential element of the process in any of these movements, even if they may be accompanied by some very diffuse feeling of well-being or the reverse. Possibly

[1] *The Threshold of Religion*, p. x, to which work (cf. chap. i.) reference may be made for illustrations from present-day savage life of an attitude of supernaturalism independent of animistic interpretations.

'the arc of stimulus and reaction is completed through lower brain centres, unconnected with consciousness.' [1] No infant was ever born into the midst of 'a great, blooming, buzzing confusion,' [2] to borrow an often-quoted picturesque phrase, for the simple reason that the sensory equipment of a child at birth is not sufficiently developed to perceive the world as such. 'Rather does the babe drift slowly in among phenomena, wrapped away from their impact in a dim cloud of unconsciousness, through which but the simplest and faintest gleams and echoes make their way to him. Then month after month the multiplex vision without clears itself from the background of cloud, bit by bit, everything grouped and ordered for him in the very process of coming to his consciousness—a wonder and a joy to him, and the most beautiful of all unfoldings to see.' [3] And it may even be that certain marked characteristics that begin to develop towards the close of the first year in connection with the advent of sleep, to wit, the intensified disposition towards confidingness and affection, and the evidence of timidity and loneliness that takes the form of piteous wild crying both before going to sleep and upon awaking —what Miss Shinn calls 'an unaccountable sort of distress' [4]—are associated, particularly in the waking moments, with 'a disturbance of the feeling of bodily identity and of relation to the external world—feelings as yet but feebly established, and liable to confusion from alterations in cerebral circulation.' [5] It is a process of gradual integration of sensations that are external in their causation with those of directly somatic origin that tend to group themselves around the conscious-ness, *e.g.* of muscular control—an integration that passes by way of slow appreciation of a distinction between self and not-self at last into vivid self-consciousness.

[1] Milicent W. Shinn, *Notes on the Development of a Child*, ii. **18**.
[2] William James, *The Principles of Psychology*, i. 488.
[3] Milicent W. Shinn, *op. cit.* ii. 144.
[4] *Op. cit.* ii. 214.   [5] *Op. cit.* ii. 214.

The later months of this period are marked by the definite reference of the child to itself in the third person ; it does not yet know itself as an ego, or individual. ' The fact that a child, even towards the end of his second year, will offer his foot a biscuit, shows that he still looks upon it as an independent being.' [1] And in other cases—where, for example, a child in its third year, who has certainly shown evidence of a dawning sense of individuality, will yet dress up her own foot as a doll, and converse dreamily with it in her hand before she falls asleep, as if it were another person—no better proof could be forthcoming of the incipient vagueness of that sense. In the ebb and flow of this gradual attainment of self-consciousness, with its consequent instability of the feeling of personal identity and relation to the exterior world, the sense of wonder and of awe in face of that world is very easily awakened.

Now, to this phase in the life-history of the individual there corresponded a period in the racial history—pre-animistic and penumbral—when as yet there was little more than a community consciousness, so to speak. The word for the first personal pronoun was not in existence, for a person, not to speak of a first person, did not exist : man was still the animal with incipient personality— the sub-personal *Homosimius*. Professor F. B. Jevons is clearly justified in his contention [2] that the existence of fetishism implies a developed sense of the individual, since the function of a fetish is to fulfil the desires of the individual owning it, apart from, in opposition to, or in a special degree in participation with, the desires of the community as a whole, which, on the other hand, are made known to the Power (or Powers) superior to man in which the community has come to believe. During this long period of slow development towards individual self-consciousness, possibly representing tens of thousands of years of racial history, the sense of awe and wonder,

---

[1] H. Höffding, *Outlines of Psychology*, p. 6.
[2] *The Idea of God in Early Religions*, pp. 4-8.

which constitutes an elemental factor in this most rudimentary pre-animistic form of religious consciousness [1] or experience, began to emerge.

To this deep-set apprehension of transcendent Power manifesting itself in the world, and the feeling and emotion excited thereby, the descriptive term 'numinous' has recently been applied, and an analysis furnished on the subjective side which holds in a measure throughout the later development of religion.[2]   Thus attention is directed, amongst other elements, to the pervasive, overwhelming, and solemnising sense of awefulness and dread, even to 'absolute unapproachability,' in 'the presence of that which is a *Mystery* inexpressible and above all creatures';[3] as also to the feeling of its 'absolute overpoweringness' and '*urgency* or *energy*' producing a reflex, abased 'creature-consciousness' in the subject of the experience.   The sense of the Mysterious or 'wholly other' may be excited in many ways, by different kinds of objects or circumstances, all of which have in some degree or other about them that which fascinates, allures, or enthrals the subject, casting a spell over him, in spite of the dread aroused.   The feeling of the 'beyond' or 'wholly other' thus aroused becomes heightened and clarified in manifestation, and in the process gradually tends to 'set the numinous object in contrast not only to everything wonted and familiar (*i.e.*, in the end, to nature in general), thereby turning it into the "supernatural," but finally to the world itself, and thereby exalt it to the "supramundane," that which is above the world-order.'[4]   Later, as religion involved the gradual

[1] By this term should be understood nothing other than consciousness, whatever the stage of development, as directed towards the controlling Power or Powers.   The idea of the religious consciousness as a specific *kind* of consciousness is dangerous mythology ; on the other hand, many lines of conduct tend to deaden those more exquisite sensitivities which provide content for the religious consciousness.

[2] Rudolf Otto, *The Idea of the Holy*, p. 7.   As developed in the work, however, the analysis seems to lead back into depths of subjectivity and superstition.

[3] Otto, *op. cit.* p. 13, and chaps. iv.-vi. *passim*.   [4] *Op. cit.* p. 29.

recognition of an unseen yet kindred Power or Powers manifesting themselves in the world, the attitude of the seeker became one of definite self-committal to these Powers, and acknowledgment of responsibility to them.

This may represent the line of actual later development, but from a very early stage, perhaps even in that vaguer phase of Animatism which Marett thinks of as preceding Animism,[1] the Awe-inspiring was an object of solicitude, sought after as something to be possessed or to be in relation with, in order to secure the seeker's weal. Out of this most rudimentary pre-animistic magico-religious complex there probably slowly differentiated two elements or aspects corresponding to the modern terms *mana* and *tabu*. The former is essentially a positive conception, representing especially an impersonal, awesome, ' in a way supernatural ' [2] power or influence pervading the Universe, which is there at the disposal of man. ' He may draw upon it to work his ends, as he draws on the atmosphere for purposes of respiration.' [3] Without being the particular property of definite supernatural beings, although related in origin to them, it is transmissible, and may have animate or inanimate objects as its locus or vehicle. The conception of mana in its vagueness, and yet in its association of uncanniness and traffic with the unseen, corresponds very well to what may have been the earliest subconscious philosophy of primitive man. The idea tones the primitive outlook on the world, and to-day the philological root actually sustains a great many Polynesian words expressive of psychical states or activities. It is in virtue of resident mana that any degree of success above the ordinary in natural process or human achievement comes about ; on the other hand, it may be latent or dormant. It is

[1] R. R. Marett, *The Threshold of Religion*, pp. 14-19.
[2] R. H. Codrington, *The Melanesians*, p. 119 *n*.
[3] R. A. S. Macalister, *A Textbook of European Archaeology*, p. 135, who also speaks of it as ' something perhaps similar to what is expressed by the word " virtue," as used in Luke 8 [46] (A.V.), " I perceive that *virtue* is gone out of me." '

not mere physical energy or power, but something that influences this so that it is manifest in it, whether the activity be that of unusual fruitfulness, or strength of arm : in short, it corresponds essentially to the idea of the immaterial and supernatural. Impersonal to begin with, the conception of mana in relation to a living man may ' come very near to meaning " soul " or " spirit," though without the connotation of wraith-like appearance ' ;[1] yet animism is always the larger and a more discrete individual conception. Doubtless the primitive conception of mana developed into that of animism, with which it was able to coexist, and even combine. In the end, however, animism never succeeded in completely driving mana from the field, and it is probable that the conception survives even in civilised countries to this day.[2]

Tabu, on the other hand, represents awareness of a mysterious power or influence also impersonally conceived, which it is better not to meddle with, otherwise trouble is likely to follow : in a general sense it may be thought of as the negative mode of mana,[3] and involving, accordingly, a kind of negative sacrifice and even self-denial. So certain things come to be avoided : certain other things are not done. Like mana, that is to say, the conception of tabu has its field of action within the sphere of the magico-religious. Man is aware of himself as in contact with a Power whose behaviour is not altogether intelligible to him ; it transcends his reasonable expectations, and this calls for heedfulness on his part. Tabu accordingly represents the feeling, engendered by awe, that certain actions on his part may be followed by reprisals or punishment for some infringement of a rule. It is ' the dangerousness of a person, or thing, or action, or word, conceived of as a motive for not touching or uttering or meddling therewith. The dangerousness may either lie in the nature of a person or thing, or be

[1] Marett, *op. cit.* p. 118.　　　　[2] Cf. Ps. 62 [11].
[3] But cf. R. R. Marett, *E.R.E.*, viii. 377, art. ' Magic.'

imposed upon it.' [1]   Whatever the individual may feel,
however, the tribe as a whole is very susceptible to the
spiritual peril that may follow on the infraction, and the
tabu-breaker may suffer in any case directly at the
hands of the community, quite apart from the specific
punishment that may fall on him through the agency of
the offended Power.   The community as a whole, largely
owing to the conservatism of the primitive mind, is not
so willing to run risks as the individual may be.   Tabu
may be represented as the self-protective attitude of
avoidance or shunning of that which has mana.   Both
terms are, to begin with, at any rate, devoid of all moral
significance.   This comes out clearly in the case of what
are known as the major tabus of the unknown stranger,
the isolated chief, the dead, and woman, even when these
are occasionally and avowedly ' sympathetic.'

There would be, however, little, if any, systematic
thought behind all these earliest vague experiences,
simply because there was not as yet a human mind that
could systematise in abstract fashion :   the interests of
primitive man then, even more than is the case to-day,
would be with the concrete and practical.   As Marett puts
it, ' savage religion is something not so much thought
out as danced out,' [2] and, we might add, played and
acted out.   It is a group or social consciousness in which
the predominant note is feeling or emotion, in a lesser
degree will, and, vaguest of all, systematic thought.
There is a wealth of feeling with the faintest background
of connecting idea, which, however, leads to action.
Reverting to the hints that may be gathered from the
study of the child mind, we may also posit a vividness of
imagination in the picture-thinking, and a total lack as
yet of any criterion by which to judge the soundness or
otherwise of these imaginative beliefs.   Hence the conditions permit of a high degree of suggestibility, and
provide a suitable atmosphere for an exuberant develop-

[1] Carveth Read, *The Origin of Man and of his Superstitions*, p. 131.
[2] *The Threshold of Religion*, p. xxxi.

ment of magical practice. In this stage of pre-animism or animatism we may therefore perhaps think of a general vague feeling of awe and wonder produced in reaction to the awe-inspiring manifestations of the Power (or Powers) of the world around, which transcended any capacity to explain it, yet prompted a desire to come into some relation with it which would suffice to keep it as protector rather than have it as enemy. The root idea underlying the conceptions both of mana and of tabu is power, more especially perhaps in the vague sense of will-power or psychic energy, yet exercised in a wonder-compelling way. It is impossible to exclude the suggestions of magic and the mysterious, indeed of the supra-sensible or supernatural, from either of the terms.

It seems most probable, then, that in the early phases of the racial history, magico-religious practice or ritual would be associated mainly with the ideas grouping themselves round the primitive conception of mana and its correlative tabu. The modern savage, transferring what he believes aetiologically with regard to his own exercise of magical power to any manifestations of the supernatural, supposes these to be caused directly by the activity of some sort of will—controlled, that is to say, as he believes that he himself controls. Mana is attributed to the Powers that he recognises as at work in these natural phenomena that overawe him by their incomprehensibility. So there followed, we may imagine, the natural step of the magician as anxious to supplement what he felt to be his limited command of mana by drawing on the unlimited resources that he knew to be there, beyond him, at the command of those mysterious natural Powers. Indeed, the general purpose and aim of primitive religious practices were probably, as has been shown in Melanesia,[1] in great part the desire to obtain mana, this power of magical work, for purposes either of good or evil, even if it is doubtful whether the idea presents itself thus definitely and abstractly to the more modern Melanesian mind.

[1] R. H. Codrington, op. cit. p. 119 n.

Fundamentally the magical act is apparently conceived, in Marett's words, as 'an inter-personal, inter-subjective transaction, an affair between wills—something, therefore, generically akin to, if specifically distinct from, the relation which brings together the suppliant and his god.' [1] Religion, however, proved itself to be the broader and more complex element of the two ; magic for a long time had its place *within* religion.

Such are some of the circumstances that we may think of as providing at once the background and content to that far-reaching magico-religious aspect of the life of primitive man. Attempts to discriminate between these two elements from the very earliest stages have not proved particularly successful.[2] The expression or manifestation of this aspect of human life in ritual or cult affected every side of tribal welfare, *e.g.* the chase and all that related to the prime and ever-pressing necessity of the search for food, primitive marriage, and so forth. It is not improbable even that primitive man, in his desire to propitiate the Power or Powers surrounding him, which he thus conceived of as essentially creative, first represented them to himself, when personalised, in female form, being himself still fundamentally ignorant of the rationale of procreation. In this way may be explained the scattered objective evidence that is adduced for an early belief in a Great Mother.[3] Naturally, at the earliest stage, the practical ritualistic aspect would claim most attention on the part of man, for there would always be things that he felt he could *do*, even when he had reached the limit of his powers of thought and emotion ; yet it was inextricably and always associated with reflection in some degree. In this way the priest or sorcerer proved himself, by the measure of his control over these unseen Powers, to be the thinker *par excellence*

---

[1] *Op. cit.* p. 71.

[2] For a classical example, cf. Sir J. G. Frazer, *The Golden Bough* (abridged edition), chap. iv.

[3] Prof. G. Elliot Smith, *The Evolution of the Dragon*, p. 151.

in the childhood of the race. Later, indeed, a distinction begins to emerge. Magico-religious practices tend to group themselves round one of two centres—those that are in the interests of the community and on the whole beneficent, and those that are devised in the interests of an individual as against the community. Yet at first the distinction is not always clear so far as either ritual or agent is concerned ; the priest and sorcerer often meet in the person of the medicine-man.[1] In the more purely religious aspect, the relation growingly becomes one of trust and self-committal. The Power is not normally conceived of as hostile, although it may be rendered so, and man is submissive, seeking to conciliate by righteous conduct rather than by ritual, for life is a good, and he begins to feel that there must be a way of life. Magic, on the other hand, rather implies distrust of the unseen powers ; man is rebellious and endeavours to outwit or thwart or coax the Power (or Powers) into conformity with his will.

At the same time Prof. Gwatkin was surely right in maintaining that ' the earliest stage of religion . . . cannot have been one of continual terror. Even the beasts are above this ; and primitive man must have been as good as they.' [2] No truly religious relationship has ever been born of fear in itself, for the essence of religion is trust, which expresses itself in fellowship ; it springs rather from a sense of need and dependence, and of the mystery in things. Fear may enter in because of ignorance or a bad conscience—conscience, as that term is ordinarily understood, being a somewhat late development; but in itself and by itself, fear can never have constituted the one vital element in religion. Such fear as there was—and its representative phase is apparent in the attitude of young children towards the darkness—was largely due to such circumstances as the apprehension of encounters by night with the disembodied spirits of the

---

[1] R. R. Marett, *E.R.E.*, ' Magic,' viii. 250.
[2] H. M. Gwatkin, *The Knowledge of God*, i. 263.

dead, particularly of those who had been objects of dread during their lifetime. The Universe, at whatevei stage man has thought about it, is doubtless a vast and awe-inspiring environment, and religion at its broadest is man's reaction to that Universe so far as he understands it. But through it all, with the progress of the centuries, that reaction has shaped itself as if in response to an increasingly clear, revealing message from the heart of the Universe itself, ' Be of good cheer : it is I ; be not afraid.' [1]

In all this, to begin with, we may suppose, the community acts together, and for the good of the community. It was only as the sense of individuality began to emerge, as the third personal pronoun, so to speak, became replaced by the assertive first, and the asserting ego began to realise that he might use this power—which he believed he controlled in the rite—in his own interests as against those of the community or a fellow-tribesman, that magic began to develop that more sinister atmosphere in which it became increasingly enveloped. Magic in the history of the race corresponds originally to the child's power of make-believe in the development of the individual. Just as the child identifies itself with its dolls, carrying on by itself a conversation in which it assumes in turn each of the imagined personalities as it moves them about, so in the dawn of the racial history, in magical practice or, later, in totemistic ritual, man realised his primitive ideas and desires in action. And if in his vivid dream-life primitive man was apparently capable of intense action at a distance in time and space, why should this not be possible for him in imagination on his return to his immediate surroundings from that far country ? Magic, whether in pictograph or cult, is projected will or desire, the end sought being the control of another's will, or of the actions of some animal form desired as food or feared as predatory, or, it may even be, simply of the weather. The magician imagines

[1] Mark 6 50.

that his pretence is the action of his will, converted into very deed. The desire may be further expressed in the spoken word, and the spell becomes the vehicle of the desire—a spoken prayer. This prayer may be addressed to the dimly conceived agency that is thought of as working in the spell, or to any object or symbol that is associated with the spell. The 'hand of might,' worn as a charm by men, women, and children, the conception of the creative potency of words, quite apart from their meaning, due to their being regarded as actual 'soul-stuff that animates the body,'[1] and the magical power of a name, are different forms of such primitive belief. Of a similar character is the strain of thought underlying the adornment of man's person with the teeth or claws of wild animals, or, in the case of woman, the symbolism of the cowrie shell.[2] The faith in such power when secured, for example, in an amulet or charm is even to-day unlimited. A West African negro of a Yoruba tribe, who was wearing a protective charm against gunshot wounds, picked up a missionary's[3] revolver and handing it to him, challenged him, though unsuccessfully, to shoot at him at close range, as a test of the potency of the charm.

Religion, then, clearly characterised the stage when man in his development first began to be aware of himself, and likewise had a dawning sense of certain courses of action as binding him to the tribe or alienating him from it, more vaguely as relating him favourably or unfavourably to the dimly conceived Power (or Powers) behind things—in short, an incipient sense of courses of action as right and wrong. While it is patently incorrect to say with Crawley that 'religion is an adult growth,'[4] still it seems certain that we must think of the religious sense as only very gradually being awakened

[1] Prof. M. A. Canney, *Givers of Life*, p. 71, where various examples are cited. See also *infra*, p. 59 *n*.
[2] Cf. Prof. G. Elliot Smith, *op. cit.* p. 150 ff.
[3] Rev. Dr. S. S. Farrow, MS. of *Yoruba Paganism*.
[4] A. E. Crawley, *The Idea of the Soul*, p. 296.

in the childhood of the race : religious ideas and impulses do not characterise the very young child, yet are awakened before adolescence. Such behaviour or particular manners or morals could only characterise relations between a group of individuals, *i.e.* they imply a gregarious being, while the natural affection which was stimulated by the long period of human infancy gave wider scope for the stricter demarcation of those lines of action that were found to be injurious to the degree of social life attained. Already in the Mid-Palaeolithic, man had not merely acquired sufficient working knowledge of Nature to enable him to succeed in the struggle for existence ; he had also reached a certain vague theory as to himself and the world around him. In this definitely animistic stage he ascribed all movement, whether in river or tempest, tree or animal, to the will of some independent spirit resident in the moving object. Many of these spirits were obviously more powerful than he : they could put his companions into that condition of un-responsiveness which we know as death. So it was only natural that, more than ever, man should desire to reach some condition of security in relation to these spirits, which in some instances he may have thought of as hostile, though assuredly not in all.

We are justified in supposing that in the development of the race a time would come when this ability to traffic with the unseen world would be first realised to be more characteristic of some individuals than of others, and later when it would become restricted to a coterie or certain individuals. There would be those who through unusual ability or by social precedence or by age came to be looked on as the guardians of the mysteries of the tribe. Probably in time they became little more than human repositories, with no ability to explain the customs which they were there to enforce, other than by saying, So was it done of old.[1] The rites, the mysteries

[1] A good example of the persistence of a practice, the meaning of which is not understood by the participant, is seen in a ball game still

are there, and their origin is forgotten; and in order to satisfy the curious, myths or explanations are invented. Primarily, then, the sacred becomes a locus of tabu practices; the negative aspect develops an attitude of humility and submission. In presence of the sacred the sense of awe overcomes the inquirer, and in the weakening of his power of self-assertion, humility is begotten.[1]

On the other hand, in the case of some minds the failure of magic would not necessarily drive them towards definitely religious relationship to the mysterious, for very often the use of it was for anti-social ends, private advancement, or the satisfaction of a private grudge. It would rather mean closer examination of the reason of that failure, more intent observation of things as they actually were ; in such deliberate application of common-sense, which was gradually to free itself from the attendant trappings of magic, are to be found the beginnings of science. The desire to control the course of events, to bend Nature to his use in the interests of his everyday life, apart from the more critical occasions when he attempted to come into contact with the invisible Power to ensure the success of herds and flocks, of crops, and irrigation needs, has been there in one form or another from a very early stage in man's active response to his environment. Whenever he sought to do this in itself and for itself, regardless of the opinions and customs authorised by those who were looked on as the tribal authorities on such matters, and considered themselves as the repositories of the tribal lore, it was obvious that differences were likely to occur, and the struggle between science as untrammelled investigation and the authori-

---

played by Scottish children. Throwing the ball against a wall, a girl will clap her hands together before catching it on the rebound after the first throw. After the second throw she will turn lightly round before catching it, at the same time exclaiming ' merry-me-tanzy.' This mystic word is known to be a corruption of *Admirez me danser*—one of the many relics of the former close association of France and Scotland.

[1] R. R. Marett, *The Threshold of Religion*, p. 169 ff.

tative tradition that was associated with the institutional aspect of religion began. And just in the degree that recourse may have been had by tribesmen to some other 'medicine-man' to counteract the suspected malign activities of some dealer in magic, the tendency would be to keep the development of whatever primitive discoveries were made in the hands of a definite caste. Indisputable evidence of the later break, so far as Europe is concerned, is reached with the earliest scientific developments in Ancient Greece, although it was probably in process in Egypt and Babylonia even earlier.

Thus, we may suppose, there commenced that estrangement on the part of Religion and Science due to the failure, initially born of human selfishness, to recognise that the Reality which both were seeking to understand, although approaching it from different aspects, was one and the same.

CHAPTER II

AMONGST man's earliest interrogations were his wondering questionings about the stars. Probably one of the first great contrasts or differences of which he became conscious was that between day and night. This he must soon have connected in some way with the daily journey of the sun : there was also the lesser luminary that usually shone out when the greater disappeared. In time there came to be little of importance in his life that was not related in some way to the sun, moon, or stars. In Egypt, as originally in Babylonia, the temples were observatories. Astrology (which preceded astronomy) and religion were closely linked because of their bearing on the practical needs of the life of the people, but such association tended to keep scientific knowledge as part of the professional occupation of the priesthood. Of these earliest Babylonian and Egyptian watchers of the skies no individual names and discoveries are known.[1] Since, however, exact dates and calendar determinations are already on record from about the middle of the fifth millennium B.C., it is obvious that they must have been preceded by a long period of observation and record. It is probable that we are only at the beginning of understanding how ancient civilisation actually has been.

Exact astronomical science on any considerable scale is first associated with certain Greek names, but it has yet to be determined to what extent the Greeks learned

---

[1] At least one name of a later Babylonian astronomer is known.

19

from the Egyptians, and the latter in turn from Babylonia.[1] It becomes increasingly impossible to think in the old manner of the Babylonians as mere star-gazers whose whole interest lay in the recording of motions, and who had no gift for speculation and never indulged in cosmological thinking. If, as Professor Burnet insists, ' there are insuperable difficulties in the way of assuming any Aegean influence on India or any Indian influence on the Aegean '[2] in the sixth century B.C., the case will probably prove to be different so far as Babylonia is concerned. In days when, owing to the remarkable discoveries of Sir Arthur Evans at Knossos in Crete, the direct contact of the Egypt of the Eighteenth Dynasty with the Minoan[3] culture of the fifteenth century B.C. (Late Bronze Age) has been made out, as also the steps linking the latter with the civilisation of the First Dynasty at Mycenae on the Greek mainland, which in due time had its direct share in that renaissance which proved to be the unfading glory of classical Greece, it becomes increasingly difficult to suppose that the intercourse between Babylonia and Egypt was on a negligible scale, so far as cultural influence goes. The brilliant if highly speculative theory about an ' Archaic Civilisation ' presumably of late Neolithic times, characterised by irrigation, the rearing of megalithic monuments, the polishing of stone implements, the carving of stone images, and the working of metals, which came into existence in Egypt during the Age of the Pyramids

---

[1] The statement of Eudemus that ' Thales, who went to Egypt, first brought this science (geometry) into Greece,' is well known. With regard to his prediction of a solar eclipse, which was probably that of May 28, 585 B.C., Sir T. L. Heath states : ' Now, the Babylonians, as the result of observation continued through centuries, had discovered the period of 223 lunations after which eclipses recur. It is most likely, therefore, that Thales had heard of this period, and that his prediction was based upon it.' (*The Legacy of Greece*, edit. R. W. Livingstone, p. 106.) Similar connections are shown with regard to Natural Science and Medicine, *ibid.* pp. 181, 204, 205, 208.

[2] *The Legacy of Greece*, p. 65.

[3] From Minos, the semi-legendary king of Crete, who first consolidated the power of this Aegean empire.

and spread thence throughout the world,[1] is likely to meet with even more significant qualification than that contained in the simple fact reported by Professor Langdon to the effect that ' records found at Nippur and Ellasar agree in making Kish the oldest of historical cities,' or the most recent discoveries on which he bases the far-reaching conclusion that it is to the Sumerians, whose true *métier* was letters and art rather than war, that ' the ancient world owes its first spiritual inspiration.' [2] It is just as probable in the light of present-day knowledge, to say the least, that Sumeria [3] gave originally to Egypt, perhaps through later Semitic contacts, as that Egypt gave originally to Sumeria.[4] But further, there is a vast and important sweep of years between the dim twilight records of observation in Babylonia and Egypt in the middle of the fifth millennium B.C., and that momentarily more distinct outline of knowledge that is associated with Greece supremely in the fifth century B.C., even if the preparation for it commenced some two hundred years previous to that date. It seems, therefore, certain that in the decades to come, as the result of further excavations especially in Mesopotamia, there will be a gradual but far-reaching alteration of perspective, and the science of Greece and the early religious literature

[1] Cf. in particular Prof. G. Elliot Smith, *Ancient Egyptians*, and W. J. Perry, *The Children of the Sun* and *The Origin of Magic and Religion*. The prime motive of this movement is found in the elaboration of Egyptian ideas about immortality, their expression in mummification, and the consequent search for ' givers of life ' such as gold, pearls, jade, and cowrie shells, which it was believed would be found, together with eternal youth, in some earthly paradise.

[2] ' The Excavations at Kish, 1923-1924 ': Lectures at the School of Oriental Studies, *Times* report, 20th and 27th June 1924.

[3] The old native term for Babylonia. The pastoral Semitic peoples of Arabia seem to have poured out from their country in all directions in migratory overflow on at least four major occasions. Cf. Prof. J. L. Myres, *The Dawn of History*.

[4] This probability is unaffected by the recent remarkable communication by Sir Flinders Petrie about the existence of a skilled civilisation in Egypt, at Badari and in the Fayum, which apparently must be dated previous to 10,000 B.C. It is described as having come into Egypt from the outside (*Brit. Assoc. Report*, 1925).

of the Hebrews, which have hitherto been vaguely associated with the dawn of history, will find a truer but
none the less significant place about half way down the
span of time separating us to-day from the most recently
ascertained beginnings of human history.

The statement is sometimes made that science was
first pursued for its own sake in Greece. As a matter
of fact, antiquity had very little, if any, idea of the
value of knowledge for its own sake ; that is rather something characteristic of our own civilisation.[1]   Observation
and experiment are essentially modern in any thorough-
going sense of these terms. Greek civilisation was
primarily literary and rhetorical as compared with our
modern scientific civilisation ; and while the Greeks started
with observation, their fondness for unverified hypotheses, and their liking for logical theories of things that
hung well together, often resulted in those theories rapidly
passing over into literary traditions. If these traditions,
e.g. the theory of pores in the skin, were plausible, the
Greeks were satisfied with them, handed them on, and
did not think it necessary to investigate further. None
the less, Greece was the home of a liberating movement
in thought which inaugurated the study of things as they
were, away from the shadow of the temple ; the glow of
individuality and a certain superlative energy radiate
from all the varied masterpieces of her sons. If some of
the older claims made on behalf of the Greek genius, as
e.g. that ' it was Ionia that gave birth to an idea which
was foreign to the East, but has become the starting-
point of modern science—the idea that Nature works
by fixed laws,' [2] may have to be modified in face of more
recent knowledge concerning Babylonia, yet the distinctive
Greek interest in Nature and desire to understand and
interpret her, productive of many strange fancifications

[1] Cf. W. James, *Principles of Psychology*, vol. ii. p. 640, for an interesting Eastern excerpt on the vanity of knowledge. I am indebted to
Dr. Edwyn Bevan both for the reference and for some direction at
this point.
[2] S. H. Butcher, *Some Aspects of the Greek Genius*, p. 10.

and ' anticipations ' of Nature as it undoubtedly was, will always mark a very definite stage in that intellectual and practical conquest of her through sympathy and obedience that is the glory of Science.

The Greek tendency towards abstract generalisation and deductive reasoning is already evident in Thales of Miletus (c. 624-547 B.C.), the first, and in some respects the greatest, of the Ionian philosophers. It is interesting to note that on certain fundamental matters, details of his cosmogony correspond to those which have been described in connection with the Biblical cosmogony, although his interpretation has nothing in common : the same holds true with regard to other aspects in the case of Anaximenes (c. 588-524 B.C.). With the Greek philosophers, inquiry was primarily directed towards the endeavour to find out the ultimate nature of the world as it is, and the manner of its working. In some cases, e.g. that of the Epicureans, the desire to banish the popular fear of the supernatural had entered in as motive to such inquiries ; if they could only show that things were natural in their causation, the basis for this fear would vanish. Gradually the older conceptions of causality, conveyed in tales of arbitrarily acting deities, were replaced by those of impersonal causes working according to law.

Pythagoras (c. 582-500 B.C.), through the observation of eclipses, had determined the spherical form of the earth, which occupied the central position in a living spherical Universe composed of the four elements. Members of his school, a century later,[1] considered that the heavenly bodies, including the earth, moved round a ' central fire,' in which resided the directing principle of the Universe ; while Hicetas of Syracuse (4th cent. B.C.) thought of the earth alone as in motion, and further producing by its revolutions the same impression as if the heavens moved and it alone stood fast. These views,

---

[1] But, apparently, *not* Philolaus ; cf. J. Burnet, *Early Greek Philosophy*, p. 345.

if never very widely held, by loosening the earth, as it were, from its fixed central position, were probably factors that aided Heracleides of Pontus (*c*. 388-315 B.C.) and Aristarchus of Samos (310-230 B.C.) in reaching the heliocentric hypothesis. Yet the statement of his ideas laid Aristarchus open to the charge of blasphemy, while owing to the reversion of Aristotle to the geocentric point of view, and the influence exerted by his name, the work of Copernicus, some two thousand years later, was virtually of the nature of a discovery rather than a rediscovery.

Any attempt to estimate to what extent the scientific views of the Pythagoreans influenced the religious thinking of their time must always be attended with great difficulty. The esoteric character of their teaching, with the consequent reluctance to publish, largely accounts for the scrappy form in which it has been preserved. Yet the general fact of such influence remains. Pythagoras, indeed, so far from ignoring religion, ' founded a society in southern Italy which was primarily a religious community. . . . If the doctrine which Plato makes Socrates expound in the early part of the *Phaedo* is Pythagorean, as it is generally supposed to be, we may say that what Pythagoras did was to teach that, while the ordinary methods of purification were well enough in their way, the best and truest purification for the soul was just scientific study. It is only in some such way as this that we can explain the religious note which is characteristic of all the best Greek science.' [1] In the case of his later followers, however, it seems clear that no such practical harmonising of the two disciplines was effected. Some pursued their scientific inquiries with lessening interest in what may have seemed to them a blend of superstition and mythology ; others who went by the same name were primarily interested in a ' Way of Life,' and had no mind for the understanding or interpretation of Nature.

In the main succession of investigators and thinkers

[1] J. Burnet, in *The Legacy of Greece*, pp. 64, 66.

whose collective work constituted the Golden Age of Grecian culture stand several whose contributions were in one way or another to furnish elements in the impending struggle between science and theology. At once the names occur of Democritus of Abdera (*c.* 420 B.C.), whom, on account of the views held by, but not original with, him of the origin of the world from a fortuitous concourse of atoms, Dante singled out, amongst a great company of the unbaptized relegated by him to the first circle of Hell, as ' Democritus, who sets the world at chance ' ;[1] of Plato (427-347 B.C.), whose cosmology rather than his mathematics, and his general philosophy more than either, so influenced Christian thought latterly that even the translation and interpretation of passages in the New Testament were affected detrimentally thereby ;[2] and of Aristotle (384-322 B.C.), ' the master of them that know,' whose texts were regarded in the Middle Age by some philosophers and theologians as possessing well-nigh the same infallibility as that of Holy Scripture itself.[3] With the name of Eudoxus, the ' god-like ' (408-355 B.C.), is associated an attempted systematic explanation of the apparent motions of the heavenly bodies by means of a theoretical system of concentric spheres, whose actual existence was apparently first maintained by Aristotle, and that too on an even more complicated scale. In the belief of the Pythagoreans of his day, the motions of the heavenly bodies were productive of musical notes. By this time, further, the spherical character of all the stars was accepted, and a fair estimate of the circumference of the earth had been arrived at, together with some appreciation

---

[1] *Inferno*, iv. 132 (Carey's translation).

[2] *E.g.* in connection with the idea of the inherent immortality of the soul ; cf. the Greek text of Luke 9 [25] with A.V. and R.V., bearing in mind Matt. 10 [28]. There is also little doubt that serious injury was done to Christian thought by some of its early exponents through their too placid acceptance and assimilation of Platonic doctrines on such issues as the independent existence of matter and the source of evil in the world.

[3] Cf. *infra*, chap. vi. The other reference is to Dante, *Inferno*, iv. 128.

of its small mass as compared with that of other of the heavenly bodies. If all their orbits were circular, that was simply because the motions of the planets as divine beings could only partake of this perfect orderly form. Nevertheless, the anomalies in their motions soon began to attract attention, and instigated attempts to provide an explanation.

With the subjugation of Greece by Alexander the Great in 330 B.C., the further development of Greek scientific and philosophical inquiry was checked on its native soil, and so far as the first Christian teachers began to be conscious of contemporary doctrine—apart from their knowledge of the early Greek philosophies—that seemed seriously to counter the cosmological outlook of the Hebrew Scriptures as they understood them, Alexandria was the principal centre of dissemination. On the death of Alexander in 323 B.C. his empire was divided amongst his generals. Egypt fell to Ptolemy Soter, his half-brother, who made Alexandria his capital, and by his beneficent rule attracted Greeks and Jews to the city in large numbers. He founded the Museum in 300 B.C., and it was completed by his son Ptolemy Philadelphus. Its institution was a direct result of the stimulus to the acquirement of knowledge consequent on the Asiatic campaigns of Alexander, from which the learned men who had accompanied him brought back in more definite form then ever before the intellectual treasures of Babylonia—knowledge, it may be added, that quickly passed into the category of long, unquestioningly accepted tradition. Built for the preservation, the increase and diffusion of knowledge, this world-famous school poured out a steady stream of light, especially upon the pathways and structure of the heavens, as from the white-marbled Pharos at the harbour mouth was illumined the course of the coasting vessels. It comprised the most famous library in the world (700,000 manuscripts), as also zoological and botanical gardens, astronomical observatory, and chemical and physical laboratories. From the point of view of research and instruction, this Museum-University originally had four faculties — literature, mathematics, astronomy, and medicine ; it is worth while noting the comparative importance attached to astronomy. As many as 14,000 students, young and old, were sometimes in attendance in a single year, amongst whose number at one time or another might have been found Clemens Alexandrinus, Origen, and Athanasius. No school in the world has ever had such a galaxy of talent associated with it. The names of Euclid (c. 330-275 B.C.), Archimedes (287-212 B.C.) and Apollonius (260-200 B.C.) are in a general way synonymous with elementary plane geometry, mechanics, and analytical geometry respectively, while the librarian Eratosthenes (275-194 B.C.) was the first to put geography upon a scientific basis, giving, incidentally, an amazingly close approximation to the correct circumference of the earth. In astronomy and natural science generally, the summed results of the previous ages were at the disposal of investigators, and formed the basis of continuous fresh discovery. Chief amongst the former for this purpose were the discovery of Heracleides of Pontus that the earth rotated on its own axis once in twenty-four hours; the hypothesis of Aristarchus of Samos that the earth and the other planets revolve in circular orbits round a central stationary sun ; while the wonderful star catalogue of Hipparchus of Rhodes (c. 161-126 B.C.), which led to his discovery of the precession of the equinoxes, provided in turn a substantial basis for the work of his most distinguished successor, Ptolemy.

Claudius Ptolemaeus, to give him his full name (c. A.D. 125-151), stands out by reason of his monumental ' Syntaxis,' also known as the ' Almagest,' which was in effect A Treatise on the Mathematical Construction of the Heavens, and, although the result of investigations carried on in the second quarter of the second century of our era, it continued to dominate scientific thinking for

the next fourteen centuries, and some theological thinking
up to the present day. According to Ptolemy the earth
was spherical and situated in the centre of the heavens :
it had no motion of translation, nor did it rotate upon
its axis. Around it revolved at increasingly greater
distances the Moon, Mercury, Venus, the Sun, Mars,
Jupiter, and Saturn.[1] Beyond the Saturnian orbit lay
the firmament of the fixed stars. By means of complicated systems of excentrics and epicycles, Ptolemy
was able to explain the apparent motions of the various
heavenly bodies. Every one of these statements was
accompanied by good reasons that carried conviction to
many at the time, even if he himself realised that it would
simplify matters very greatly if only the earth did spin
upon its axis. It was no fault of Ptolemy's, however,
that the fanciful Pythagorean conception of the harmonic
spheres was later worked into his sober observational
' construction of the heavens '; nor was the spirit of many
who in later days appealed to the authority of his name
the spirit of the man himself, for Ptolemy was always
ready to face the facts. Similarly, in medicine, the almost
Paleyan pronouncements of Galen (c. A.D. 130-200), based
on his own work and that of his illustrious predecessors
Alcmaeon of Croton (c. 508 B.C.), Hippocrates of Cos
(c. 460-400 B.C.), as also Herophilus and Erasistratus,
both of whom belonged to the School of Alexandria
(c. 300 B.C.), sufficed for the next thousand years, during
which Theology ruled proudly as Queen of the Sciences.

How far even the rudiments of this wealth of knowledge entered into contemporary Greek cultural thought
it would be difficult to say, but it is almost certain that its
effect upon the intelligent lay mind was comparatively
slight compared with the influence of the dominant

---

[1] From the names of the days of our seven-day week, it is evident
that they were all derived from these heavenly bodies on relationships
involved in the Ptolemaic system. They presided in succession over
the hours of the day. If the first hour is assigned to Saturn, the
second to Jupiter, and so on, the twenty-fifth falls to the Sun, the second
day of the Hebrew week.

Stoic philosophy, whose cosmology was of the nature of a reversion to primitive conceptions. Stoicism, with its appeal to the human will and its stout assertion of freedom, helped to drill the soul into serene detachment from circumstance, and into the pursuit of virtue. But it had its roots in a fixed belief in Providence, which was unaffectable by the growing knowledge of the world, and engendered an uncomplaining acceptance of what is. A particularly interesting *résumé* of this point of view on its cosmological side may be found in the little treatise entitled *De Mundo*,[1] supposed to be of date either early in the second half of the first century A.D. or the first half of the second century, and to be based upon two works of Poseidonius of Rhodes (*c.* 135-51 B.C.). A few passages will suffice to show its general drift. ' The Universe then is a system made up of heaven and earth and the elements which are contained in them. But the word is also used in another sense of the ordering and arrangement of all things, preserved by and through God. Of this Universe the centre, which is immovable and fixed, is occupied by the life-bearing earth, the home and the mother of diverse creatures. The upper portion of the Universe has fixed bounds on every side, the highest part of it being called Heaven, the abode of the gods. Heaven is full of divine bodies, which we usually call stars, and moves with a continual motion in one orbit, and revolves in stately measure with all the heavenly bodies unceasingly for ever. . . . Now the number of the fixed stars cannot be ascertained by man, although they move in one surface, which is that of the whole heaven. But the planets fall into seven divisions in seven successive circles, so situated that the higher is always greater than the lower, and the seven circles are successively encompassed by one another and are all surrounded by the sphere containing the fixed stars. . . . Thus then five

---

[1] *The Works of Aristotle: De Mundo,* trans. by E. S. Forster, The Oxford Translation, vol. iii. I am indebted to Prof. James Moffatt for directing my attention to this work.

elements, situated in spheres in five regions, the less being in each case surrounded by the greater—namely, earth surrounded by water, water by air, air by fire, and fire by ether—make up the whole Universe. . . . Yet some have wondered how it is that the Universe, if it be composed of contrary principles—namely, dry and moist, hot and cold—has not long ago perished and been destroyed. It is just as though one should wonder how a city continues to exist, being, as it is, composed of opposing classes—rich and poor, young and old, weak and strong, good and bad. They fail to notice that this has always been the most striking characteristic of civic concord, that it evolves unity out of plurality, and similarity out of dissimilarity, while it admits every kind and variety. It may perhaps be that nature has a liking for contraries and evolves harmony out of them and not out of similarities. . . . Thus then a single harmony orders the composition of the whole—heaven and earth and the whole Universe—by the mingling of the most contrary principles. The dry mingling with the moist, the hot with the cold, the light with the heavy, the straight with the curved, all the earth, the sea, the ether, the sun, the moon, and the whole heaven are ordered by a single power extending through all, which has created the whole Universe out of separate and different elements—air, earth, fire, and water—embracing them all on one spherical surface and forcing the most contrary natures to live in agreement with one another in the Universe, and thus contriving the permanence of the whole. . . . Nature teaches us in the greater principles of the world that equality somehow tends to preserve harmony, whilst harmony preserves the Universe which is the parent of all things and itself the fairest thing of all. . . . Thus an unbroken permanence, which all things conspire to secure, counteracting one another—at one time dominating, at another being dominated—preserves the whole unimpaired through all eternity. . . .

'There still remains for us to treat briefly . . . of the cause which holds all things together. . . . The old explanation which we have all inherited from our fathers, is that all things are from God and were framed for us by God, and that no created thing is of itself sufficient for itself, deprived of the permanence which it derives from him. . . . God is in very truth the preserver and creator of all that is in any way being brought to perfection in this Universe ; yet he endures not all the weariness of a being that administers and labours, but exerts a power which never wearies ; whereby he prevails even over things which seem far distant from him. . . . When, therefore, the ruler and parent of all, invisible save to the eye of the mind, gives the word to all nature that moves betwixt heaven and earth, the whole revolves unceasingly in its own circuits and within its own bounds, sometimes unseen and sometimes appearing, revealing and again hiding diverse manners of things, from one and the same cause. . . . That this force is unseen stands in the way neither of its action nor of our belief in it. For the spirit of intelligence whereby we live and dwell in houses and communities, though invisible, is yet seen in its operations. . . . Thus, too, must we think of God, who in might is most powerful, in beauty most fair, in time immortal, in virtue supreme ; for, though he is invisible to all mortal nature, yet is he seen in his very works. For all that happens in the air, on the earth, and in the water, may truly be said to be the work of God, who possesses the Universe. . . . To sum up the matter, as is the steersman in the ship, the charioteer in the chariot, the leader in the chorus, law in the city, the general in the army, even so is God in the Universe ; save that to them their rule is full of weariness and disturbance and care, while to him it is without toil or labour and free from all bodily weakness. . . . God is to us a law, impartial, admitting not of correction or change, and better, methinks, and surer than those which are engraved upon tablets.' Finally, after showing

how God, though one, has many names, ' being called after
all the various conditions which he himself inaugurates,'
and after identifying him with Necessity, Fate, Nemesis,
and so on, the writer concludes : ' God, then, as the
old story has it, holding the beginning and the end and the
middle of all things that exist, proceeding by a straight
path in the course of nature brings them to accomplish-
ment ; and with him ever follows Justice, the avenger
of all that falls short of the Divine Law—Justice, in
whom may he that is to be be happy, be from the very
first a blessed and happy partaker ! ' [1]

Upon such a world outlook, with its remote, almost impersonal, yet lofty conception of Deity, the discoveries of
science could have little effect, because there was little to
affect. ' The earth and the things upon the earth,' says
the writer of the *De Mundo*, ' being farthest removed from
the benefit which proceeds from God, seem feeble and in-
coherent and full of much confusion ; nevertheless, inasmuch as it is the nature of the divine to penetrate to all
things, the things also of our earth receive their share of
it, and the things above us according to their nearness to
or distance from God receive more or less of divine
benefit.' [2] He cannot get away, however, from the sense
of distance from God, and unconcern on His part with
mundane affairs. ' The objects of sense which are held in
the highest esteem occupy the same region '—he is speaking of Heaven—' to wit, the stars and the sun and moon.
For this cause the heavenly bodies alone are so arranged
that they ever preserve the same order, and never alter
or move from their course, while the things of earth,
being mutable, admit of many changes and conditions.' [3]
Very different was the feeling in the case of a people who
believed that God had indeed come nigh to men, and had
further given to them in His revealed word knowledge
concerning the world, its creation and ordering.

Now, it was most probably in this same city of

---

[1] *Op. cit.* 391 [b], 392 [a], 393 [a], 396 [a, b], 397 [a, b], 399 [a, b], 400 [b], 401 [b].
[2] *Op. cit.* 397 [b].   [3] *Op. cit.* 400 [a].

Alexandria that at any rate the earliest part (probably comprising the Pentateuch) of that translation of the Old Testament from Hebrew into Greek, popularly known as the Septuagint, was carried out in the first half of the third century B.C., and, as legend affirmed, at the command of Ptolemy Philadelphus. Of the historicity of this instruction, indeed, there is little likelihood, for the language of the Septuagint constitutes the most vivid extant reflection of the spoken Greek of the Alexandrian streets, so suggesting rather that the translation was made directly in the interests of the Jewish settlers in that city. The lack of polish, the popular style reminiscent, grammatically, of ' the kind of thing you get in the papyri by the hundred,' [1] ill accord with the idea of a scholarly rendering done at a royal command. There is no reason to suppose that the whole work was carried out at once. Rather did it grow up to serve the needs of the very numerous Jewish residents, the task of translation being continued over a long period. No one knows who had a share in what was a very remarkable piece of work, in spite of its repeated disagreement with the Hebrew text. We have even less reason to suppose that a single individual of the mythically numbered Septuagesimi, or actual translators, ever had the interest to cross the threshold of the Alexandrian Observatory. Perhaps if he had done so, the bitterness of the forthcoming struggle between science and Christian theology might have been mitigated from the first. Nevertheless, in the early Christian passion for definition, as in other regards, may be traced something of the influence of contemporary Greek scientific and philosophical thought upon Christianity.

With the conquest of Greece finally accomplished by Rome in 146 B.C., there came a most effective dampening down and, in the end, extinction of the fire of the creative Greek genius. On the other hand, few circumstances are

[1] For these expert details the writer is indebted to Prof. H. A. A. Kennedy.

more remarkable in the history of science than the comparative failure of the Roman mind to adapt itself to the task of attempting experimental or theoretical understanding of the world. Inclined to rhetoric, and further expressing itself through a long line of purely literary men and of historians, Roman constructive genius displayed itself, apart from the realm of jurisprudence, especially in the broad field of civil and military engineering. Lucretius' monumental work *De Rerum Natura* (*c.* 95-55 B.C.) is, after all, very largely an exposition of Greek philosophy ; in medicine, apart from Celsus (*c.* 30 B.C.), there is no name of outstanding distinction, for Galen was no Roman. Strabo (63 B.C.-A.D. 24) as a geographer is almost solitary in his eminence; and Pliny the Elder (A.D. 23-79) in the thirty-seven books of his encyclopaedic *Natural History*, throughout which he sought to indicate how all natural objects have really been created in the direct interests of man, draws most largely upon Greek sources.

Upon religion such an undeveloped, nerveless system of scientific thought could have no effect, particularly since Roman religion was little more than a round of ceremonial resting upon a minimum of dogma. The simple countryman's beliefs in the localised spirits (numina) of the field, the grove, the spring, the household—truly, if ever there was such, a ' natural piety ' —developed into the more sublimated Paganism of the city-state. Yet the former, meaning more to its devotees, proved the more enduring, and still survives in considerable measure, transmuted or disguised, in the Roman ritual of to-day. The hospitable and tolerant Roman Pantheon lost in influence just because of its indiscriminate assimilation, although the ever-growing number of welcomed extraneous divinities, conquered with their people or adopted for their own supposed worth, involved an increasingly elaborated hierarchy : in the case of the Olympians, it became a matter of identification with, or even of substitution for, the corresponding, less sophisticated Roman tutelary deities. To the really thoughtful Roman there was something strangely sympathetic in the Stoic world-philosophy : indeed, in the cultured Roman mind religion and philosophy were markedly confluent. But in any case such a self-contained system as Stoicism provided little motive for the acquisition of knowledge that seemed devoid of practical value.

Possibly the one direction in which there was an active and direct influence of science, or of what passed for science, upon Roman religious life and thought was in the exotic practice of astrology, which began to spread in Rome during the first century A.D. 'There are others,' says Pliny, 'who . . . assign events to the influence of the stars, and to the laws of our nativity. They suppose that God, once for all, issues his decrees, and never afterwards interferes. This opinion begins to gain ground, and both the learned and the unlearned vulgar are falling into it.' [1] The practice was opposed by early Christian writers, inasmuch as it seemed the negation of the doctrine of freewill. But, further, the whole astrological system originally represented certain primitive beliefs concerning the structure and ordering of the Universe. It was the science of its day, and, just in the degree in which it was replaced by more exact knowledge, left correspondingly less room for the activities and even the existence of the anthropomorphic ' numina,' whose organised priesthood still sustained the people in their beliefs. As for the more thoughtful and more instructed, they seem in some instances to have been led towards a conception of a divinely interrelated Universe which they vaguely equated with God. In one rare passage, Seneca (3 B.C.-A.D. 65) reaches a clarity of conclusion far in advance of any of his contemporaries and many of his successors :

' God has not revealed all things to man. How small a portion of His mighty work is entrusted to us ? But

[1] *Natural History*, ii. 5 (Bohn Trans.).

He who directs them all, who established and laid the foundations of all this world, who has clothed Himself with creation, and is the greater and better part of His work, He is hidden from our eyes, He can be perceived only by thought.

'Many things, moreover, akin to highest deity, or holding power near it, are still obscure. Or, perhaps, one may be still more surprised to find that they at once fill and elude our sight. Either their subtlety is too great for human vision to grasp, or such exalted majesty conceals itself in the holier sanctuary, and rules its kingdom, which is itself, without permitting access to any power except the spirit.' [1]

Yet others, reacting against the confining, hopeless, and unrelenting grip of the system of things in which they had thus become involved, sought freedom and solace in Christianity.

[1] *Physical Science in the Time of Nero*, being a translation of *Quaestiones Naturales* of Seneca, by John Clarke, p. 305.

CHAPTER III

COSMOGONIES ANCIENT AND MODERN

THE Biblical cosmogony reflects the primitive geocentric outlook on things which the Hebrews held in common with Babylonian, Phoenician, and other peoples, their religious interpretation of which, however, differed in a way that was as unique as it was sublime. Of its particular relation, for example, to the Babylonian Epic of Creation, ' undoubtedly written in the period of the First Babylonian Dynasty, 2225-1926 ' B.C.,[1] the scholarship of the future will have much to say in the light of the new knowledge which is now accumulating year by year as the result of continuous systematic exploration in Mesopotamia. To the Hebrew mind the earth and its attendant sky practically constituted the world ; other sidereal systems were unknown. Situated at the centre of the universe, the earth was thought of as a disc-like body, its upper surface sculptured by wind and rain and other physical agencies into the familiar features of mountain and plain, river and sea—' It is He that sitteth above the *circle* of the earth . . . that stretcheth out the heavens as a curtain, and spreadeth them out as a tent to dwell in.' [2] The earth rested upon, and was surrounded by, the ' Great Deep ' or watery abyss (*Tehom*), by which is to be understood what remained of those primeval waters which had engulfed the earth previous to its separation out of them. ' The earth is the Lord's . . . for He hath founded it upon the

---

[1] S. Langdon, *The Babylonian Epic of Creation*, p. 10.
[2] Is. 40 [22]; cf. also Job 14 [18, 19].

seas and established it upon the floods.' [1] From these
waters 'under the earth,' by way of subterranean
passages, the lakes, ponds, and springs were supplied,
which in their turn fed the rivers. So Basil says in
his *Hexaemeron*, 'the earth is all undermined with
invisible conduits, where the water travels everywhere
underground from the sources of the sea.' [2] It must
be so in that arid Mesopotamian climate, for since 'all
the rivers run into the sea, (and) yet the sea is not full,'
this can only be because in some way 'unto the place
from whence they come, thither they return again.' [3]
So also as a factor in the causation of the Flood, according to the version in the Priestly Document (P), 'were
all the fountains of the great deep broken up'; [4] that
is to say, there were preternatural upwellings of the
waters of the Great Deep upon which the earth was
supposed to rest ; the regular channels were 'broken up.'
It is further interesting to note that the dark, mysterious
water-depth under the earth was sometimes represented,
consonant with Semitic mythology, as a sea-monster
or dragon, *Rahab*, the 'Tiamat' of the Assyrians and
Babylonians, that had engaged in conflict with Jehovah,
and been worsted by Him.[5] Indeed, Professor J. P.
Peters,[6] taking *Tehom* (the Deep) as a proper rather
than a common noun,[7] identical with the Babylonian
Ti'amatu or *Tiamtu*—for in Hebrew it is never preceded
by the article—affirms that the two opening verses of
Genesis virtually tell of the same victorious struggle of
God with the monster of chaos as is narrated in the

[1] Ps. 24 [2]; cf. also Gen. 1 [9], 49 [25]; Ps. 104 [6], 136 [6]; Ex. 20 [4]; Deut.
4 [18], 5 [8], 33 [13]; Ezek. 31 [4]; Am. 7 [4].
[2] Hom., iv. 6.   [3] Eccles. 1 [7].
[4] Gen. 7 [11]. In the parallel version by J, the secondary cause of the
Flood is found in excessive rain. Cf. J. Skinner, *I.C.C.*, 'Genesis,
pp. 150-181.
[5] Ps. 89 [10] ; cf. also 74 [12-17]; Is. 51 [9]; Job 9 [13], 26 [12]. In certain other
passages, *e.g.* Ps. 87 [4] and Is. 30 [7], the name is employed to designate
Egypt : perhaps this is also the case in Is. 51 [9].
[6] *Bible and Spade*, pp. 59-61. Cf. *E.R.E.*, art. 'Cosmogony,' iv. 154.
[7] Cf. Gen. 49 [25] : Deut. 33 [13].

Babylonian Creation Narrative, the monster being in both cases overcome by the aid of a rushing wind, while its carcase was made use of in the creation of heaven and earth.

In the opposite direction, high over the earth—and yet not so high but that heaven might be reached through it by a bold and skilfully constructed tower [1]—extended the firmament, which originally was formed to ' divide the waters from the waters.' [2] It was thought of as a solid vault—' Canst thou with Him spread out the sky, *which is strong as a molten mirror ?* ' [3]—something like a gigantic round dish-cover set over the flat disc of the earth. It was supported upon mountains that are varyingly conceived as rising either all round the extreme edge of the disc, or beyond the waters ; outside it was darkness. ' He hath described a boundary upon the face of the waters, unto the confines of light and darkness. The pillars of heaven [*i.e.* the mountains, as above] tremble, and are astonished at His rebuke.' [4] It is probable that the roots of these great mountains were considered as extending deeply downwards into the abyss of waters under the earth, and so in turn aiding in supporting the earth.[5] If the question be raised, But upon what did the Great Deep rest ? an answer might be rendered in terms of the passage in Job 26 [7]—' He stretcheth out the north over empty space, and hangeth the earth upon nothing '—where the idea of the earth as suspended *over* nothing is on the whole preferred by Driver and Gray [6] to the idea of it as hung with its inconceivable weight *upon* nothing. It may, however, be doubted whether out of the scant references in Scripture an absolutely consistent cosmological system can be constructed. We have continually to recollect how much of poetry there is in the sacred story, and be

---

[1] Gen. 11 [1-9].   [2] Gen. 1 [6].
[3] Job 37 [18] ; cf. Prov. 8 [28].   [4] Job 26 [10, 11] ; cf. Am. 9 [6].
[5] 1 Sam. 2 [8] ; Job 9 [6], 38 [6] ; Ps. 75 [3], 104 [5] ; Prov. 8 [25] ; Jon. 2 [6].
[6] *I.C.C.* in loco.

rigidly on our guard against reading modern ideas into
its ancient phraseology.　On the other hand, it becomes
increasingly evident that the Hebrew cosmogony is
a distinctive modification of that of the Semitic
Babylonians, who in turn inherited from their Sumerian
predecessors.　Now, ' from the fact that planets and
stars disappeared below the horizon and rose again, the
Sumerians inferred that their spheres extended under
the earth as well as above it, so that there were under-
hemispheres that were the exact counterparts of the
upper-hemispheres.' [1]　The probability therefore is that
the visible hemisphere of the firmament was conceived
of as continued downwards in another hemisphere which
held in the ' waters under the earth.' [2]

Above the firmament were the ' upper waters,' [3] held up
by the clouds, likened to waterskins that do not burst ; [4]
there also were the ' treasuries ' of the snow and of the
hail.[5]　In it were set windows—' the windows of heaven
were opened, and the rain was upon the earth forty days
and forty nights ' ; [6] and also two doors, through one
of which—that in the east—the sun appeared in the
morning ' as a bridegroom coming out of his chamber,' [7]
disappearing in the evening by means of the other into
his tent or canopy where he spent the night.[8]　The
creation of the firmament preceded that of the luminaries
or lamps which were set upon its *lower* surface, each with
its prescribed course.　It is for this reason that darkness
was supposed to reign outside the vertical walls of the
firmament.　Somewhere beyond the horizon, also, presumably near to where the firmament reaches the level of the
earth, were the storehouses of the winds : in Scripture

---

[1] Prof. L. B. Paton, *Archaeology and the Book of Genesis*, ' The
Biblical World,' xlv. 204.　Cf. also his *Spiritism and the Cult of the
Dead*, chap. vii.

[2] Gen. 49 25 ; Ex. 20 4 ; Am. 7 4.

[3] Cf. Ps. 104 3, 148 4.

[4] Job 26 8.　　　　　　　　　　　　　　[5] Job 38 22.

[6] Gen. 7 11, 12, 8 2 ; cf. also 2 Kings 7 2, 19 ; Is. 24 18 ; Mal. 3 10.

[7] Ps. 19 5 ; cf. 78 23.　　　　　　　　　[8] Ps. 19 4 ; Eccles. 1 5.

there are several references to the ' four winds of heaven.' [1]
They are respectively the north wind, the south wind,
the east wind, and the west wind, each with its special
characteristics.   The passage in Rev. 7 [1] is very vivid :
' After this I saw four angels standing at the four corners
of the earth, holding the four winds of the earth, that
no wind should blow on the earth, or on the sea, or upon
any tree.'   One can almost see the four winds, like
chained-up dogs, each straining at the leash in the angel's
hand. [2]

To the disc of the earth below there corresponded
ocularly, amongst the clouds of waters that were above
the firmament, a heavenly disc : ' He walketh on the
circle (vault) of heaven.' [3]   With this region also were
directly associated certain of the concrete elements
in those prophetic visions of the indescribable—the
' paved work of sapphire stone, and as it were the very
heaven for clearness,' [4] upon which were set the feet of
God Himself ; or the ' crystal firmament ' above which
was ' the likeness of a throne, as the appearance of
a sapphire stone.' [5]   Meanwhile, with the developing
thought of the divine transcendence, correspondence
began to be found in the old idea of a plurality of heavens.
' Behold, unto the Lord thy God belongeth the heaven
and the heaven of heavens,' [6] i.e. the highest heaven,
perhaps, more specifically, the heaven of the fixed stars.
This conception of a plurality of heavens, which corresponded originally to the seven heavens or concentric
spheres of the planets, and was shared by the Jews with

[1] Jer. 49 [36] ; Ezek. 37 [9] ; Dan. 7 [2], 8 [8] ; Zech. 2 [6], 6 [5] ; Matt. 24 [31] ;
Rev. 7 [1].
[2] Euroclydon (Acts 27 [14]) or Euraquilo (R.V.) is a particular typhoon
well known to Mediterranean sailors.
[3] Job 22 [14] ; cf. Prov. 8 [27], where the vault is said to rest on ' the face
of the deep.'
[4] Ex. 24 [10].
[5] Ezek. 1 [26] ; cf. 28 [14] ; Job 37 [18] ; Am. 9 [6].
[6] Deut. 10 [14] ; cf. 1 Kings 8 [27] ; Neh. 9 [6] ; Ps. 68 [33], 148 [4].   Prof.
J. E. M'Fadyen suggests that in the last two passages the sense may be
simply that of a superlative, as in the title ' The Song of Songs.'

the Babylonians and other Eastern peoples, having come down from Sumerian times, held its place in Rabbinical and Apocalyptic literature, and is found in the New Testament. ' I know a man in Christ,' said St. Paul, ' fourteen years ago (whether in the body, I know not ; or whether out of the body, I know not : God knoweth), such a one caught up even to the third heaven. And I know such a man (whether in the body, or apart from the body, I know not : God knoweth), how that he was caught up into Paradise, and heard un-.speakable words which it is not lawful for a man to utter.' [1] Here we have very pronouncedly this conception of a plurality, perhaps a hierarchy, of heavens, seven in all, Paradise being situated, according to the most general rendering of the passage, in the third heaven, although, apparently, according to later Judaism it was localised in the fourth heaven.[2] Although there is no mention of Paradise in the Pentateuch, the Jews speculated about it as they liked ; Apocalyptic and Rabbinical writers wandered about its imaginary purlieus and premises at their sweet will. The solidity of the firmament had gone with the retreat of the stars deeper into space, leaving more open than ever the possibility of a series of heavens. With the lowest heaven somewhat near the clouds, and these in turn often wrapping around the summits of the highest hills,[3] the framework of conception within which much Scriptural truth is set becomes even more closely knit together.

Somewhere inside or beneath the earth lay Sheol.[4] Primarily Sheol is a definitely cosmological conception of Sumerian origin, rather than a purely Semitic idea

[1] 2 Cor. 12 [2-4] ; cf. Heb. 4 [14], 7 [26] ; Eph. 4 [10], 6 [12].
[2] Cf. S. D. F. Salmond, ' Heaven,' *H.D.B.*, ii. 322 ; R. K. Abbott, *I.C.C.*, ' Ephesians and Colossians,' pp. 116, 184. This distinctively later Christian conception is a return to a primitive view. Paradise is no longer a department of Sheol, considered as the intermediate state, as in Luke 16 [23], 23 [43]. Cf. John 20 [17] ; Acts 2 [31].
[3] Ex. 24 [10] suggests that heaven was thought of as very close to, if not actually at the top of, Mount Sinai.
[4] Num. 16 [30-33] ; Deut. 32 [22] ; Job 26 [6] ; Is. 7 [11], 14 [9] ; Am. 9 [2], [3].

about a future existence. ' The bowl under the earth that
corresponded to the dome of the sky above it was Aralu,
the under-world, the abode of spirits of the dead ; and
there were seven hells just as there were seven heavens.' [1]
Man might reach these nether regions directly, as when
in the case of Korah and his fellow-conspirators ' the
earth opened her mouth, and swallowed them up. . . .
So they . . . went down alive into Sheol.' [2] More
usually the route was indirect, and the souls of the dead
were thought of as passing on their way to Sheol, like
flighting birds, over the intervening seas, towards that
same western gate in the firmament where the sun had
made his exit—' for it is soon cut off, and we fly away.' [3]
This subterranean cavernous abode was connected with
the grave, but, as a matter of fact, the exact relations
of Sheol and the grave are never quite straightened out
in the Old Testament. At first Sheol is simply the
abode or country of the dead, *i.e.* of the good and bad
alike ; but later its topography underwent differentiation
with the growing sense of individuality and that moral
estimation of life that involved the idea of rewards and
punishments.[4] In the parable of the rich man and
Lazarus,[5] Our Lord employs the current Jewish conception of that differentiation—the place of torment
separated by an impassable chasm from ' Abraham's
bosom,' though here not actually designated Paradise. It
is peculiarly instructive to trace the development within
Scripture itself of how Sheol becomes emptied, as it were,
and heaven peopled. Originally the home only of Enoch,
Moses, and Elijah amongst the sons of men, while Sheol
was still the destination of the good and bad alike,
heaven became the final abode of the righteous, until,
in contrast with the nearest access to God that was open
to the Hebrew under the Old Testament economy, a

---

[1] Prof. L. B. Paton, *op. cit.* p. 204. It is very doubtful if the belief
occurs in this form in the Old Testament.

[2] Num. 16 [32, 33].   [3] Ps. 90 [10].

[4] These, however, are late developments, later even than the Book
of Job   [5] Luke 16 [19-31].

New Testament writer could say, ' but ye are come unto mount Zion, and unto the city of the living God, the heavenly Jerusalem, and to innumerable hosts of angels, to the general assembly and church of the firstborn who are enrolled in heaven, and to God the Judge of all, and to the spirits of just men made perfect, and to Jesus the mediator of a new covenant, and to the blood of sprinkling that speaketh better than that of Abel.' [1]

How firmly this cosmogony maintained itself, as also the nature of the modifications forced upon it as the result particularly of the increase in geographical knowledge, may be gathered from a comparison with that propounded by Cosmas Indicopleustes, its greater consonance with known facts giving it an established position for many centuries. Indeed, it held its place as the popular form of the flat-earth doctrine until the voyages of Columbus and Magellan showed its untenable character.

Cosmas Indicopleustes,[2] originally a merchant, who was probably born in Alexandria, perhaps of Greek parents, about the close of the fifth or beginning of the sixth century, travelled widely in connection with his business, and later in life became a monk. His Christianity, which was fervent, had a Nestorian cast. His *Christian Topography* was published probably about the middle of the sixth century, and is, as numerous readers have found, a somewhat tiresome and repetitious medley, containing, however, many valuable first-hand geographical and other observations. Its main purpose was to refute the conception of the pagan philosophers that the earth is a sphere, round which the heavens revolve as another sphere inset with the celestial luminaries. He develops, *per contra*, the theory that the Tabernacle in the Wilderness, designed by ' the divine

[1] Heb. 12 [22-24]; cf. Rev. 7 [9].
[2] *The Christian Topography of Cosmas Indicopleustes*, by E. O. Winstedt (Camb. Univ. Press, 1909). Cf. also J. W. M'Crindle, *The Christian Topography of Cosmas, an Egyptian Monk* (Hakluyt Society, 1897), and C. R. Beazley, *The Dawn of Modern Geography*, i. 273-303.

cosmographer Moses,' [1] was in fact a model of the universe.[2] As ' heavier than all other bodies, God placed the earth as the foundation of everything, having made it steadfast in virtue of its own inherent stability.' [3] The two storeys of Cosmas' rectangular, vaulted, box-like universe are separated by the firmament, and in the upper storey are located the two heavens, supported by four walls at the confines of the earth, and ' welded ' to it. According to its ' pattern,' the table of the shew-bread, the surface of the earth was flat, and its length twice its breadth : the ' waved moulding ' [4] that ran round the edge of the table typified the encircling ocean, beyond which lay remoter territory on every side, and to the east, in particular, the Land of Paradise, the abode of man previous to the Deluge. It was to the limiting vertical extremities of this outer ' earth ' that the nether extremities of the firmament were welded.

Phenomena like the size of the sun, its nightly disappearance and journey round a huge conical mountain that rose somewhat far up in the north-west and from which the earth sloped downwards towards the south, the eclipses of the sun and moon, the stars and their courses, are all noted and explained in accordance with the theory of a flat earth and the supposed teaching of Scripture. The angels he conceived as concerned with the task of moving and guiding the stars in their courses, an operation which they performed ' by day and by night unceasingly,' [5] yet from the terrestrial side of the firmament, to which they were restricted in their toil on behalf of mankind until the resurrection. But they were not limited to this work, for ' God again provided rains for

[1] Edit. Winstedt, ii. 76 A.
[2] There is little doubt that this particular fancy, which was not original with Cosmas, arose from a literal interpretation, on the part of some of the Church Fathers, notably Theodore of Mopsuestia, of certain phrases in Heb. 9 [23-24]. It is also worthy of remark that ' both the shape of the world and the comparison to a place of worship were old Egyptian traditions.' (E. O. Winstedt, op. cit. p. 6, n. 1.)
[3] Op. cit. ii. 80 B.   [4] Op. cit. iii. 160 D.   [5] Op. cit. ii. 128 D.

the good of the earth through the angelic powers, who
with the utmost exertion bring them up from the sea
into the clouds, and in obedience to the divine command
discharge them wherever the divine command directs.
For saith Scripture by the prophet Amos, He that
calleth forth the water of the sea, and poureth it out
over the face of the earth.' [1] They are also entrusted
with the guidance and guardianship of every human
being. His invective against the idea of the heavens
(conceived as distinct from the stars) as spherical and
in constant revolution, was motived by his fear that to
admit these propositions would dispose of a future life
and render the resurrection of Christ of no avail.

More particularly, while fiercely combating certain
views that he considers subversive of particular Christian
beliefs, he evidences in his description of the earth as
oblong—even if he speaks of ' having learned ' the fact
' from Moses ' [2]—a concession to the growing knowledge
of the earth's surface, which contrasts with the older
view that considered it more of a square, with Jerusalem
in the centre. The idea of the Antipodes—' an old
wives' tale ' [3]—where, if the earth is a sphere, men
must be standing head downwards and rain falling
upwards, proves as much of an irritant to Cosmas as it
did to some of the Early Fathers, and only needed, in his
opinion, to be stated or, better, pictured, to carry its
own refutation. In general he is thoroughly impatient
with the views of the philosophers ; as he says, ' if any
one should wish to examine the Hellenic (pagan) theories
he will find them to be entirely fictions and mythical
sophistries and thoroughly impossible.' [4] His method
is often to hurl a series of questions at them on the basis
of their theories, which he believes to be unanswerable,
and then crown it with some such explosion as, ' Stop
talking worthless nonsense, O wiseacres, and learn, even
at this late date, to follow the divine oracles and not

---

[1] *Op. cit.* ii. 129 B.   The reference is to Amos 9 [6].
[2] *Op. cit.* ii. 81 B.   [3] *Op. cit.* i. 67 C.   [4] *Op. cit.* i. 56 A.

your own baseless fancies.' [1] Yet it is not in any mere
spirit of scorn that he writes. What hurts him is that
'those who are decked out with the wisdom of this
world, and are confident that by their daring reasoning
they can get hold of its form and position, scoff at all
the divine writing as a collection of myths, slightingly
calling Moses and the prophets, the Lord Christ and the
apostles, idle babblers ; [2] while raising their eyebrows,
as they enunciate a great sophistry, they present as a gift
to the rest of mankind a spherical form and a circular
motion for the heavens, and by geometrical methods
and calculations of stars, and by gambling with words
and by cosmical craft, attempt to grasp the position
and form of the world by means of the solar and lunar
eclipses, leading others astray and being led astray
themselves in maintaining that such phenomena could
not take place in any other kind of form.' [3] He attacks
their statements, sometimes successfully, on the double
ground that what they maintain are ' absurdities in-
consequent and contrary to nature.' [4] What impresses
him, on the other hand, and compels his adherence to
the statements of Scripture rather than to those of the
philosophers, is the attestation of Moses by God Himself [5]
and Jesus Christ, and the agreement with Mosaic statements on the part of other divinely inspired prophets and
apostles. In the face of such a situation, ' in very truth,
to express myself more warmly, I maintain that unless
one fights against God, he will not be able to gainsay
this.' [6]

This ' last of the old Christian geographers, and in a
sense, too, the first of the mediaeval,' as Professor Beazley

---

[1] *Op. cit.* i. 64 A.

[2] Prof. H. A. A. Kennedy points out that the word here rendered
' idle babblers ' (σπερμολόγος) occurs in Acts 17 [18], where, according
to Sir William Ramsay, ' the nearest and most instructive parallel
in modern English life . . . is "Bounder."' (*St. Paul the Traveller*,
p. 243.)

[3] *Op. cit.* i. 59 D.   [4] *Op. cit.* i. 65 A

[5] Cf. Ex. 33 [11]; Deut. 34 [10].   [6] *Op. cit.* iii. 164 B.

has designated him,[1] is further interesting in that he not merely summarises the knowledge of his day, but describes with vividness his own considerable travels. He is also very honest : ' This animal,' he says in description of his drawing of the Monoceros or Unicorn, ' is called the unicorn, but I have never seen it. But I have seen four brazen figures of it set up in the four-towered royal palace in Ethiopia. Wherefore I drew it in this way ' : [2] an account that contrasts sharply with the succinct note upon the Choerelaphus or Hog-deer, which runs, ' The hog-deer I have both seen and eaten.'

To-day the outlook of the astronomer is upon a totally different kind of Universe ; the world of the modern geographer is likewise very unlike the scheme of things detailed by Cosmas. In the opinion of one of the most brilliant of modern investigators, ' the galactic system is more than a hundred thousand times as large as we formerly believed it to be.' [3] Far beyond our earth-moon system, and the solar system itself, the astronomer reaches out through time and space into the complexities of the sidereal system. He presents it to us in the form of a flattened disc or lens, at least 300,000 light-years [4] in diameter and some 6000 in thickness, while grouped around and outside it as possibly dependent sub-systems are the ' globular ' star-clusters. It is estimated that this disc comprises some 1500 million stars, amongst which our system occupies, in the opinion of Professor H. N. Russell, a position which would appear on any page diagram about half way between the centre and the left-hand periphery of the disc.[5] The great mass of the stars goes to compose the Milky Way, constituting that periphery on which we look out, as

[1] C. R. Beazley, *The Dawn of Modern Geography*, i. 33. Elsewhere he refers to him as ' the first scientific geographer of Christendom ' (i. 40).

[2] *Op. cit.* xi. 444 B.

[3] Dr. Harlow Shapley, *Journ. Brit. Astron. Assoc.*, vol. xxviii. p. 149.

[4] A light-year is an astronomical unit of measurement, equivalent to nearly six million million miles, representing the distance traversed by light travelling for a year at the rate of 186,000 miles per second.

[5] Other views place it nearer the centre.

it were, from a position within. The actual centre of
the sidereal system is placed by Shapley in the densely-
crowded constellation Sagittarius. The farthest object
whose distance is known with any real accuracy is the
star-cluster N.G.C. 7006, computed by Shapley to be
220,000 light-years away. That is to say, we see it to-day
as it was 220,000 years ago ; of its present conditions
we have no means of knowing. Some recent research
indicates afresh the possibility of the Milky Way itself
being a vast stellar procession in a spiral of two turns,
and only one of 900,000 other spiral nebulae that have
been observed and catalogued. On the other hand,
Kapteyn's picture of the Milky Way as constituted by
two intermingling star-streams moving in opposite
directions, and probably themselves derived originally
from two or more spiral nebulae, is still the most
generally accepted view.

Overwhelming as these considerations are, it is still
always with a system, or rather a system of systems, that
we find we have to deal—in short, with a Universe, not
with a multiverse. Everywhere the impression left is
of infinite and eternal energy, of unity and of order. The
Universe is a unity in the sense that throughout it we find
the same elements. It is the same Universe because it
is composed of the same matter ; yet amongst these
stars which have been examined spectroscopically no
two have identically the same physical constitution ;
verily, ' one star differeth from another star in glory.' [1]
It is also all related—a connected whole—because it is
all in space, and, *pace* the Relativists, in the same
ether of space. In many of the minds most qualified
to judge, the conclusion has been reached on various
grounds that the sidereal system is finite ; it ' thins
out perceptibly within distances reached by telescopes
of very moderate size.' [2] A corresponding conclusion
has been reached along other lines. ' Though four-

[1] 1 Cor. 15 [41].
[2] J. H. Jeans, ' The Origin of the Solar System,' *Nature*, cxiii. 329.

D

dimensional space-time is of infinite extent, its three-dimensional space section, of which we perceive a small part, is mathematically speaking finite in its volume, and, using Silberstein's value of R, that volume would be something of the order of one thousand million times the size of the galaxy of stars around us.'[1] On the other hand, the fact of the existence of the star-cloud N.G.C. 6822, calculated by Shapley to be about five times as far away again as N.G.C. 7006, as also of the existence of dark obscuring nebulae,[2] serves to keep in mind the enormous difficulty of acquiring the evidence that the sidereal system is finite, even if it were so. In certain regions of the Galaxy the numbers of the stars apparently show a tendency to decrease, but the astronomer can never know how much this fact may be explained by the absorption of light. For aught he knows, behind those seemingly scantier regions there may be an infinite number of stars which are blotted out.

Further, in this sidereal system the direction of evolution, with a few enigmatic exceptions (*e.g.* planetary nebulae, long-period variables, etc.), follows quite definitely the course of increasing density: 'it begins with nebulae of almost incredible tenuity, and ends with solid stars as dense as iron.'[3] It is supposed that, as the result of radiation of energy, the rotating mass of gas composing a regular nebula must shrink, and the rotation becomes more rapid. Up to a certain point the effect of shrinkage can be met by change of shape. In Jeans' words, ' the mass carries the same angular momentum as before, in spite of its reduced size, by the simple expedient of rotating more rapidly, and restores equilibrium by bulging out its equator.'[4] But a point is reached when further shrinkage ' involves an actual break-up of the

---

[1] A. V. Douglas, 'Measuring the Universe,' *Discovery*, vol. v. No. 57. R = curvature of space.
[2] G. E. Hale, *The Depths of the Universe*, chap. ii.
[3] J. H. Jeans, *op. cit.* p. 330.
[4] *Op. cit.* p. 331.

nebula, the excess of the angular momentum beyond that which can be carried by the shrunken mass being thrown off into space by the ejection of matter from the equator of the nebula.' [1] The passage of neighbours, whatever they are, may, it is further supposed, produce tidal irregularities in the shape of the primitive nebula, and mathematical considerations show that ' the ejection of matter will take place from the two antipodal points on the equator at which the tide is highest,' [2]—the actual state of affairs that is disclosed by the typical ' spiral ' nebula, in which are two gigantic arms or filaments, issuing from opposite sides of the nucleus, and consisting of matter flowing out of that nucleus, which itself continues to shrink. Gravitation comes into play, and the gas issuing from an arm breaks off into globular nebulous condensations which represent the first stage in the development of new stars. From a single nebula in this way may be produced millions of stars, which may remain together forming a cluster if the parent was originally sufficiently remote from the main universe of stars, or mingle with the general body.

The great interest of Jeans' investigations, [3] however, lies in the demonstration that while the above account probably represents the course of events in connection with primitive nebulae on the grandest scale, ' a nebula of mass comparable to our sun might go through the same life-history as the bigger nebula until matter began to be thrown off from its equator, but after this the difference of scale would begin to tell, and the subsequent course of events would be widely different. The ejected matter could not condense into filaments, still less into detached globules ; it would merely constitute a diffuse atmosphere surrounding the parent nebula. As such a system shrank by the emission of radiation, the constancy of angular momentum would, at first, merely

---

[1] *Op. cit.* p. 331.   [2] *Op. cit.* p. 331.
   Cf. also his *Problems of Cosmogony and Stellar Dynamics.*

demand that more and more gas should be transferred
from the centre to the atmosphere. But mathematical
investigation shows that in time, after the central star
had shrunk to a certain critical density, perhaps somewhere about one-tenth of that of water, a cataclysmic
period would ensue, from which the mass would emerge
as a binary star — two stars of comparable masses
revolving about one another nearly in contact and in
approximately circular orbits.' [1] Of such binary stars
millions have been recorded, so that this stage in stellar
evolution seems a normal development. The driving-
force in this long process appears as ' increase of rotation
consequent on the shrinkage produced by emission of
radiation. When the shrinkage has proceeded a certain
length, solidification sets in ; the rotation can increase
now no further, and evolution, in the physical sense, stops.
The distance along the course to which any particular
system proceeds depends in effect on the amount of
rotation with which it was originally endowed.' [2]

There is no reason to suppose that many systems
stay out the whole course, and Jeans shows reason for
believing that our sun has never had ' more than a
fraction of the angular momentum necessary for a
rotational break-up into a binary star.' [3] Further, our
solar system exhibits no plane of symmetry such as
would naturally have been maintained had it developed
out of some undisturbed rotating nebular mass. As a
matter of fact, the orbits of nearly all the planets and their
satellites do lie very nearly in one plane, but ' the sun's
axis of rotation is not perpendicular to this plane,' [4]
as would be expected. The sun has its own plane of
symmetry in its equator, which we may naturally suppose
to represent the plane of rotation of the original system,
and this is inclined at an angle of seven degrees to the
plane of the planetary orbits. Now, in striving to
explain the origin of the planets and their satellites—in

[1] *Op. cit.* pp. 335-336.   [2] *Op. cit.* p. 336.
[3] *Op. cit.* p. 336.   [4] *Op. cit.* p. 338.

endeavouring to account for the fact, as Jeans has stated it elsewhere, that ' the earth-moon system is exceptional in the system of the planets, just as the solar system to which it belongs appears to be exceptional, and for aught we know may be unique, in the system of the stars,' [1] having been apparently thrown out of the main line of evolutionary development towards binary formation,—observation gives no aid; at any rate, no system corresponding to our solar system is anywhere visible.[2] The disturbing influence on the planetary orbits is attributed by Jeans to some star or stars passing near our system in some early stage of its thousand, or maybe thousands of millions of years of history, when, being of enormously lower density than to-day and of correspondingly greater size, it was not much beyond the stage of a condensation in the arm of a primitive spiral nebula, and so peculiarly liable to suffer gigantic disruptive tidal effects under the pull of passing stars. A filament of gas set free by such a tidal cataclysm ' might easily be of sufficient substance for its own gravitation to hold it together as a compact whole,' [3] or break up the filament comparatively rapidly into a small number of unequal masses, *i.e.* the planets.[4] On the other hand, if Professor Eddington's conclusion that the luminosity of a star depends almost wholly upon its mass is confirmed, the consequent deduction that the Universe formerly consisted of much more closely packed stars suggests conditions under which the apparently unique method of formation of our solar system may have been more common than has hitherto been supposed. But on the scale of things with which we have here to do,

---

[1] *Problems of Cosmogony and Stellar Dynamics*, p. 290.

[2] While differing from Jeans on several points of detail, Dr. Jeffreys also considers it ' probable that systems of the type of the solar system are the exception in the universe and not the rule.' (*The Earth*, p. 258.)

[3] J. H. Jeans, *Nature*, cxiii, 339.

[4] For further details reference should be made to the works of this investigator, already cited; for a short résumé, see his article ' Cosmogony ' in *Evolution in the Light of Modern Knowledge*.

the normal, when clearly understood, is no less wonderful than the unique, and the unique mayhap owes its temporary significance precisely to the circumstance that it is not clearly understood.

Nevertheless, in all this we seem to move in the region of ultimate forces — Infinite Immeasurable Power or Energy, in virtue of which primitive nebulae or the primitive nebula are invested with an ' amount of rotation,' and something that looks like a directive, if not a selective, factor in the agelong process. There is a permeating unity and strangeness and far-reachingness of influence, like that of causes that simultaneously produce spots on the sun and magnetic disturbances upon the earth. Lalande might still sweep these larger heavens with his telescope and find no sign of God, who is invisible like all the forms of energy of which He is the Ultimate Source, but he could not, with any mental satisfaction, set down the scheme of all these new heavens upon paper, and the *événement* of the process in human minds upon this planet that can weigh the farthest stars and predict their courses, and merely say, ' It has all happened so,' for unreason has never yet produced reason.

In an article on the Ascension,[1] Principal Denney remarked that ' to talk about Copernicanism in this connection, and to object to the whole idea of the Ascension because we cannot put down the heaven into which Jesus entered on a star map, is to misconceive the Resurrection and everything connected with it. The Lord of Glory manifested Himself to His own, and at last put a term to these manifestations in a mode as gracious as it was sublime ; but the whole series of events is one with which astronomy has nothing to do.' There is a very profound sense in which this is undoubtedly true, but the statement takes no account of the fact that the thought of the average man upon this matter, so far as he thinks at all, is not even Copernican : it is

---

[1] *H.D.B.*, i. 161.

crudely Ptolemaic. It further disregards the circumstance that just as we cannot thoroughly understand
a man's religious outlook until we know something also
about his world outlook, so we cannot say that we
really understand his world outlook until we have some
conception of his general astronomical conceptions,
vague as these are inevitably bound to be. In other
words, are the sun, moon, and stars—this sidereal system
that we are just beginning to understand—mere background to human history worked out on a fixed flat
disc whose limits are roughly a thousand miles from
Alexandria in every direction ; or is the earth an element
in that system—necessarily to us the most important
element, yet only an element—whose motions, both in
themselves and in their relations to other heavenly
bodies, compel us to realise that Ptolemaicism and
Copernicanism alike are insufficient as a framework
for a world outlook, and that a religious system, the
setting of some of whose basal conceptions is still that
of the fourth century, is certain, if left confined in
mediaeval thought forms, to prove in the long run more
of a hindrance than a help to the present generation ?
We cannot get away from the fact that in the text-books
of to-day we are taught one astronomy, while the terminology of Scripture in great part depends upon another,
and even mediaeval theology had no conspicuous success
in its attempted development of the old world outlook.
In fact, as E. T. Brewster says, ' our traditional theology
rests on an astronomy which we have not believed for
two hundred years and shall never believe again. Therefore, our religion hangs in the air. That is, in no small
part, what is the matter with us all.' [1]

There are, however, fortunately, more fundamental
aspects of the matter. In the first place, the story of the
Ascension helps us to understand how limited and indeed
misleading are our conceptions in so far as we speak
of the spiritual world as the ' next ' world. In reality,

[1] E. T. Brewster, *The Understanding of Religion*, p. 61.

as Sir Oliver Lodge so rightly urges,[1] there is no ' next '
world, save subjectively. ' The Universe is one : it is
not so much a sequence as a co-existence.' The ' next '
world, *i.e.* the spiritual world, is here and now, surrounding and simultaneous with us who have to live under
strictly limited space-time conditions, until, through the
releasing agency of death, spirits that have laid hold
upon the Eternal, in fuller union with Him, enter upon
an existence in which they can exercise powers, even of
manifestation, transcending those of human life. And,
in the second place, the fact remains that the spiritual
leaders of a people whose religious sensitivities were
the most exquisite that the world has ever known,
took the inherited cosmogony of their racial group,
and in the purified interpretation of it, under the illumination of the inspiring and enlightening Spirit of God,
made of it a vehicle for the proclamation of eternal
truths that are at once independent of the categories
of any age, and yet must be re-presented through those
of each particular age in order to be made real to that
age. No doubt the Universe looked several thousand
times larger in Alexandria than it did in Jerusalem,
but in Judaea were men who had understood the inwardness and meaning of it as no Alexandrian searcher
of the skies had done. The race which has done most
for religion had, in its best days, neither theology nor
philosophy nor science, as we understand these words
to-day, but they knew what religion was. Their hearts
cried out for the living God, and He was found of them.
They used such science, even more than philosophy,
as was open to them, making of it a vehicle, as every
generation must do, for the conveyance of truth as that
was revealed to them. There was in them a sense of
need, a desire that went out to that in the Universe
which, they felt, justified both that Universe and their
place in it, and with which they wished to come into
harmonious relationship ; to this outgoing of the human

[1] *Making of Man*, p. 32.

spirit God made answer.   Finally, the cosmogony of
Scripture is in great part the common-sense outlook of
the pre-scientific age in the modern acceptance of the
term 'science'; it is the cosmogony of the childhood of
the race.   Yet it also corresponds to the science of that
age, for the Creation Narratives embody definite attempts
at explanation of how all things came into being.   At
the same time they show the transforming Spirit of
God at work upon myth and naïve observation, even
as it works upon the heart of man.   The water-lily may
have its roots in the mud, yet through its wider relationships with the water and the air transforms elements
out of the mud into the gracefulness and beauty of
its life.

CHAPTER IV

CREATION, HUMAN AND DIVINE

(a) *Human*

IN thinking of Creation, by which may be understood the bringing into existence of that which apart from the exercise of specific activity would not have existed or begun to be, the human mind quite naturally moves along three different lines, each of which seems to merit the application of the term. We may think, for example, of the process whereby a new life comes into existence, and speak of the creation of a child. More usually the term employed in this sense is procreation, where the prefix has the significance of ' forth.' Such pro-creation or generation, however, is bi-parental, as the biologist says, and in its actual results is more correctly described as reproduction, although on the other hand we must always remember that there is no absolute duplication. The figure of birth in illustration of creation is familiar in Greek and Hebrew thought alike from the earliest times. The Book of Genesis is the book of begetting, both of the inanimate and of the animate. Thus the Second Creation Narrative begins, ' These are the generations of the heavens and of the earth.' [1]

Or we may think of some tool or implement of wood being fashioned under the skilled hand of a craftsman. The whittling and carving of a shepherd's crook out of some specially selected branch of a tree suggests creation in a sense ; and this carpenter-like conception of creation —the forming out of pre-existent material—is also very

---

[1] Gen. 2 [4]; cf. also 5 [1], 6 [9], 10 [1], 11 [10], 11 [27], 25 [12], 25 [19], 36 [1], 37 [2].

old. Yet in both of these instances we feel an insufficiency in the outcome that makes it fall short of our conception of what creation is. That thought includes in some sense the idea of the absolutely new. Thus there was a stage in organic history when as yet there were no birds. The first organism recognisable as a bird was something distinctly new; that kind of life-form had not been in existence before. Again, in the case of the carved crook there is definite manipulation of already existing material other than the agent, whereas a conception which has filtered into the minds of many generations, e.g. of Presbyterians, is that which was summarised in the Answer to Question 9 of the deservedly famous Shorter Catechism of the Westminster Assembly (1648)—' What is the work of creation ? '—which runs, ' The work of creation is God's making all things of nothing, by the word of His power, in the space of six days, and all very good.' For the opening phrase, the sole ' proof-text ' given was Gen. 1 [1].

There is a third and closely related sphere of activity in connection with which the conception of creation inevitably suggests itself, viz. the production of a poem or other work of art. Perhaps the former corresponds most closely to the idea of creation as we ordinarily think of it—visibility or materialisation or objective expression of a thought synchronising with the thought itself : ' He spake and it was done,' [1] or made. For to us moderns creation is essentially an energetic process, and even in the physical world it is an expression of something, e.g. a materialisation of energy. In the spiritual world, or the world of mind—in the so-called ' creative imagination '—the process is still energetic, perhaps to some degree even in the same kind of way ; but it is even more an expression of something, and

---

[1] Ps. 33 [9]. Cf. also of Thoth who made the world by speaking it into existence—' That which flows from his mouth, happens, and that which he speaks, comes into being.' (Quoted in E.R.E., iv. 227, from P. Le Page Renouf, *Origin and Growth of Religion of Ancient Egypt.*)

coherent, continuous, logical in that expression. The poem or picture is a realisation of the power—of the very being—of the poet or artist ; it is an expression of himself. In the previous examples, likewise, we have to come back eventually to mind operative at some stage in the process, or continuously throughout. Thus, in the case of the carved crook, the idea of the whole lay in a mind which conceived and controlled the entire activity. In the case of procreation, the material, to begin with, is part of the very agents themselves, but the idea of the child again lies first in the minds of its parents.

If, however, we examine a little more closely, something of the sharpness in our conceptions of creation begins to disappear. Thus Evolution has taught us that while, when we look at the record of life over long stretches, there certainly was a period previous to which there were no birds, yet birds did not come into existence, like Athena from the head of Zeus, with full-fledged avian equipment, but came to be what in the end we recognise as typical birds by a slow process of development, with modification, from a reptilian stock. Organic creation, that is to say, so far as we have actual experience of it, is transformation or transmutation of something previously existing, by addition, or it may be in some rare cases by subtraction, of germinal elements or genes. It is important to note this element of addition—the result ultimately of some definite environmental relationship expressing itself in a modification of the germ cell [1]— for it disposes straight away of the misapprehension that may follow the use of the term 'potentiality': evolution does not proceed *in vacuo*. There is also the element of 'emergence' to be taken into account at various stages—the fact that the qualities, previously unknown, displayed by some new integral entity, cannot always be wholly explained as mere fresh resultants of qualities and

[1] For further data in connection with this vexed biological question, reference may be made to *The Spiritual Interpretation of Nature*, pp. 170-173.

properties that were familiar before.[1]   Creative transformations, whether physical or spiritual, are ultimately
environmental in origin, the result of stimulation, through
directly energetic relationships or spiritual suggestion,
working through, or upon, pliable matter or responsive
organism.   As the mind puts itself in direct relationship
with its environment, physical, spiritual, or social, there
come about definite enrichment and moulding that are
something more than the mere activity of the self.   For
the mind that is in living relationship with that truest
and most Ultimate Environment which is God, this may
well result in the awakening of creative genius.   On every
hand we are driven back to mental activity as the most
creative process that we know—that one which supplies
most directly a satisfactory idea of creation, particularly
in the form of Imagination.

Inasmuch as man himself is a genetic product of the
evolutionary process as we know it, his creative moments
in the realm of imagination may reasonably be expected
to yield some analogies however faint that may perhaps
aid our finite minds in attempting to represent the
infinite.   And, as a matter of fact, it is really instructive
in this connection to listen to the testimony of living
creative artists themselves, and attempt to understand
something of the conditions under which their work is
done, as also to enter into their conception of the character
of the creative movement.   It has been possible to
set down the following experiences only as the result
of sympathetic and generous co-operation on the part
of those to whom application for assistance was made.
So Mr. John Duncan, R.S.A., a well-known representative
of the Scottish imaginative school, represented the
situation as follows :—

' Plato says somewhere that man has a double origin,
that he is a creature of heavenly as well as of earthly
birth, and I believe that Art too has a double source :
one stream coming directly from man's centre meets

[1] Cf. C. Lloyd Morgan, *Emergent Evolution*, passim.

another from Nature. Sometimes the child of the
union, Art, favours the father, and sometimes the
mother.

' All artists speak of a certain feeling of excitement
accompanying the inception of the idea—for the first
impulse comes from within—and then they express it
differently. But you *have* to work or draw. An itch
or desire possesses you ; it is compelling—this force that
moves you to expression. There is nothing vague or
unimportant about the feeling ; you are full of excitement
about it. I just start to draw and the thing comes. The
first scratch is the whole thing ; everything else is detail.

' When the idea is very vivid, the expression of it
is a finished thing, and you do not touch it.' And then
the artist told of a waking vision of a radiant figure that
had once come to him, exalting him, taking him out of
himself, and giving him a new conception of Beauty.
' It was so vital—an objective vision of a being, standing
by something that looked like a loom. The figure was
very detailed, yet left no impression of sex about it.
I remember in particular the feeling of joy and uplift
that remained with me for some days after, as if some
good fortune had come to me. The vision was not
simply glimpsed and forgotten. What made the special
impression was the circumstance that I had always
adored Botticelli and Burne-Jones, but this vision
liberated me from the lachrymose and devitalised art of
these painters : hence the feeling of surprise and also
of joy and liberation. I did not attempt to reproduce
the figure at the time, feeling that it was beyond me to do
so. I thought, "If I try to paint it, the process of painting
will shut it out of my mind—come between me and the
vision." Years after I did make the attempt, but with
no success. Very often the idea at which the artist tries
to work is something vaguely seen—glimpsed. But this
particular vision was perfect ; there was nothing for
me to do. On the other hand, you think about the
glimpsed idea, and more and more comes ; it grows.

' Modern painting is not very creative. It is in the earlier stages of Art that you find it at its creative stage. When religious life is at its fullest—when, for example, the Greeks really believed in their gods, then they reproduced them in great works of Art. Creative Art in Greece had really expended itself before Pheidias, but he still had the fire at his heart ; he still believed in the gods when his contemporaries in Art no longer did so. The moral energy that burned in his Zeus and his Athena was something that belonged to an earlier age, which his contemporaries had lost. He was a master of his technique, with the old fire at his heart.

' The artist must identify himself with his work—the object of his endeavour. His knowledge of Nature must be something very deep and long-standing. In Japan some artists paint merely *one* thing, *e.g.* cherry blossoms, and keep to that. While the artist's knowledge of Nature must be very intimate and deep, yet he does not necessarily paint directly from Nature. Even when his inspiration comes from Nature, he reshapes it in his own spirit ; from Nature to the human spirit and back to its manifestation in a material form—the complete circuit is necessary. The great artists have learned their facts from Nature, but draw from memory or sketches. Michael Angelo had made such a practical study of human anatomy that he did not need to draw from sketches ; he knew the machine of the human body so thoroughly that he rarely worked directly from the model, doing it by a species of unconscious memory. Even when engaged on landscape work to-day, a man will spend perhaps three months amidst the scenery that has appealed to him, and then return to the city for the other nine, drawn indeed by the need for human society but also by the necessity of getting away from the compelling scene, in order to be able to think over it and, so to speak, digest it. There are the two types of artist : he who, sympathetic and reflective, holds the mirror up to Nature, and he who stamps his own values on things, and creates the type that he admires and desires.'

Even more emphatically is any mere imitative theory of Art rejected by another distinctive artist — Miss Katharine Cameron, A.R.E.—and the emphasis laid on the creative side. 'You see something. The beauty of it fills you with enthusiasm, and the enthusiasm inspires you to paint it. I once saw a landscape of mountain and loch in the West Highlands of Scotland at dawn. It was like a pearl in all its soft beauty. The hour was 5.45 A.M. No one was about. It was an extraordinarily exquisite morning under which the whole landscape was enchanting and inspiring. I felt I must grasp it, but it is impossible to make a transcript of anything so fleeting. The enchantment increases and inspires a rush of creative work. I must take down what I can, and do the rest from memory. In such ways can poems be painted. Or I may see the peak of some great mountain appearing from the mist, blue as a hyacinth. I must paint it, but it is gone before I can complete it, so again memory must finish the picture.

'Great scenes in Nature must be studied constantly. It is best not to move about too much, but to become steeped in one district, beautiful and congenial, or in a flower, such as the rose. The moods of flowers and of landscape must be studied from early morning till evening—in every light that one can think of, in every season that is beautiful. It seems to me that, with the one rare exception of Turner, the greatest painters painted at home and in their own country. The artist thus becomes able to take beauty of varying character from the country he knows best. He becomes accustomed to extract the very essence of beauty out of his environment. Great art is always simple and sincere; it eliminates the unnecessary or the trivial.

'There are passages in Whistler's *Ten o'Clock* that express what I mean. "The artist is born to pick, and choose, and group with science, these elements, that the result may be beautiful—as the musician gathers his notes, and forms his chords, until he bring forth from chaos glorious harmony.

' " To say to the painter, that Nature is to be taken as she is, is to say to the player, that he may sit on the piano. . . . .

' " To him (the artist) her secrets are unfolded, to him her lessons have become gradually clear.   He looks at her flower, not with the enlarging lens, that he may gather facts for the botanist, but with the light of the one who sees in her choice selection of brilliant tones and delicate tints, suggestions of future harmonies. . . .

' " Through his brain, as through the last alembic, is distilled the refined essence of that thought which began with the gods, and which they left him to carry out." [1]

' Surely in all this, Art is somewhat like Poetry.

' A lovely line in a poem may be an inspiration, for it opens a gate, and your brain, as it were, runs down the pathway.   Take, for example, William Blake's line, " The honeysuckle sleeping on the oak."   To me this suggests a dusky woodland, through which the wind sighs, swaying the honeysuckle against the trees.   Sometimes great art is produced by impulse.   Sometimes the impulse is hewed or modelled into shape by thought.   I mean that at times one works out the idea in one's brain until it begins to revolve with such rapidity that fire is created, and then the careful thought becomes an insistent desire to record in line and colour the idea which has grown in power and speed.

' You cannot do great work consciously ; you have to forget yourself.   You think the whole thing out first. In the production of a picture, three-quarters of the time may be spent in thinking about it, and a quarter in actually painting it.   Of course, in water-colour painting you have to be quicker than with oils, hence the liquidity and transparency of such pictures.   Yet everything comes from thinking : you must think hard or you cannot

[1] *The Gentle Art of Making Enemies*, pp. 142-146.

E

do good work, or anything that will abide. The great artists of old must all have been great thinkers, and time was nothing to them. In those days also a stern apprenticeship eliminated the unfit.'

In the realm of music the situation is not otherwise with regard to the conditions under which real creative work is done. ' I incline to think,' said Professor Tovey,[1] ' that the conditions of artistic productivity have very little to do with the merit of the result, beyond what the worst rubbish produced under healthy conditions, i.e. in good mental athletic form, has in common with great art. Arnold Schönberg has written a treatise on Harmony in which he puts his own development on a theoretical basis (quite as arbitrarily an *a priori* affair as the obsolete theories he very rightly ridicules)—but he falls back upon the undoubtedly correct theory that the only real thing is *der Einfall*—the idea that comes into your head. Everything you work upon afterwards, I would add, is of the nature of confirming and refreshing *den Einfall*, and the genius is the person whose afterwork, though it may expand or change the first *Einfall* to unrecognisability, does not falsify it or drop to the plane of a sense of duty. Beethoven's innumerable sketches, and his frequent starting from a very commonplace sketch, afterwards refined to his most original ideas, are quite consistent with this view : the *Einfall* is a soul waiting for a body—a mood which may be conveyed in terms of art. Any old cliché may serve to mark out the region of the requisite terms ; and some of the sublimest flights of genius have consisted in recognising that in this or that case the oldest cliché is exactly right as it stands. No safe inference, therefore, can be based on the apparent methods of great composers as shown in the way their works are written. The writing of music, plus the getting it into terms which can be played as well as written, is probably the most voluminous technical

[1] Donald Francis Tovey, Reid Professor of Music in Edinburgh University, and well-known composer.

process in all the fine arts ; and the composer's problem
is to ensure that every stage of this process shall keep
him realising *Einfälle* the whole time.   Hence the distinction between a sound and an unsound way of revising
one's work.   A work needing revision (*i.e.* left in a state
in which much had to be executed by logical inference—
always a hopelessly loose method in the fine arts—
instead of having time to " wait for inspiration ")
can always be perfected so long as the composer is still
in sympathy with its style.   He has only to do, on a
higher intellectual plane, but on paper, what he would do
in conducting a rehearsal by an orchestra that couldn't
read perfectly at sight—remove whatever was not an
Einfall, and substitute something that does *einfallen*.
The only difficulty comes when he encounters an *Einfall*
(instead of an absence of idea) of which he is ashamed.
He must then choose between two evils, (1) the danger
of a conflict of styles, and (2) leaving the original *Einfall*
alone.   The one inadmissible thing is to do something
merely inferentially right with his greater knowledge ;
and, whatever he really does, that is what he will be
accused of doing.   For he alone can judge (and that
solely by his own sensations) whether he is or is not
in that mental athletic form in which one has *Einfälle*.
Other people call his work " inspired " when they like
it, and " uninspired " when they do not.   What seems
to me quite certain is that the worst of best-sellers owes
his or her popularity to inspiration (the fountainhead,
therefore, flooding a large and low-lying tract) by just
the same mental musculature as that by which Bach
earns his immortality ; and so, I suppose, if you boiled
it down to ultimate shreds, whenever two people get the
length of understanding each other, it is by inspiration.

' In all musical teaching and analysis, I confine myself
rigorously to the facts of the form.   A musical sentence
in a piece of instrumental music is of an obviously
rhetorical form, but that kind of form cannot be
dissociated from the art of composition as a whole.

What Professor Bradley says of poetry in his essay on
" Poetry for Poetry's Sake ' is true of music. The
meaning and the sounds are one. You cannot separate form and substance. There is no such thing
as mere form, for all form is expressive. Form and
substance or meaning are one thing from different points
of view. Just as in a poem the true content and the true
form neither exist nor can be imagined apart, so in a
musical composition it is not a matter of sound on one
side and a meaning on the other, but of " expressive
sound." When music, like poetry, is true to its idea,
you have identity of form and content. Poetry, in so
far as it succeeds, completely digests its material, and
we realise the folly of trying to separate the meaning
from the poem. I am opposed to the pure formalist
heresy—to the idea that the meaning of the poem would
be the same if you turned it into prose. It is simply
an illusion that because musical forms can only be
described in technical language, the technical description
gives much information. The information is of the order
of a mathematical demonstration of the shape of a
generalised human face. People really remain at present
incapable of judging of the art of musical composition
except in narrowly stereotyped forms. Until you can
judge composition in music as you would judge it in
prose, you have no criterion at all. Music is a rhetorical
art, and all the genuine new art-forms are going to be
worked out first, and un-" absolutely," in the laboratory
of drama, or of otherwise setting words to music. To
fall back on descriptive titles for instrumental music is
a natural symptom of order in the chaos of a transition
period. Half the bad things in music have come from
the *a priori* " art for art's sake " idea. As in science,
you get much further on a basis of observation, and it is
the biggest stimulus towards generalising. Every art
tends to make itself free, but that is not best done simply
by the process of cutting adrift.

' To try to describe the conditions under which actual

creation or composition takes place, is like trying to
remember a dream. Sometimes one musical idea can
be traced to another musical idea. Effects in Nature
also prompt ideas : thus the rising of a particularly
gibbous moon suggested the idea of soft trumpets in a
certain passage in one of my symphonies. Or once again,
the experience of standing on a hill in an extremely high
wind, and happening to think of Beethoven's D Major
Trio, reproduced itself in a movement in another work ;
but which of the two elements in the experience was
the primary cause would be impossible to say. Musical
ideas might become symbolical (using " symbolical " in
a proper psychological sense, *i.e.* not as the conscious
devices of the composers, but as Freudians discuss
dreams) to any extent. On the other hand, the more
significant symbolism is in music, the less you can trace
the etymology, as it were, of a musical phrase or idea,
and life isn't long enough to explain the associations.
You really would be at a loose end in trying to do
this, although occasionally you do come across enormously interesting origins. Thus there is a passage in
Mendelssohn's Letters where he says something to
this effect : " People say that words are definite and
music is indefinite : I say it is just the other way about." [1]
And there is also Beethoven's self-revealing comment
on his Pastoral Symphony : " Mehr Ausdruck der
Empfindung als Malerei." '

[1] The reference is to *Briefe aus den Jahren 1833 bis 1847*, by F. M.
Mendelssohn, p. 337, where, in answer to a correspondent who had
asked what some of the ' Songs without Words ' meant, the composer
replied : ' Es wird so viel über Musik gesprochen, und so wenig gesagt.
. . . Die Leute beklagen sich gewöhnlich, die Musik sei so vieldeutig ;
es sei so zweifelhaft was sie sich dabei zu denken hätten, und die Worte
verstände doch ein Jeder. Mir geht es aber gerade umgekehrt. Und
nicht blos mit ganzen Reden, auch mit einzelnen Worten, auch die
scheinen mir so vieldeutig, so unbestimmt, so missverständlich im
Vergleich zu einer rechten Musik, die Einem die Seele erfüllt mit
tausend bessern Dingen, als Worten. Das was mir eine Musik ausspricht
die ich liebe, sind mir nicht zu unbestimmte Gedanken, um sie in
Worte zu fassen, sondern zu bestimmte.' The whole letter repays
perusal.

Something of the same sense of illumination or revelation, and of being near to the heart of things, would also
seem to be characteristic of creation in poetry. ' There
are moments in life,' said Mr. Alfred Noyes, ' when you
feel, as in your deepest conscience, the touch of the
Eternal ; when out of some incident or clash of incidents,
or the silent majestic drama of Nature, the Divine Reason
seems to shine, and for a moment the Universe explains
itself. To every one such moments come : it is only
a question of the power of expressing the experience.
It is this experience that gives real significance to the
phrase, " the artistic conscience," over and above its
technical application. It is just when such a creative
moment comes that the task of the poet begins. His
problem, as Browning said,[1] is to put the infinite into
the finite. The poet who has once caught these glimpses
has the supreme concern of giving them such form that
they will be visible to other people. He is, in Dante's
words, " the scribe of Love ; and, when He breathes,
takes up his pen ; and, as He dictates, writes." [2] You
might almost say, modifying the line in the *Midsummer
Night's Dream*, he " gives to a spiritual everything a
local habitation." [3]

' The chief necessity for the poet is to be in touch with
the reality and its laws through which alone that Voice
is heard—in the city as on the mountain or by the sea.
If his mind is full of trivialities, it is fatal so far as poetry
is concerned. The arrival of these creative moments
is totally unexpected. The occasions may even be during
something so apparently commonplace as riding on the
top of a 'bus. Once when I happened to go on a 'bus
ride into the country, a young man evidently in an
advanced state of tuberculosis was helped on to the

---

[1] Letter, quoted in biography by Mrs. Sutherland-Orr.
[2] *Purgatorio*, canto xxiv. lines 52-54.
[3]   As imagination bodies forth
The forms of things unknown, the poet's pen
Turns them to shapes, and gives to airy nothing
A local habitation and a name.—Act v. sc. i.

'bus by his wife, who also had to look after two little children. There was, as it happened, only room for one on the top, and after his wife had helped her husband up, the conductor, somewhat harshly, sent her below with the two children. Later they were able to join him on the top. When they came to the point where they had apparently arranged to have a meal in a field, the conductor helped the sick man off, then dived back under the steps leading to the top, and, producing an orange, went after the sick man once again, saying, " Do you like oranges, friend ? " The incident moved me to expression in "The Conductor." [1]

' The only things that interest one from the point of view of writing are those things that present themselves as images of something much bigger—in short, of eternal, spiritual things. One sees them often in Nature. So an old sailor holding up bread to the gulls at the Serpentine—this picture of a city dweller pining for the sea, and happy in the discovery of his friends of the sea—suggested to me the exile from the spiritual world longing for that world, and envying the little things with wings.[2] So also the subject of Dick Turpin's Ride from London to York, proposed as the subject of a poem, seemed all unpromising until the idea came to me of the famous highwayman as pursued and overtaken by *himself*. I saw him riding "like a dark thief in the night," arriving at the gates of York only to meet himself —" Thou has outstript all but me." ' In glimpses such as these, in nearness to Reality, in the sensitivity of mind that responds to the ultimate truth in things, lies the real difference between true poetry and the machine-made thing. In his most creative moods the poet feels that he is directly but an agent, whose source of inspiration is other than himself. Yet these ideas grow and develop in his mind in the degree in which they represent living truth, and are nourished by contact with reality.

[1] *Songs of Shadow-of-a-Leaf*, p. 53.
[2] ' Seagulls on the Serpentine,' *op. cit.* p. 81.

In the authorised English translation of the works of
Nietzsche there is given in what is his autobiography,
'*Ecce Homo,*' [1] the following description of the manner
in which he experienced the creative activity of the poet.
It is to be remembered that he conceived that the
world is to be justified only as an aesthetic phenomenon. Speaking of the origin of his work, *Thus spake
Zarathustra*, probably the most popular and best known
of his writings, he says : ' The fundamental idea of
the work, the *Eternal Recurrence*, the highest formula
of a Yea-saying to life that can ever be attained, was first
conceived in the month of August 1881. . . . It was
on these two roads that all *Zarathustra* came to me,
about all Zarathustra himself as a type—I ought rather
to say that it was on these walks that he waylaid me. . . .

' In order to understand this type, you must first
be quite clear concerning its fundamental physiological
condition : this condition is what I call *great healthiness*.

' The idea of revelation, in the sense that something
which profoundly convulses and upsets one becomes
suddenly visible and audible with indescribable certainty
and accuracy—describes the simple fact. One hears—
one does not seek ; one takes—one does not ask who
gives : a thought suddenly flashes up like lightning, it
comes with necessity, without faltering—I have never
had any choice in the matter. There is an ecstasy so
great that the immense strain of it is sometimes relaxed
by a flood of tears, during which one's steps now involuntarily rush and anon involuntarily lag. There is
the feeling that one is utterly out of hand, with the
very distinct consciousness of an endless number of fine
thrills and titillations descending to one's very toes ;—
there is a depth of happiness in which the most painful
and gloomy parts do not act as antitheses to the rest,
but are produced and required as necessary shades of
colour in such an overflow of light. There is an instinct

---

[1] The references, for which I am indebted to Prof. John A. MacIntosh,
are to pp. 96 ff.

for rhythmic relations which embraces a whole world
of forms (length, the need of a wide embracing rhythm,
is almost the measure of the force of an inspiration, a
sort of counterpart to its pressure and tension). Everything happens quite involuntarily, as if in a tempestuous
outburst of freedom, of absoluteness, of power and
divinity. The involuntary nature of the figures and
similes is the most remarkable thing ; one loses all
perception of what is imagery and metaphor ; everything seems to present itself as the readiest, the truest,
and simplest means of expression. It actually seems,
to use one of Zarathustra's own phrases, as if things
came to one, and offered themselves as similes. (" Here
do all things come caressingly to thy discourse and
flatter thee, for they would fain ride upon thy back.
On every simile thou ridest here unto every truth. Here
fly open unto thee all the speech and word shrines of the
world, here would all existence become speech, here
would all Becoming learn of thee how to speak.") *This
is my experience and inspiration.'*

These accounts which come from very different quarters
yet have certain elements in common. There is agreement
that in the highest forms of Art we are face to face with
that which is not so much imitation as interpretation,
and definitely involves creation, — as when an artist
studying some deep set river valley in varying lights,
at different hours of the day, from points now higher up,
now lower down, so that his foreground varies it may be in
relation to some bend in its course, yet in the end succeeds
in portraying something which is not any one of these
particular impressions, but rather a combination or
synthesis of them all, which commands instantaneous
recognition as having ' caught the spirit ' of the valley.
There is also the testimony to the external or environmental stimulus, to the overwhelming possession and
loving compulsion of the creator by the creative impulse,
to the un-selfconscious character of the operation, to the
sense of wholeness and indivisibility in the perfect,

finished thing, to the ecstasy and feeling of uplift in completion of the toil as when ' the morning stars sang together and all the sons of God shouted for joy,' [1] what time the foundations of the earth were laid. The satisfaction, the joy, in such creatorhood is its own sufficient reward.

and (b) Divine

In thinking of Creation, however, the mind inevitably turns, sooner or later, to the two Narratives in Genesis. Of these, the Second (Gen. $2^{4b}-3^{24}$) is the older, the simpler, the more vivid, and the more direct. According to its account, at the time when Jahveh ' made ' earth and heaven, the former was barren and dry, for ' Jahveh had not sent rain upon the earth, and there was no man to till the ground. But a stream used to come up from the earth, and water the whole face of the ground.' [2] As a result, but also under the direct agency of Jahveh, a beautiful garden or park appeared, fit home for the man, beasts, and birds whom He had alike ' moulded out of the ground.' The setting of the picture is perhaps suggested by the Bedouin outlook on the world—an oasis in the desert, the home and resort of life and civilisation as they knew it. The freedom, warmth, and personal relationships of such a life are reflected even in the literary style. The conception of the Creation of Man—for earth and heaven are assumed as already in existence, and the cosmogonic element is of the slightest—is very simple and naïve. Jahveh creates man out of the damp dust of the ground as the potter fashions a vessel out of the clay. He breathes into man's nostrils the breath of life, and he becomes a living being. The leading suggestion is that nothing in the very natural sequence

---

[1] Job 38 [7]. Cf. also *Timaeus*, Jowett's trans., iii. 456, ' When the father and creator saw the creature which he had made moving and living . . . he rejoiced.'
[2] Based on trans. by A. R. Gordon, *The Early Traditions of Genesis*, p. 233. Cf. also T. K. Cheyne, *E.B.*, i. 949.

of events has merely happened so ; it is all the doing of Jahveh alone, all orderly and progressive.

The First Narrative (Gen. 1-2 [4a]) is different in style and character, though not in main tendency and purpose. If the older Narrative—that from the Jahvistic source designated J—may be dated from somewhere in the kingdom of Judah about 850 B.C., the other—that from the so-called Priestly Code (P)—was only committed to writing some four centuries later, although the oral tradition is much older. It is from a source that always tends to be schematic and precise, orderly and dignified in its statements, but with less glow of human feeling. The conception of God in this later Narrative is more abstract and transcendent than in the earlier one, where He is represented in a quite anthropomorphic manner, entering into free and friendly relations with His creatures. The First Narrative details a progressive, punctuated, stately sweep of creative activity. ' In the beginning,' we may read with Professor A. R. Gordon,[1] ' God fashioned the heavens and the earth. Now (before it was fashioned into shape) the earth was waste and void, and darkness lay upon the face of the abyss, and the spirit of God brooded over the face of the waters.' In the beginning, that is to say, of that phase or economy of things which has culminated in the appearance of man, God fashioned the heavens and the earth, the latter, previous to this particular active divine movement, being a waste, formless mass, thought of as engulfed in the primordial watery Deep (abyss), the whole enveloped in darkness. It is to this primordial relationship of the elemental earth and sea that the somewhat over-driven term Chaos is applied,[2] for it is apparent from the circle of ideas reflected in that very remarkable commentary upon this Narrative, viz. Psalm 104, that the earth when ' covered with the deep as with a garment ' was figured as possessing developed physical features ;

---

[1] *Op. cit.* p. 245.
[2] A view that seems supported by Is. 45 [18].

'the waters stood above the mountains.'[1] Creation, in the First Narrative, then, consists to some degree, at any rate, of separation and differentiation of what is already existent. Quite evidently, therefore, this Creation Narrative does not refer to any absolute beginning. It starts at a certain point in what, for all that is said, may be an infinite and eternal process.

It has been maintained[2] that the idea of absolute creation (*i.e.* creation out of nothing) 'appears to have been a peculiarity of Christian thought,' and further that 'the idea of absolute creation, which is implicit in the highest teaching of the Hebrew prophets, is entirely absent from the philosophical reflection of the Greeks.' Both statements seem open to modification, particularly if under 'Christian thought' is included Biblical statement. According to Skinner, the sense of the word (*bara'*), usually translated 'create,' 'stops short of *creatio ex nihilo*—an idea first explicitly occurring in 2 Mac. 7 [28].'[3] The word is used many times in the Old Testament,[4] but never with the sense 'out of nothing,' although always of God in the originative effortless production of something new. Thus in the obviously poetic passage, 'I am Jehovah, and there is none else. I form the light and create darkness : I make peace and create evil ; I am Jehovah that doeth all these things,'[5] although the

---

[1] Ps. 104 [6].

[2] *E.g.* by W. R. Matthews, *Studies in Christian Philosophy*, pp. 194-196 ; cf. also J. Oswald Dykes, *The Divine Worker in Creation and Providence*, chap. iii.

[3] J. Skinner, *I.C.C.*, 'Genesis,' p. 15; apparently the etymology of the word suggests the meaning to *cut, carve*, or *hew*. For *creatio ex nihilo*, cf. also *Pastor of Hermas*, 2 Com. I. E. Hatch (*The Influence of Greek Ideas and Usages upon the Greek Church*, pp. 195-197) seems to attribute the idea to Basilides the Gnostic. For a discussion of the whole question, cf. A. S. Pringle-Pattison, *The Idea of God*, Lect. xvi., and C. M. Walsh, *The Doctrine of Creation*.

[4] Is. 45 [6, 7] ; cf. also 40 [26, 28], 42 [5], 45 [12, 18] ; Ps. 104 [30], etc.

[5] Is. 45 [6, 7]. Professor J. E. M'Fadyen informs me that the word rendered 'evil' is better translated 'disaster.' The writer is making a metaphysical point out of what he probably knew as historical fact. The real interest of the Hebrews was in facts; hence the very large proportion of history, compared with other forms of literature, in the

idea certainly is that there is no kind of existence which is not ultimately the result of the creative power of a Sovereign God, there is no suggestion of creation out of nothing ; the idea of absolute creation is nowhere explicitly or implicitly stated in Scripture.[1] We owe the development of the doctrine to St. Augustine, who built it into a scheme, although statements of it are found even earlier, *e.g.* in Irenaeus.[2] In support of the second statement, Professor Matthews quotes from Brandis to the effect that ' the notion of absolute creation is unknown to Plato, as it is to all Grecian and Roman antiquity,' [3] a position that seems somewhat too uncompromising in view of such passages as the following in the *Sophist*, put in the mouth of the Stranger : ' We said, if you remember the beginning of our discussion, that every power which is the cause of that which formerly was not, afterwards coming into being, was creative. . . . All living things that die and all plants, all that springs upon the earth from seeds and roots, and all lifeless bodies, whether capable or not of being melted, that exist as conglomerates in the earth—surely we must say that it was by the creative agency of none other than God that they, which formerly were not, afterwards came into being. Surely this view is simply that which is commonly held and expressed. . . . We, I suppose, and the other living things and the natural materials out of which they are composed, fire, water, and all their kin, these, we know, and every species of them, have come into existence by the activity of God.' [4] It may

Bible. The Hebrews found God in the facts of history rather than through finely-spun metaphysical theories.

[1] Heb. 11 [3] simply means that the visible has its ultimate origin in the invisible. On the basis of such passages as Rom. 11 [36], 1 Cor. 8 [6] and 11 [12], it might even, perhaps, be maintained that a doctrine of emanation is more Biblical than a doctrine of creation out of nothing.

[2] Cf. M. L. Burton, *The Problem of Evil*, pp. 14-18, 57-60, for the principal passages in the writings of St. Augustine. For Irenaeus, cf. *Haer.* II. x. 3 and 4 : (reference in W. R. Matthews, *op. cit.*).

[3] *Op. cit.* p. 195.

[4] The references are to 265 B, C ; 266 A. For the translation I am indebted to Prof. H. J. Rose.

perhaps be urged that the first of these passages indicates no more than that something which was, for example, a tree after the action of creative power, was not a tree previous to that exercise of power, and that there is no positive suggestion of *creatio ex nihilo* ; that in the second passage the phrase ' which formerly were not ' likewise implies no necessary conception of creation out of nothing ; and that in the third passage the phrase ' have come into existence ' means no more than ' have come into their present state of existence.' But if this be so, there does not appear any valid reason for interpreting such a Scriptural passage as Gen. 1 [1] in any different way. Indeed, the famous ' probable explanation ' of creation given in the *Timaeus*, where a disordered protyle is represented as already in existence, really corresponds in some respects to the situation as viewed by the writer of the First Narrative in Genesis,[1] and may perhaps be supposed to refer in either case to the beginning of a later phase in the process.

None the less, ' Chaos,' in the Creation Narratives, is conceived of as so subject to the control of the Sovereign God that if we elect to speculate about its origin, of which nothing is said in the text, we can only represent it as in some manner dependent upon God, pliable and responsive to His will. The actual creative process is associated in the First Narrative with two types of manifestation of the Infinite Divine Energy. The ' Spirit of God '—His energising, life-giving Power— is spoken of as ' brooding over the face of the Deep,' [2] awakening in the lifeless mass the springs of life and movement. There may be a suggestion of the widespread conception of the world-egg in the phrase, but the word translated ' brooding ' is also rendered ' hover,' as of an eagle over her young,[3] which suggests something

---

[1] As indeed some of the Early Church Fathers, *e.g.* Justin Martyr and Clement of Alexandria, recognised. (For references cf. *E.R.E.*, art. ' Creation,' iv. 229.)

[2] Gen. 1 [2] ; cf. Is. 40 [12, 13].   [3] Deut. 32 [11].

akin to the modern idea of vibration—rapid motion
without change of position.[1] The second type of manifestation is through the ' word ' of God, who speaks and
the thing is done,[2] thus emphasising ' the effortless
expression of His thought and purpose,' [3] even when, as
in the case of the firmament, the two great lights, the
sea-monsters, and the beasts of the earth, it is also stated
that God ' made ' or ' fashioned ' them.[4] In the mind of
the writer the relation between God and Nature is of the
closest ; the order of Nature is simply the efficacious
expression of the Divine wisdom and will.[5] When the
earth ' puts forth verdure,' or ' brings forth living
creatures after their kind,' [6] it is God who is the efficient
agent. Whether regarded in terms of natural process
or direct action, Creation, in the view of the First Narrative, is in effect the result of the ' Word ' or expressed
thought and will of an omnipotent God, and in this basal
idea both Narratives agree. It may be a universe of
discrete elements and sharply distinguished contrasts ;
the creative activity is that of God.

In the fact of this close creative relationship of God
to Nature, as also of God to man, is to be found the
explanation of the singular *rapport* between Nature and
man that is so much in evidence in the Hebrew literature. God is the author of Nature, and so must have
given of Himself in her, and the Old Testament writers,
being poets, attribute life to the earth and appeal to it

[1] In *Bible and Spade*, pp. 53-59, Professor J. P. Peters reaffirms the
translation already given by him in ' Cosmogony and Cosmology '
(*E.R.E.* iv. 154) : ' the wind of God was rushing upon the face of the
waters,' which harmonises with a causal factor in the annual disappearance of the Tigris-Euphrates inundations. (See *infra*, p. 82.)

[2] Ps. 33 [9] ; Heb. 11 [3]. In 1 Kings 13 [9] the ' Word of the Lord ' is
almost hypostatised. The Hebrews were not philosophically inclined,
and between this and their comparative lack of vocabulary, what
appear to be inconsistencies in statement occasionally occur. Cf. also
p. 59, n. 1.

[3] J. Skinner, *op. cit.* p. 7.

[4] Gen. i. [7, 16, 21, 25]. Cf. Ps. 121 [2], 146 [5-6] ; Prov. 3 [19, 20] ; Jer. 51 [15].

[5] Cf. Ps. 104, 136 [5] ; Prov. 8 [22-32] ; Job 28 [23ff.]

[6] Gen. 1 [11, 24].

as a living thing.[1] They think of it as sensitive and
sympathetic, and so responding to the divine appeal,
and sharing in the varying fortunes of man. ' For ye
shall go out with joy, and be led forth with peace : the
mountains and the hills shall break forth before you
into singing, and all the trees of the field shall clap their
hands.' [2] Similarly the earth reflects varying phases
of human distress in face of man's failure or the divine
wrath. ' The earth is utterly broken, the earth is clean
dissolved, the earth is moved exceedingly. The earth
shall stagger like a drunken man, and shall be moved
to and fro like a hut.' [3] The same point of view domin-
ates the minds of some of the New Testament writers.
So St. Paul speaks quite definitely of the sympathetic
co-experience of Nature with man. He does not think
of her as inert or unresponsive or unrelated to human life,
but in true Old Testament fashion as sharing in the
hopes and strivings of man. Nature as well as man is
regarded as expectantly looking and working towards
a day of emancipation ; for both there is in process a
winning of freedom which will one day be attained.
And he adds that ' to this day, we know, the entire
creation sighs and throbs with pain.' [4] In the reality
of his own struggle he feels sure that this is true of all
Nature. He feels that his ultimate interpretation of his
own life cannot be correct unless it also holds true of her.

In the First Creation Narrative, the creative process
is further viewed as a series of distinctly related stages,
marked even by a certain degree of correspondence or
parallelism between a first and second group of three days
each. Thus on the first day light is called forth, possibly
from the primeval darkness—' as the spark from the
flint,' says Gregory of Nyssa,[5] ' although we cannot
explain the process in the one case, any more than in the
other '—and corresponding to it, on the fourth day,

---

[1] Jer. 22 [29], Hos. 2 [21, 22].   [2] Is. 55 [12].
[3] Is. 24 [19, 20]. Cf. Jer. 10 [10].   [4] Rom. 8 [19-21] (Moffatt's trans.).
[5] *Hexaemeron*, Migne, i. 71 D.

are formed the sun, moon and stars, the future recep-
tacles or bearers of light.   In the Scriptural narrative
the heavenly bodies are lamps, whereas in the Babylonian
cosmogony they are gods.   On the second day the firmament is created, and the waters beneath it are separated
from those above, while on the corresponding fifth day
these tenantless domains are populated, the first with birds
which 'fly above the earth in front of the firmament'—
to the writer of this Narrative, heaven was comparatively
near—the second with marine forms of life.   The third
day sees two creative works—the separation of the
land from the sea, and the production of vegetation
whereby the land was rendered habitable; while on the
corresponding sixth day it is stocked with animals, and
by a second creative act, man, *i.e.* the human race,[1]
is likewise formed, after express deliberation—man,
towards whose creation the whole scheme had progressively moved.   It is the Second Narrative alone
which tells the story of 'our first parents.'   Then the
Creator rested on the seventh day, looking with satisfaction upon His work.[2]   He had joy in His climactic
process of creation; 'behold, it was very good.'[3]

In seeking for hints as to this author's thought with
regard to the method of Creation, we have seen a suggestion of a conception of separation and even of differentiation in connection with the appearance of the dry land
from the water, and possibly in the case of the creation
of light and darkness: the earth 'brings forth' grass,
herb and tree, and living creatures after their kind, as
also the waters.[4]   It is permissible to suppose that the
conceptions were suggested in some degree by what

---

[1] Just as birds, creeping things, etc., had been created previously.

[2] Into the author's interest in the institution of the Sabbath, and the
basal sublimity and purity of his monotheistic teaching as compared
with that of the related polytheistic Babylonian and other cosmogonies,
it is beside our purpose to enter.   However definite some of the
points of resemblance may be, the differences are even more noticeable
and profound.

[3] Gen. I [31].   [4] Gen. I [12, 21, 24].

reflecting men saw enacted before their eyes. Thus the description of the appearance of the dry land corresponds with phenomena with which the dwellers in Mesopotamia were familiar in connection with the annual inundations caused by the great Tigris - Euphrates system, or the growth of its delta, the dry land appearing from out of the waters when these were seemingly gathered together as the spring floods subsided. The idea of one stage in the creative process as providing material for further advance has been stressed by some commentators, and carried through the whole series of creative acts. Thus, for example, Professor A. R. Gordon interprets the firmament as ' made from part of the solid substance of chaos,' and the heavenly bodies as ' made of light-substance concentrated and bounded.' [1] But there is always the danger of reading later ideas and modes of thought into primitive accounts, and striving to find a definiteness and precision of statement upon problems that may never have been, and in some cases could never have been, before the mind of the writer in question. The conception of Chaos is ordinarily held to cover the ideas of primordial, pre-existent Darkness, possibly with Light thought of as still imprisoned within it; [2] the Deep, containing engulfed within it the already, in some measure, shapen earth, [3] but also possibly other substance from which the solid firmament was formed; and the suggestion of Confusion or Indefiniteness en-

[1] *Op. cit.* p. 129, with a reference to the Babylonian Creation Tablet. Cf. also *The Book of Wisdom*, xi. [17], ' Thy almighty hand, that made the world out of formless matter '; and Dr. Henry Cotterill, *Does Science aid Faith in regard to Creation ?*, pp. 152, 153.

[2] To the Hebrew mind Light and Darkness were distinct ' physical essences,' each with its own dwelling-place (Job 38 [17]) from which it periodically issued and to which it returned. Of the origin or creation of Darkness thus conceived, nothing is said in the Genesis record, and it has been suggested that Is. 45 [6, 7] may have been inspired by the challenge of seeming dualism in the First Narrative. Cf. J. P. Peters, ' Cosmogony and Cosmology,' *E.R.E.*, iv. 155.

[3] The author of 2 Peter 3 [5] evidently understood from the Genesis Narratives that ' heavens existed long ago, and an earth which the word of God formed of water and by water ' (Moffatt's trans.).

shrouding the undifferentiated whole. But whether in a certain degree there be a vague partial conception of the sorting out of elements from a pre-existent complex, or the actual production of later elements from earlier ones, all under the influence of the omnipotent Divine Energy, or whether the main idea be that of a Creative Will expressing itself with the ease of a spoken word, certain it is that the main purpose of this Hymn of Praise to God in Creation is to affirm the majesty and omnipotence of the Creator over against the creature, to establish a point of view which would make impossible any merging of the world in God, still more of God in the world, and of rendering it clear that He alone is the Power in whom and by whom all things—and the writer makes a sort of rough inventory of created things— and all process ultimately consist. Nevertheless, if any one feels constrained to maintain that Evolution is the divine method of creation, there is nothing in the first chapter of Genesis to hinder him in that faith, and even something to support it. From the standpoint of Religion it does not make any vital difference whether the divine activity is conceived in terms of discrete act or continuous process. There remains, on either view, a conception of what in finite terminology we can only refer to as Infinite Energy, expressive of Infinite Mind. And for many, the evidence of process has enormously added to the sense of wonder in its extended revelation of the divine working. The heavens still declare the glory of God, but in a degree undreamed of by the Psalmist.[1] There can be no quarrel between Science and Religion until Science, passing beyond her field of description, endeavours to deny the interpretation of her facts by Religion in terms of the efficacy of the Spirit or of the Word of God, and challenges her insistent declaration that the world and all things therein depend ultimately upon God as well in origin as in orderly maintenance. And this she is increasingly un-

[1] Ps. 19 [1].

likely to do. ' Of absolute origins,' as E. W. Hobson
truly says, ' Science knows nothing, and we can form no
conception.' [1]

Nor is there anything in the Narrative that forbids
us to think, with Origen, St. Augustine, St. Anselm,
John Scotus Erigena, and Thomas Aquinas,[2] of God's
work of creation as an eternal work. In God there can
be nothing accidental, therefore; ' if He is Creator, He
is not so accidentally ; it must be of the essence of His
nature to be Creator ; and, therefore, He is Creator
eternally. That which is eternal, therefore, and that
which has come to be, are not diverse, but are one and
the same : in the Word of God, the Universe is eternal,
and yet it is at the same time a process of becoming.' [3]
In all this they but followed the teaching of Jesus ;
' My Father worketh even until now,' He had said,
' and I work.' [4] There is no reason to suppose that
Scripture postulates an absolute beginning.[5] Creation
is ultimately a divine energetic activity depending on
the Will of God [6]—the bringing into being of that, conceived by the Divine Mind, which had not hitherto been
in existence, or as itself begun to be—an expression of
His nature who is the World-Ground and its active
and efficient Cause ; which makes it difficult to think
of this self-expression of the Eternal God as having had

---

[1] *The Domain of Science*, p. 315.

[2] For Origen's views, cf. *De Princip.*, **III.** v. 3-4 ; for statements by
St. Augustine on this point, cf. *De Genesi contra Manichaeos*, lib. prim.
cap. iii. and vii. : ' Non ergo possumus dicere fuisse aliquod tempus
quando Deus nondum aliquid fecerat. Quomodo enim erat tempus
quod Deus non fecerat, cum omnium temporum ipse sit fabricator ?
Et si tempus cum caelo et terra esse coepit, non potest invenire tempus
quo Deus nondum fecerat caelum et terram.' For Thomas Aquinas,
cf. *Summa Phil. c. Gent.*, ii. 38 ; *Summa Theol.*, i. 46, 104.

[3] G. J. Blewett, essay on Erigena in *The Study of Nature and the Vision
of God*, p. 295. The references to the *De Divisione Naturae* are iii. 16, 25.

[4] John 5 [17].

[5] In Is. 46 [10] the same word (*bara'*) is used of the commencement of
a series.

[6] As C. M. Walsh puts it, ' We will, and it *is done*. God wills, and
it *is* ' (*op. cit.* p. 156).

an absolute beginning *in* time, or even to have been the beginning *of* time. Phases or cycles of such partial self-manifestation there may be. Indeed, we are driven to think of phases of creation, of temporal expressions being given to eternal meaning, while yet insisting that both the meaning and the power of expression are inherent in an Ultimate Source or Ground of all. But that there ever was a time in which there was no willed self-expression of the eternally active and loving God— no out-going and out-giving of Himself in the creation of, and establishment of relations with, things and beings other than Himself—seems almost a derogatory conception.

Such ultimate reference of creation to the divine activity also serves, however, to make the evidence of imperfections and dysteleologies in the process only stand out in bolder relief. Particularly in face of the refrain which rounds off the Hymn of Praise, and is repeated no less than five times—' God saw that it was good ' [1]—the problem of these seeming imperfections was very real for some of the Church Fathers, who made the quaint suggestion that the consequences of the Fall extended even to the animal creation, so that forms originally gentle and harmless became beasts of prey and possessed of death-dealing weapons of offence.[2] Even in the otherwise attractive interpretation of the World as Imagination offered by Mr. Douglas Fawcett— ' Divine Imagining,' he says, ' creates as the lark sings, and is immanently teleological withal ' [3]—the struggle and pain accompanying such efforts of Divine Imagining as the python and the tiger are left wholly unrelieved. ' In the interests largely of finite sentients there has to be a world, and in the divisions of this world dawns an unavoidable tragedy. Imagining runs amok discretely and unforeseeably. It invents, we may say, in piece-

---

[1] Gen. I [10, 12, 19, 21, 25].
[2] Cf. A. D. White, *op. cit.* i. 28.
[3] *H.J.*, xxi. 586.   Cf. also his *Divine Imagining*.

work, wherefore infernoes of contention have to arise.
The world, in short, can only be initiated at a great risk
and price. It is experimental. And yet at long last
it may prove worth all its pains. Creation, whatever
betide, must be untrammelled, and in the end only its
real successes endure.' [1] Such an account seems like
the imagery of despair. The process must perforce be
recognised as an essentially reasonable process, since
at no point does it put us to lasting intellectual confusion. Reason, that is to say, must have in it a more
commanding, controlling place—forming the very tissue
of the Divine Creative Imagining—for otherwise it is
difficult to see how Mr. Douglas Fawcett ' accepts fully
Goethe's "Bond of Love" which " gives direction to the
Whole." ' On the contrary, when we bear in mind the
conditions under which the world may reasonably be
conceived as in process of becoming, and in particular
the implications involved in the measure of growing
freedom attained at every stage in the organic process
from the dawn of life—in short, the whole conception
of ' Evolution as the winning of freedom '—we may find
in the sadly frequent misuse of that freedom some
explanation of the cul-de-sac, arrested developments,
dysteleologies, parasitisms, and other features that seem
to constitute blemishes or imperfections in the process
as a whole.[2] Undoubtedly a world of spiritual beings
with the definite attainment of individuality as their
goal must be a world with possibilities of initiation,
adventure, trial and error, sympathy, self-sacrifice.
In Professor J. S. Mackenzie's words, ' a world without
these would seem to me to be a much poorer world than
the world we know. And I do not see,' he continues,
' how any of these ingredients in its composition would be
possible without something of the nature of what we call
evil—some pain, some eating of one's bread with tears,

[1] *H.J.*, xxi. 586.
[2] Cf. *Man and the Attainment of Immortality*, chap. xi., and the
references there given.

some regret, some anxiety, even some remorse, and, in general, some room for progressive achievement.'[1] Accordingly, to arraign the divine omnipotence on the basis of the world process as it actually presents itself to us can only be possible upon some misunderstanding of what the term ' omnipotence ' does, and does not, imply,[2] as also of the character of that process itself. In any case it is only a jaundiced eye that can see evil in the world in excess of, and overcoming, the good. On the contrary, the world presents itself as a Universe in process of becoming, and being made, perfect; in which process we can co-operate, to our spiritual advantage, or temporarily dislocate and hinder, to our lasting and vital hurt. We co-operate in the degree in which we have learned that self-realisation is never secured by self-assertion alone.

That the question of creation is beset with difficulties of every type is one of the few things of which we can be sure, yet this need not surprise us in connection with an activity so ultimate. In the end we cannot lift ourselves by our own boot-straps; and in face of our inability not merely to explain, but even to describe with any satisfaction, the action of the human will upon muscle tissue, to attempt to formulate the divine creative activity suggests presumption. We cannot create as God creates, but then it is no part of our argument that we are gods. ' God,' says Dr. Cadoux, ' does not limit Himself by bringing into being something external alien to Himself (a meaningless thought), but by an inward movement, in the recession from each other of elements otherwise to be thought of as co-extensive, with the result that a stress is created under which the evolu-

---

[1] ' The Idea of Creation,' *H.J.*, xxi. 218. He adds to these ingredients ' effort ' and ' free choice.'

[2] Cf. J. S. Mackenzie, *op. cit.* p. 219 : ' I am pretty fully convinced that there *are* conditions implied in the creation of an intelligible world ; and that it is mere nonsense to think of an omnipotence that could override such conditions ' ; and W. R. Matthews, *op. cit.* p. 210, ' for religion, omnipotence means that the world depends upon God.'

tionary process proceeds. This is, of course, merely figurative speech, but if we use spatial figures at all (and they are difficult to avoid) something of this sort is preferable to that which makes God and the material Universe external to each other.' [1] Certainly we cannot rest content to think of God in relation to the creative process, as some mere noumenon behind phenomena. If one of the characteristic features of the evolutionary process is the broadly progressive development of novelty, this seems to demand something more than merely a new disposition of the already given. It involves some definite development by assimilative intake from, and energetic relationship with, an activating environmental Ground. It is probable, accordingly, that when we wish to picture to ourselves that which is inherent in the process—its directive cause and driving energy—we shall be nearest truth and clarity in thinking of that which is subject to no human limitations of mind and character, and is fullness of power. The evolutionary process, at whatever stage it is examined, gives an impression of deep-laid purposiveness,[2] and an examination of alternative explanations serves only to bring out the greater worth and satisfactoriness of that solution which regards it as a voluntarily initiated phase of manifestation of a transcendent Being who is not exhausted by His Universe—by that particular expression of Himself which we happen to know in time and space.

On the other hand, objections are sometimes raised against the conception of Divine Creation which admit of being considerably relieved. Thus it is often urged that the idea of a creative God is incompatible with that of free spirits. It is suggested that it is impossible that a *free* will in finite beings can be willed by an Infinite Will—the idea is a contradiction in terms ; the Infinite Will

[1] A. J. Cadoux, *Essays in Christian Thinking*, p. 65.
[2] For discussion of this particular point reference may be made to *The Spiritual Interpretation of Nature*, chap. xi. ; *Man and the Attainment of Immortality*, chap. i.

must will the details.[1] As Professor Matthews points out, however, ' the higher we rise in the scale of the subject-matter within which the will is exercised, the more persistently does freedom enter into the end which is willed and form an essential element in it.'[2] And he illustrates by the wise statesman who has created a nation, and has ideals for it which he suggests but will not press, preferring that the people should choose them themselves in their good time, and themselves make them real. ' He wills freedom for his community as a fundamental element of the end itself. . . . It is, therefore, so far from being true that to will freedom for others is impossible, that the higher acts of will include the creation of freedom as part of the end willed.'[3]

Further, when we consider the actual relationships between an individual and the community of which he is a member, we see a relative independence which helps us by an analogy to resolve any supposed contradiction between a creative God and a creative world of spirits in process of attaining freedom. For even in a great drama the writer introduces us to certain characters which are, as we say, the creation of his genius, and the power and truth of the drama for us are in exact proportion to the degree in which within a certain area of freedom we feel that they carry out lines of action concordant with their character. There is a point of development after which, however, the dramatist cannot just do *anything* with them : they are themselves in a relative semi-independent sort of way, and their actions are in a secondary degree their own. But if we feel that this may be true of creations of the human mind, is it impossibly true of the creations of the Divine Mind ? ' For we are also His offspring,'[4] and if like Cretans we are liars, it is not because of anything in our blood, but

---

[1] Cf. B. Bosanquet's view that belief in a Creator who ' creates creators ' is self-destructive, in *Value and Destiny of the Individual,* p. 136.
[2] *Op. cit.* p. 209.   [3] *Op. cit.* p. 210.   [4] Acts 17 [28].

because we have deliberately said, 'Evil, be thou our good.'

For the motif of Creation we can only fall back, with any mental satisfaction, on the Christian conception of God as Love, or even suppose with Plato that God being ' free from envy ' ' sought to " create creators " as like Himself as possible. For this purpose it was necessary to provide a world not yet fully ordered ; '[1] or rather such elements as in their development and unfolding should furnish the definite objective environmental opportunity in reaction with which spiritual beings could come into existence, and win their freedom. Such creation would imply a self-limitation, even, it might be said, a form of kenosis,[2] on the part of God, purely voluntary, yet an expression of His inmost nature. This does not in the least imply that such created spirits are necessary to God, but it does mean that they are ultimately dependent on Him. On the other hand, their existence is so real, and the individuality that they can attain so objective and discrete, that abstract conceptions of the Absolute as that which is outside of and beyond all relations, or that of which such individual selves are ultimately mere absorbable elements, come to have little convincing value for thought or reality, and certainly would not permit of the idea of creation at all. In order to attain the goal of its being, each spiritual self must, in a partially analogous way, go out of itself in service and sacrifice for the fellow-man ; there must be an individual kenosis. In short, for all life, ' dying to live ' is the fundamental law of progress, and this was objectively and supremely revealed to men at the Cross of Christ.

[1] Professor J. S. Mackenzie, *op. cit.* p. 217. The reference is to the *Timaeus*, 29.

[2] Lit. emptying. Originally the term was used of the Son of God, from the phrase, ' but emptied himself ' (Phil. 2 [7]).

CHAPTER V

THE EARLY CHURCH FATHERS AND SCIENCE

To what extent actual conflict developed between the
Early Christian writers and the exponents of the science
of their day could only be determined by intimate
knowledge of the works of all the Early Church Fathers.
It may be doubted whether during the first three centuries
of the Christian era theologians generally were sufficiently
interested in the teachings of natural science on its own
account to care very much about the natural philosopher's
interpretation of the world. As a matter of fact, the
conditions of acquiring recorded knowledge were so
tedious and troublesome, being so vastly different from
those that are to-day at the disposal of the citizens of
any moderately sized town, that we need not be surprised
at the scant degree of acquaintance with contemporary
science shown by some of the Church Fathers. On the
other hand, the Gnostic heresy compelled others of them
to examine the pagan cosmologies and anthropologies.
Tertullian (c. A.D. 155-222) and Origen (c. A.D. 185-254),
for example, striving to elucidate the problem of the
origin of evil, devoted careful attention to the Greek
philosophers and men of science.

One fact, however, stands out in connection with these
Early Christian centuries in sublime impressiveness,
viz. the absolute and unquestioned authority of the Old
Testament Scriptures in relation to all questions of
cosmology, geography, anthropology, and history for
those communities out of which the Christian Church
developed. This rigidity of attitude was the main
element in provoking the inevitable struggle during the

succeeding centuries. The fact is there, but it has never yet been wholly explained, and it is all the more remarkable because the Canon of the Old Testament had not even yet been closed. From the fifth century B.C. the group of writings containing the five books of Moses, and known as The Law, had held undisputed supremacy over the minds and hearts of the godly in Israel, having been represented to them, possibly by such an one as Ezra, as the very Word of God Himself. If this generally received view is correct, the date would be about 444 B.C., after the return from the Babylonian exile,[1] though this does not necessarily imply that there was no development in The Books of the Law subsequently; most probably there was. Religion had been for the Hebrew, from the beginning, something of the nature of a covenant between God and the people of his race, and The Books of the Law were the formulated and directly inspired terms of that covenant. Just because God loved His chosen people, He had laid many commands upon them. This deep impression may very well have begun to form even earlier, stimulated, if not created, by the events connected with the discovery and promulgation of the Deuteronomic Law under Josiah in 621 B.C.[2] Later, to The Books of the Law were added The Books of the Prophets.[3] ' That these writings were immediately inspired by God,' says Dr. Skinner, ' was certainly the belief of the post-exilic Church (Zech. I [5f.], 7 [12], 8 [9]). But inspiration was not yet equivalent to canonicity.'[4] Accordingly, it was somewhere towards

---

[1] Cf. Neh. chaps. 8-10.

[2] Cf. 2 Kings 22-23 [25]. It should be mentioned that certain scholars dispute the statement that The Book of the Law discovered in the Temple in 621 B.C. was the Deuteronomic Law. Cf., e.g., Prof. A. C. Welch, *The Code of Deuteronomy*, to whom I am indebted for some direction at this point.

[3] These consisted of two groups: (a) the former Prophets, comprising Joshua, Judges, 1 and 2 Samuel, and 1 and 2 Kings; and (b) the Latter Prophets, including Isaiah, Jeremiah, Ezekiel, and the twelve Minor Prophets.

[4] In A. S. Peake's *A Commentary on the Bible*, p. 38.

the close of the third or the beginning of the second century B.C. before the actual incorporation took place, although the greater part of these works had been already in the hands of the scribes in the fifth century. The decisive impulse, apparently, towards the canonisation of this class of writings was ' the cessation of the living voice of prophecy in the Jewish community.' [1]

With regard to the remaining books of the Old Testament, known collectively as the Hagiographa,[2] the fact seems to be that, although in existence for some time previously, its constituent elements only gradually acquired canonicity individually during the two centuries succeeding the canonical recognition of The Prophets, and that it was already towards the end of the first century A.D. before the Old Testament, as we have it, was firmly established. Indeed, the desirability of the recognition of Canticles, Ecclesiastes, and Esther was still debated in the Jewish schools in the beginning of the second century A.D., and this suggests, although the argument is by no means conclusive, that the Canon had not yet been closed as the result of the decision of any authoritative assembly. At the same time, ecclesiastical authority was more loose under Judaism than under Christianity, and the circumstance that individual men continued to argue about the rightful canonicity of certain books does not necessarily imply that the Canon was not generally accepted. Such a decision seems, however, to have been taken by the Synod or Sanhedrim of Jamnia near the end of the first century A.D.,[3] and thereafter generally accepted, although, here again, there is apparently nothing to show that this Synod had any strictly representative authority. The important point in this connection is, however, the fact

---

[1] J. Skinner, *op. cit.* p. 38, who gives references to Zech. 13 [4-6]; Ps. 74 [9]; 1 Mac. 4 [46], 9 [27], 14 [41].

[2] *I.e.* Psalms, Proverbs, and Job ; Canticles, Ruth, Lamentations, Ecclesiastes, and Esther ; Daniel, Ezra, Nehemiah, 1 and 2 Chronicles.

[3] The date usually given is *c.* A.D. 90.

that the fundamental Jewish criterion of canonicity was conformity to The Books of the Law.[1] That is to say, apart from the consideration whether or not its production fell within a certain time limit, extending roughly from the Age of Moses (c. 1230 B.C.) to the reign of Artaxerxes (Longimanus, 464-425 B.C.), who was generally identified with the Ahasuerus of the Book of Esther, the principal title to canonicity of all the other books rested upon the consensus of their teaching with that of The Books of the Law. If, therefore, the Pentateuch was the criterion for the other books of the Old Testament, how much greater must have been the authority of its teaching when opposed to that of any extra-Biblical or secular writing.

The Pentateuch, then, as divinely inspired, contained not the words of men, but the very words of a holy and transcendent God. The general attitude of the Jews towards their Scriptures was that of literal interpretation, although there were individual exceptions like Philo, who took his symbolical and allegorical conception of things from the Stoics.[2] The cosmology of the Pentateuch accordingly represented for the Jews a revealed account from God Himself of the creation of the world and of man, and it continued to be so for the first generations of Christians. Read by the latter in the form of the Septuagint, the Old Testament writings made their direct appeal, and the impression of authority in their pronouncements, together with the truth of their prophecies concerning Jesus, was instrumental in the conversion of men like Tatian and Justin, Athenagoras and Theophilus of Antioch. ' While I was giving my most earnest attention to the matter, I chanced to meet with certain barbarian writings, too old to be compared with the opinions of the Greeks, and too divine to be

---

[1] J. Skinner, op. cit. p. 39. Whether this was the criterion avowedly adopted at Jamnia is not known.

[2] The Stoics explained the mythology of the gods in a symbolical way Euhemerus deliberately applied the method to all mythology.

compared with their errors ; and I was led to put faith
in these by the unpretending cast of the language, the
inartificial character of the writers, the pre-knowledge
which they displayed of future events, the excellent
quality of their precepts, and the declaration of the
government of the universe by one Being.' [1] But when
the Hellenists or foreign Jews began to influence the
presentation of Christian truth by the forms of thought
that they brought with them into the Christian Church,
and, more definitively, when Gnosticism began to offer
its semi-pagan compromise with Christianity, the teaching of the Church Fathers on the great cosmological
and anthropological issues tended to assume a distinctly
' apologetic ' cast. The Apologists directed their work
largely to the philosophers, and they were individually
more or less successful ; but it remains something of a
problem to understand how their teaching, containing,
as it often did, so much admixture of error on questions
of science, came to exert such authority that in turn their
interpretation of Scripture became the criterion and
code of all knowledge, by conformity with which the
views of scientific investigators many centuries later
continued to be judged. Possibly the wild speculations
of the Gnostics and Manichaeans, together with the only
less unsatisfactory hypotheses of the Greeks, tended to
strengthen literal acceptation of the Mosaic account of
Creation, and apologetic based upon such an attitude.
There was no alternative interpretation, for the findings
of the science of the day seemed just as far-fetched and
improbable as those of the heretical thinkers. Thus
early there developed that disastrous water-tight com-
partmental attitude to truth on the part of most of the
theologians and the men of science and philosophers—
that estrangement which, in default of any attempt at
mutual understanding, led in some instances to contempt
on the one hand and indifference on the other.

[1] Tatian, *To the Greeks*, xxix., quoted in P. Carrington, *Christian
Apologetics of the Second Century*, pp. 44, 45.

In two masterly volumes[1] Dr. A. D. White dealt at great length with the history of the conflict between Science and Theology, covering the ground in greater detail and with more perspective than had been traversed even earlier by the physiologist J. W. Draper.[2] No one can rise from the study of these volumes without a strange feeling of how easily a profound knowledge of the theology of the day may be accompanied by an utter lack of understanding of what Christianity is in practice, as also of the wantonness with which again and again throughout the ages the cause of Christ has been misrepresented by self-appointed agents. The whole question of the relationship of specific institutionalism to Christianity has yet to be worked out. For if history has made one thing clear, it is that in proportion to the degree in which institutionalism is regarded as primary, the spirit of Christianity departs.

At the same time, it is open to some question whether the severe strictures passed on official Christianity in these books have really been justified as a whole; or rather, whether the choice of those who have been singled out to support a general thesis to the effect that the Church through many centuries was not merely obscurantist and hostile to, but actively did its best to discourage and even suppress the investigation of natural causes, has been altogether fair. Thus, for example, of early Christian writers, Lactantius, or, as he is usually styled, Lucius Caecilius Firmianus Lactantius, is again and again selected as a subject for attack.[3] As a matter of fact, singularly little is known about him with any certainty.[4] He was born in North Africa, probably shortly after the middle of the third century A.D., and is definitely known as a distinguished

---

[1] *A History of the Warfare of Science with Theology in Christendom*, 1896.
[2] *The Conflict between Religion and Science*, 1874.
[3] Cf. A. D. White, *op. cit.* i. 109, 209, 375, 395, etc.
[4] Cf., *e.g.*, Introductory Notice to *The Works of Lactantius*, vol. xxi. of the Ante-Nicene Christian Library.

teacher of rhetoric in Nicomedia (Bithynia)—a post which he had to surrender on the outbreak of the persecution of Diocletian. Later he appears to have been in Gaul, in high favour with the Emperor Constantine, and entrusted by him with the education of his son Crispus. He is believed to have died at Trèves about A.D. 340. Much more of a layman than a professed theologian, he wrote with great ease, dignity, clearness, and grace, drawing largely upon his knowledge of the Greek and Roman philosophers in his defence of the Christian faith. On account of his beautiful style he was widely read, and Copernicus refers to him in the Dedication of his famous treatise to Pope Paul III.[1]

It seems, therefore, in the first place, simply a mistake to consider him in any way as representative of the recognised theological thought and attitude of mind of his day ; but it is a still more serious error to judge him by isolated sentences, and especially to judge him at all without first making some endeavour to understand his general point of view, which was not so entirely unreasonable. Thus, in his opinion, the Stoic philosophers who believed ' that all the heavenly bodies which have motion are to be reckoned in the number of gods ' were ' not only unlearned and impious, but also blind, foolish, and senseless, who have surpassed in shallowness the ignorance of the uneducated. For they regard as gods (only) the sun and moon, but you the stars also.' [2] Wisdom would long ago have been found, ' since so much time and talent have been wasted in the search for it,' if it had been possible to find it by the mere pursuit of it.[3] ' Philosophy appears to consist of two subjects,

---

[1] The reference is to the *De Revolutionibus Orbium Celestium*. The passage reads : ' For it is not unknown that Lactantius, otherwise a famous writer but a poor mathematician, speaks most childishly of the shape of the Earth when he makes fun of those who said that the Earth has the form of a sphere.' Kepler also frequently quoted him.

[2] *The Divine Institutes*, ii. 5. (Trans. as above.) He is addressing the philosophers.

[3] *Op. cit.* iii. 2.

G

knowledge and conjecture, and of nothing more. Know-ledge cannot come from the understanding, nor be apprehended by thought ; because to have knowledge in oneself as a particular property does not belong to man, but to God.'[1] Once again : ' Philosophy has been divided into many sects ; and they all entertain various senti-ments. In which do we place the truth ? It certainly cannot be in all. . . . For each particular sect overturns all others, to confirm itself and its own (doctrines). . . . If, therefore, the sects individually are convicted of folly by the judgment of many sects, it follows that all are found to be vain and empty ; and thus philosophy con-sumes and destroys itself.'[2] On the other hand, he says elsewhere : ' Nor do I now disparage the pursuit of those who wished to know the truth, because God has made the nature of man most desirous of arriving at the truth ; but I assert and maintain this against them, that the effect did not follow their honest and well-directed will, because they neither knew what was true in itself, nor how, or where, or with what mind it is to be sought.'[3] Accordingly, it is not surprising that there should develop in his mind—' I bear it with equanimity,' he says naïvely, ' that a moderate degree of talent has been granted to me '[4]—a fundamental contrast between philosophy and ' the truth,' which last ' could not have been found by the abilities of man.'[5] The ' chief good of man is in religion only ';[6] ' they who do not take up religion are of the earth, for religion is from heaven.'[7] God, when speaking to man, could not argue ; it was not befitting. ' He spoke as the mighty Judge of all things, to whom it belongs not to argue, but to pronounce sentence. He Himself, as God, is truth.'[8] It is in terms of presuppositions such as these, and certain extreme deductions from them—as, for example,

---

[1] *Op. cit.* iii. 3.
[3] *Op. cit.* iii. 1.
[5] *Op. cit.* ii. 20.
[7] *Op. cit.* iii. 27.

[2] *Op. cit.* iii. 4.
[4] *Op. cit.* iii. 1.
[6] *Op. cit.* iii. 10.
[8] *Op. cit.* iii. 1.

that ' knowledge cannot come from the understanding,
nor be apprehended by thought,—that a statement like
the following must be fairly regarded : ' To investigate
or wish to know the causes of natural things—whether
the sun is as great as it appears to be, or is many times
greater than the whole of this earth ; also whether the
moon be spherical or concave ; and whether the stars are
fixed to the heaven, or are borne with free course through
the air ; of what magnitude the heaven itself is, of
what material it is composed ; whether it is at rest and
immovable, or is turned round with incredible swiftness;
how great is the thickness of the earth, or on what foundations it is poised and suspended,—to wish to comprehend
these things, I say, by disputation and conjectures is
as though we should wish to discuss what we may
suppose to be the character of a city in some very remote
country, which we have never seen, and of which we
have heard nothing more than the name. If we should
claim to ourselves knowledge in a matter of this kind,
which cannot be known, should we not appear to be
mad, in venturing to affirm that in which we may be
refuted ? ' [1] ' It remains,' he adds, ' that there is in
philosophy conjecture only ; for that from which knowledge is absent is entirely occupied by conjecture.' [2]

It is further in terms of such a general background
that his scornful references to such ' marvellous fictions '
as the idea of the Antipodes ought to be read,[3] even if
one suspects that a measure of dissatisfaction with his
counter-statements is concealed in one of the concluding

---

[1] *Op. cit.* iii. 3.   [2] *Op. cit.* iii. 3.

[3] ' How is it with those who imagine that there are antipodes opposite
to our footsteps ?   Do they say anything to the purpose ?   Or is there
any one so senseless as to believe that there are men whose footsteps
are higher than their heads ? or that the things which with us are in
a recumbent position, with them hang in an inverted direction ? that
the crops and trees grow downwards ? that the rains, and snow, and
hail fall upwards to the earth ? ' (*op. cit.* ii. 24).   In chapter x. of his
Treatise on the Anger of God, he deals in a much more effective
way with the current philosophical views of the origin of the world,
and the nature of affairs, and the providence of God.   Cf. also *Divine
Institutes*, vii. 3.

sentences to this section: 'But I should be able to prove by many arguments that it is impossible for the heaven to be lower than the earth, were it not that this book must now be concluded, and that some things still remain, which are more necessary for the present work.' On the other hand, there is no particular point in holding Lactantius up to ridicule [1] for his inability to accept the idea of the Antipodes, since this was an inability shared by some pagan writers as well. Naturally, however, a serious-minded man who believed that he knew where truth alone was to be found, and whose main interest was the practical one of right living in a world that might come to an end at any moment, was not going to waste his time on what he believed to be merely conjectures, and so there resulted that general haziness of idea and lack of first-hand acquaintance with the science of their day that characterise so many of the Fathers. The study of physical science was deliberately neglected and sometimes even deprecated, and the rift widened. Small wonder if it led in some cases to a certain mutual impatience with, if not disdain for, one another, on the part of ecclesiastic and man of science.

Much more outstanding and representative in this respect was Basil, Bishop of Caesarea in Cappadocia, who lived during the fourth century, having been born about A.D. 329, and died half a century later. He succeeded in combining in a very remarkable way the ideals of the monastic life with those of a great ecclesiastical administrator. His influence was largely the result of his strong personality, which gave added force to his writings. Like many of the Church Fathers, *e.g.* Origen, Hippolytus, and Augustine, he wrote a commentary upon the open-

[1] Cf. J. W. Draper, *op. cit.* pp. 63, 64, and A. D. White, *op. cit.* i. 102, 103, who mentions Epicurus, Lucretius, and Plutarch (*De Facie in Orbe Lunae*, cap. vii.); but there had been others, *e.g.* Herodotus (iv. 36, 42) and, in a sense, Eratosthenes and Strabo. 'The vulgar belief in a flat plain was still the vulgar or common belief when Christianity was rising to power' (C. R. Beazley, *The Dawn of Modern Geography*, i. 276).

ing verses of Genesis, and his *Hexaemeron* is one of the best known and most admired of these treatises. The principle that he follows in this work is comparatively simple. Whenever he finds Greek science or philosophy in apparent conflict with the Scriptural narrative, he holds to the latter. At the same time, he is by no means a consistent and narrow literalist. Thus in expounding the phrase, ' And God said, Let there be light,' [1] Basil says, ' It must be well understood that when we speak of the voice, of the word, of the command of God, the divine language does not mean to us a sound which escapes from the organs of speech, a collision of air struck by the tongue ; it is a simple sign of the will of God, and, if we give it the form of an order, it is only the better to impress the souls whom we instruct.' [2] On occasion he is even ready to indulge in textual criticism and emendation. Thus he gives ' Let the earth bring forth grass, the herb yielding seed after his kind ' as his reading of Gen. I [11], adding, ' in this manner we can re-establish the order of the words, of which the construction seems faulty in the actual version, and the economy of nature will be rigorously observed.' [3]

On the other hand, he is not interested in Origen's allegorising. ' Let us understand,' he cries in another place, ' that by water is meant water ; for the dividing of the waters by the firmament let us accept the reason which has been given us.' [4] Any additional details as to the characters of living things that he wishes to make use of are taken directly from the Greek or Roman men of science. He displays a remarkable acquaintance with the science and philosophy of his day, speaking of men ' who measure the distance of the stars and describe

[1] Gen. I [3].
[2] Hom. ii. 7. The translations are all taken from the ' Library of Nicene and Post-Nicene Fathers,' vol. viii., *St. Basil : Letters and Select Works.*
[3] Hom. v. 2 ; cf. also iv. 5. In the second Homily he works with the Sept. trans. of Gen. I [2]—' The earth was invisible and unfinished.'
[4] Hom. iii. 9 ; cf. also ix. 1.

them . . . who observe with exactitude the course of the stars, their fixed places, their declensions, their return, and the time that each takes to make its revolution.' [1] Yet he is unwilling to follow their lead where it is confused. ' Those who have written about the nature of the universe,' he says, ' have discussed at length the shape of the earth. If it be spherical or cylindrical, if it resemble a disc and is equally rounded in all parts, or if it has the form of a winnowing basket and is hollow in the middle ; [2] all these conjectures have been suggested by cosmographers, each one upsetting that of his predecessor. It will not lead me to give less importance to the creation of the universe, that the servant of God, Moses, is silent as to shapes ; he has not said that the earth is a hundred and eighty thousand furlongs in circumference ; he has not measured into what extent of air its shadow projects itself whilst the sun revolves around it, nor stated how this shadow, casting itself upon the moon, produces eclipses. He has passed over in silence, as useless, all that is unimportant for us. Shall I then prefer foolish wisdom to the oracles of the Holy Spirit ? Shall I not rather exalt Him who, not wishing to fill our minds with these vanities, has regulated all the economy of Scripture in view of the edification and the making perfect of our souls ? ' [3] Or once again : ' Avoid the nonsense of those arrogant philosophers who do not blush to liken their soul to that of a dog ; who say that they have been formerly themselves women, shrubs, fish. Have they ever been fish ? I do not know ; but I do not fear to affirm that in their writings they show less sense than fish.' [4] Apart from these passages, perhaps, it would be unjust to speak of Basil as showing contempt in this treatise for the Ionian philosophers. His attitude is

[1] Hom. i. 4.
[2] Plut., περὶ τῶν ἀρεσκ., iii. 10 ; Arist., De Caelo, ii. 14. References cited in trans. as above.
[3] Hom. ix. 1.
[4] Hom. viii. 2. The references are probably to certain theories of Empedocles and Anaximander.

rather one of banter; contempt is reserved for the astrologers.[1] He feels very strongly that the Scriptural account of Creation, as he understands it, is more satisfactory than any other that he knows, and he says so, with straightforward criticism. ' The philosophers of Greece,' he remarks early in the work, ' have made much ado to explain Nature, and not one of their systems has remained firm and unshaken, each being overturned by its successor. It is vain to refute them; they are sufficient in themselves to destroy one another.' [2] When he takes up a particular problem, such as ' upon what support this enormous mass (the earth) rests,' [3] it is only after an examination of various current theories, all of which seem to him insufficient, that he suggests recourse to the religious reply, ' In His hands are the ends of the earth.' [4] There is no doubt that on some points, as for example ' the essence of the heavens,' he is too quickly ' contented with what Isaiah says, for, in simple language, he gives us sufficient idea of their nature : " The heaven was made like smoke," [5] that is to say, He created a subtle substance, without solidity or density, from which to form the heavens.' [6] He evidently had interested audiences at his early morning addresses, who asked intelligent and difficult questions about the world of Nature,[7] dealing with points upon which Scripture provides no information, and Basil was glad to read his Aristotle—for example, the *Meteorology,* and *History of Animals*—and his Pliny,

[1] Hom. vi. 5 ff. It was quite unnecessary for A. D. White to speak of ' the efforts of Eusebius, Basil, and Lactantius to deaden scientific thought' (*op. cit.* i. 109); they had neither the desire nor the opportunity to do so.

[2] Hom. i. 2.

[3] Hom. i. 8b-9.

[4] Ps. 95 [4] (Sept.). At the same time, in a later Homily (iv. 1) he refers to the ' earth, this immense mass which rests upon itself.'

[5] Is. 51 [6].

[6] Hom. i. 8.

[7] ' What trouble you have given me in my previous discourses by asking me why the earth was invisible, why all bodies are naturally endued with colour, and why all colour comes under the sense of sight' (Hom. iv 2).

in order to be able to satisfy their curiosity. Apparently a considerable proportion of his hearers belonged to the artisan class,[1] who looked in on their way to the day's work, and it is probably on this account, as Professor Thorndike suggests,[2] that Basil sometimes speaks of God as ' the Supreme Artisan ' or Artificer or Artist,[3] or bids them contemplatively ' stand around the vast and varied workshop of divine creation.'[4] ' A single plant,' he says, ' a blade of grass, is sufficient to occupy all your intelligence in the contemplation of the skill which produced it.'[5] On other occasions, he makes ' flattering allusions to arts which support life or produce enduring work, and to waterways and sea trade.'[6]

In common with his age, he believed in spontaneous generation,[7] and in face of no alternative suggestion he uses words which are clearly indicative of the idea of the fixity of species. ' All which sprang from the earth, in its first bringing forth, is kept the same to our time, thanks to the constant reproduction of kind.'[8]   He thinks of the creative fiats as being instantaneously effective. ' This short command (Let the earth bring forth) was in a moment a vast nature, an elaborate system.'[9]   A very great deal of his data and some of his reasoning are impossible, but it is the light of his day, and he is always on his guard against what he describes more than once as ' dreams ' and ' ridiculous old women's tales.'[10] ' Nothing has been done,' he says in another place, ' without motive, nothing by chance. All shows ineffable wisdom.'[11]

In breadth of outlook and genuine appreciation of

[1] Hom. iii. 1 and 10.
[2] *A History of Magic and Experimental Science*, i. 486.
[3] Hom. i. 7, 11 ; ii. 2 ; iii. 5 and 10 ; vi. 10.
[4] Hom. iv. 1.   [5] Hom. v. 3.
[6] L. Thorndike, *op. cit.* i. 486. Cf. Hom. i. 7 ; iii. 5 ; iv. 3, 4, and 7 ; vi. 9 ; vii. 6.
[7] Hom. ix. 2.   [8] Hom. v. 2.
[9] Hom. v. 10.   [10] Hom. iii. 9 ; vi. 11.
[11] Hom. v. 8.

scientific method, Gregory of Nyssa [1] stands far above either Lactantius or even his older brother Basil of Caesarea.[2] He likewise wrote an *Hexaemeron*,[3] in which he endeavours to expound points in the history of creation in terms of the knowledge of his day, and finds that this does not conflict with his understanding of the opening passages in Genesis. He has a real conception of the Order of Nature, which he presents very clearly : ' Saying therefore that " In the beginning" the world was founded, he (*i.e.* the sacred writer) means that the occasions, causes and powers of all things were created by God, and that the essence of each of existing things came into existence at the first impulse of that will—the heavens, ether, stars, fire, air, sea, earth, animals, plants, all of which things indeed were seen by the eye of God, and shown by the reason of His power, as says the prophet, " Who sees all things before their birth." [4] Now that they had been brought together by the divine power and wisdom with a view to the perfection of each of the parts of the world, a certain necessary series followed, according to a certain order, so that any one thing first arose from the whole totality of things and appeared. Then, after that, necessarily a second followed. Then as the artificer, Nature, was necessitating, a third and a fourth and a fifth and the rest after, not by chance or fortune, as according to a certain unordered and casual movement, but as the necessary Order of Nature looks for succession in the things that arise, so, he says (philosophising in a kind of statement about physical laws), individual things came into being. He assigns even certain utterances of the ruling God to the individual things which are created, and this he does rightly and in accordance with inspiration. For whatever is done

---

[1] A.D. 335-372.

[2] Yet A. D. White makes only one direct quotation from his works (ii. 175), and J. W. Draper makes no reference to him at all.

[3] Unfortunately it is not translated into English, and I am indebted to Prof. H. A. A. Kennedy for much assistance in this connection.

[4] Dan. 13 [42] (Sept.).

according to a certain order and wisdom of God, he refers in turn as if to a kind of definite utterance of God.'[1]

He is convinced of the Divine Reason as at work in all things. ' " Let there be light, and there was light," [2] for speech and reason in God, as I think, are work and deed.[3] Wherefore everything that is made is made by reason. And in those things which proceed from God, nothing unreasonable and fortuitous and spontaneous is thought of. We must believe that in each actual thing there is a certain wise and productive reason, even if it surpasses our vision.'[4] He returns to this point in dealing with verse 4 : ' Again, whatever is made by a certain natural order and harmony, Moses necessarily refers to the divine energy, teaching, as I think, by what has been said, that all things to be produced, following one another in a necessary order, were conceived beforehand by the wisdom of God.'[5] Or, as he phrases it in another passage : ' Truly everything that comes into being by wisdom is a word of God, not articulated by any vocal organs, but expressed by the actual wonders in things seen.'[6]

At the same time, he is somewhat disturbed by certain things in Nature. ' On this account it seems to me more reasonable that we speak on this wise. Since all things that God made are " very " good and beautiful, we ought to see the perfection of beauty in each thing. The addition of that particle " very," by means of its authoritative signification, clearly shows that there is nothing lacking to perfection. . . . For as in the animal creation we can find innumerable differences of kinds amongst them, still we agree to say by a general pronouncement that in each equally the beauty is " very " great. But this appro-

---

[1] Migne's edition, XLIV., Pt. i. 71 B. The trans., which is free, is based on the Greek text and parallel Latin rendering.

[2] Gen. i 3.

[3] Τὸ ἔργον λόγος ἐστί. The Latin rendering in Migne runs : ' oratio enim et ratio in Deo, ut ego sentio, est opus et factum.'

[4] *Op. cit.* i. 74 A.   [5] *Op. cit.* i. 75 B.

[6] *Op. cit.* i. 87 C.

bation is not referred to what is seen, otherwise neither
the scorpion nor the land frog nor those things which
are generated from rotting substances would be very
beautiful. For the divine eye does not look at the
appearance of things, nor is beauty defined by a certain
excellence of colour or form, but by the fact that each
thing in so far as it exists has a perfect nature in itself.' [1]
On other occasions he can be such a literalist that in order
to explain the circulation of the waters above the firmament he says that ' the back of heaven is cut up and
excavated into valleys like those which are on the earth
on account of the space between the mountains, that the
water may be confined within them.' [2]

One of his leading thoughts is that of the potentiality
in things as they were originally created. ' " In the
beginning God made heaven and earth." This we have
interpreted to mean that the word presents the simul-
taneousness of the creation of things, showing what is
contained from that which contains it ; for mediate
things are altogether contained by extremes. Now
the extremes so far as human perception goes are heaven
and earth, wherefore by these the outlook of men on
either side is bounded. . . . For it is written, But the
earth was invisible and without form ; that it be plain
from this that all things were potentially in the first
divine impulse to creation, as if a certain seminal power
were laid down for the creation of everything, but in
actual realisation individual things were not yet.' [3]

In all his references to the pagan philosophers in the
Hexaemeron, Gregory of Nyssa is respectful ; there is no
suggestion of scoffing or derision. ' For I consider the
firmament,' he says, ' whether it be one of four, or another
beyond these, as pagan philosophers have supposed, not
to be a solid hard body, but, by comparison, of an eternal
and incorporeal quality which is imperceptible to touch ;
but the extreme of being, which is perceived by the
senses, round which the nature of fire circles according

[1] *Op. cit.* i. 91 A. [2] *Op. cit.* i. 90 B. [3] *Op. cit.* i. 78 C, D.

to its ever moving power, is called the firmament of
Scripture. . . . What indeed is heavy by nature cannot
be borne aloft.'[1] Or once again : 'For those who
philosophise about celestial things show that the sun
itself is easily many times larger than the earth, so that
not even does the shadow from the earth go forth to a
great distance in the air.'[2]

Gregory presents remarkably developed views about
what might almost be called the Conservation of Matter.
' By such an experiment '—he takes up the cases of what
happens when a lamp burns, and the circulation of water
as vapour, rain, etc.—' it is evidenced that nothing
moist is consumed ; but as, at first, fire had its origin,
not by the destruction of moisture, but arose from the
same power, so this also arose according to the first composition of the element, and its continuance will be
preserved for ever, the moist nature not disturbing the
endurance of fire.'[3] This point of view is reasserted
several times: ' I, therefore, am persuaded that the
moisture in the atmosphere is consumed by fire pre-
vailing over it, considering it to be vain and contentious
to oppose what is evident : since it befits those who
search out the truth on every side not to grow weary,
I maintain that the amount of moisture in Nature is
preserved undiminished, and that what is consumed
is always replaced by what remains. . . . It is therefore
evident from these things that the moisture of the oil
was transformed into dryness, but the bulk as regards
material was not made to disappear into non-existence,
being dispersed in the air by thin and invisible particles.
This, therefore, we learned in the case of this moisture
by means of the energy of the things which have come
into being, that the moisture is only changed into dryness,
and that the material is not made to disappear entirely.'[4]
A similar idea holds of the animate world : ' For not in
not being an ox does the fact lie that a horse is a horse, but

[1] *Op. cit.* i. 79 C.   [2] *Op. cit.* i. 94 A ; cf. also 95 D.
[3] *Op. cit.* i. 94 A.   [4] *Op. cit.* i. 98 A, C.

in each of these Nature preserves herself, having obtained a proper starting-point for her own continuance or stability, holding it not by the destruction of Nature, but with a view to the power of existence.'[1] Or, once again, clinching his thesis from Scripture, he argues : ' If, therefore, the power of God delimited the heavens,[2] if His hand made the water and His fist the whole earth, if the valleys are weighed in a balance, and a base is defined for the mountains, it must be that each should abide in its own measure and position, it being neither possible that increase nor diminishing should take place in those things that have been measured by God, and those things that are contained by Him. If, therefore, as prophecy witnesses, there is no addition to or diminution in the things measured by God, each remains perpetually in its own measure, the whole of Nature to be changed being seen in the things that are, and changing all things into one another, and altering each into the other, and again leading back from that by change and alteration into its original condition.'[3]

He is quite conscious of the limitations in his explanations, and makes direct appeal to experiment. ' For we perceive by our senses that those things come to pass '— he is discussing the possibility of earth being transformed into water—' but we are unable to present the works of Nature by reason. But if any one wishes to test this opinion by experiments, we shall readily supply that by producing well-sinkers as witnesses of our contention.'[4] He then pursues a really scientific argument—for though his data are wrong, his methods are right—and concludes : ' Wherefore, since a cause must be found by which the nature of the first water is constituted, it would be much more reasonable to consider this in reference to the composition of the springs than to imagine underground lakes, for the downward course of the nature of water is contrary to the argument. For how shall it flow

---

[1] *Op. cit.* i. 91 B.   [2] Is. 40 [12].
[3] *Op. cit.* i. 104 B.   [4] *Op. cit.* i. 110 C.

upwards whose nature has its course downwards?
Besides, what immense masses of lakes will have to be
conjectured, which, since continual supplies of so many
springs flow out of them throughout all the ages, and
nothing is ever replaced, nevertheless are not emptied nor
exhausted. But it would be evident through those
things which we have examined that the rich supply
of water does not fail the rivers, because earth is changed
into water. The size of the earth is not lessened although
so much water escapes from it, since constantly it is
built up from the dried-up vapours. These things being
so arranged, no longer will a change of the elements into
one another seem to us to be improbable. For an order
is apparent by which the change of one into another is
the cause of that source. For example, water carried
aloft by vapours becomes air. Air made moist is dried up
in the higher flame. Whatever is earthly is separated
from the moist by the nature of fire, and, restored to the
earth, is changed into water through its quality of cold-
ness. From which it happens that without any hindrance,
the elements are always successively intermingling with
one another, and being carried round, and none of them
is either consumed or in superfluity; but all remain
perpetually in that measure in which at first they were
constituted.' [1]

'What,' then, he exclaims in another passage, ' is the
nature of things? Nothing of those things which are
perceived in the order of the surrounding earth has been
created constant and immutable by the Maker of all
things, but all things are mutually interchanged. For
there is a certain power in things, by a certain cyclical
movement of which all these lower things are changed
into one another and exchanged and again brought
back to their own condition. But this alteration itself
working without ceasing in the elements, it is necessary
that all things should change into one another, separating from one another, and again to an equal degree

[1] *Op. cit.* i. 112 C.

uniting with one another, for none of these things would be preserved in itself unless its mixture with that which is of a different kind should preserve its nature.' [1]

In Gregory of Nyssa, on the basis of his *Hexaemeron* alone, the Early Church possessed a teacher competent to take his place with the ablest of the pagan philosophers. He had a real idea of scientific method, and evidenced a worthy respect for the views of those from whom he was led to differ. Any first-hand acquaintance with his relevant writings must have led to some modification of the occasionally rather sweeping indictments by J. W. Draper and A. D. White of the Church Fathers as a whole.[2]

In A.D. 313, after his decisive victory over Maxentius, Constantine gave Christianity, in the Edict of Milan, a recognised place ' as one of the public worships of the empire,' [3]—the one personally favoured by himself, even if he still sustained the office of *Pontifex maximus*—thus beginning the process which ended before the close of the century in its establishment as the religion of the Empire. Gradually all official recognition of pagan ceremonial disappeared, and Christianity became the agent of imperial unification. How potent its influence had become in the State is well illustrated in the historic encounter between Ambrose and Theodosius at Milan in A.D. 390. As the state religion of the Roman Empire, its official directors found themselves in a position to vindicate its truths by force whenever they failed in argument. The Christian leaders had made a deliberate challenge in insisting that all necessary knowledge was to be found in the Scriptures and in the traditions of the Church alone, thus instituting the false contrast between profane and sacred knowledge, and reserving for the doctors of the Church the right to the promulgation and interpretation of it. The findings of ecclesiastical Councils

---

[1] *Op. cit.* i. 107 A, C.
[2] Athenagoras is also worthy of consideration in this respect.
[3] Ernest Barker in *The Legacy of Rome*, edited by Cyril Bailey, p. 81.

could be, and were, enforced by the civil powers, and Hypatia, a teacher of Greek philosophy and mathematics, was done to death in Alexandria (A.D. 415) by Cyril's mob. From 476 the framework or structure of the ' Western Empire ' was in effect that Christian society or commonwealth which proved capable of assimilating the barbarian invader, and developing along imperial lines into the institution of the Roman Church. The ' Eastern Empire ' retained in a greater degree the State organisation of the past, and its emperors, recognised by the ' Western Empire,' continued to function as head of the Church, which was simply a department of the administration of the State. ' Two parallel sovereigns of one society, the Pope at Rome and the Emperor at Constantinople—this is the theory which held in the West till the coronation of Charlemagne in A.D. 800,' [1] when Aix-la-Chapelle became the seat of the real temporal power. The authority of the Church gradually grew, till that supreme recognition of ecclesiastical dominance in A.D. 1077, when Henry IV. knelt in penitence before Gregory VII. at Canossa. Yet long after the political defeat of the Church, which came at last in the time of Boniface VIII. (A.D. 1303), her spiritual hold over the minds and destinies of men remained unimpaired.

Throughout this long period, Christian thought was dominated by the monumental formulating work of St. Augustine, the great Bishop of Hippo (A.D. 354-430). It is perhaps not too much to say that by the beginning of the fifth century the results of independent investigation in any branch of science had little chance of acceptance in Christian circles. The Book of Genesis, taken literally as an accurate record of things supernaturally communicated to Moses, had been the Patristic text-book of astronomy, geology, anthropology, geography, and chronology. ' Nothing,' said St. Augustine, ' is to be accepted save on the authority of Scripture, since

[1] *The Legacy of Rome*, p. 87.

greater is that authority than all the powers of the human understanding.' [1]   And so when any new truth was given to the world, it had henceforth to be measured up against the most relevant section in the system of thought elaborated by St. Augustine. A unique place was gradually given to his pronouncements.[2] Indeed, they became the standard of orthodoxy in science and theology alike, and were invested with an authority far exceeding anything that he would ever have claimed for them himself—much as at a later stage men made claims on behalf of Scripture to which the words of Scripture lent no support. The reverence for the authority of St. Augustine came to have more than a touch of fanaticism about it, becoming even proverbial, as in the Spanish saying, ' No " olla " without bacon ; no sermon without St. Augustine.' [3] *The City of God* was really the text-book of history in the Middle Age, and exerted tremendous influence. To St. Augustine we owe the elaboration of ' the plan of salvation ' ; and when we consider that Tertullian in his famous *Apology* made no reference to doctrines of original sin, total depravity, predestination, grace or atonement, we can understand the great advance that had been made in the development of Church doctrine.

On the other hand, St. Augustine was peculiarly sensitive to the respective claims of science (as then understood) and religion, whilst his maturest views upon the interpretation, *e.g.*, of the opening passages in Genesis, were very modern in some respects. He came to see quite clearly that the language of Scripture in these passages could not in the circumstances of the case be intended to be taken literally, but is in reality sym-

---

[1] ' Major est quippe Scripturae hujus auctoritas, quam omnis humani ingenii capacitas ' (*De Gen. ad Litt.*, ii. 5).

[2] Reference is especially intended to his different works on Genesis, and chaps. xi.-xiii. of the *Confessions*.

[3] Cf. *Cassell's Book of Quotations*, p. 833, where ' olla ' is stated to be ' a dish composed of various meats.' I am indebted to Professor James Moffatt for the reference.

bolical or ideal language, intended to convey to finite
understandings, in as direct and evident a manner as
possible, conceptions of the divine working which will
rouse a sense in the human heart of the majesty and
wisdom and power of the Eternal God, and of His immediate and special relation to man.   Thus in his commentary on Genesis I [22] he observes : ' Here plainly
any one however slow of understanding ought to waken up
in order to understand what sort of days those are which
are reckoned.   For since God has given fixed numbers
of germs to living things, preserving a wonderful constancy
in an established order, so that in a definite number of
days each genus carries what has been conceived in the
womb, and warms the laid eggs . . . how in one day
were they able both to conceive, develop, warm, and
nourish what was born, fill the waters of the sea and
multiply on the land ? ' [1]   On the other hand, he just
as clearly recognised the fact that God did reveal Himself in our growing understanding of what men speak
of as Nature, and that for Christian people either to
ignore such revelation, or set up their particular interpretations of, and conclusions from, Scripture as the
actual Word of God itself, and demand adhesion to them
upon penalty, is both mischievous in itself and no
true service to religion.   Thus, he counsels, ' in matters
obscure and most hidden from our eyes, if by any means
we read in them divine things which can give different
types of opinion without damaging the faith in which
we are steeped, let us not throw ourselves into any of
these by headlong assertion, so that if, perchance, the
truth, when more carefully examined, should rightly
upset that opinion, we should be put to confusion ; for
thus we are contending, not for the meaning of the
divine Scriptures, but for our own opinion, so that we
wish that to be the opinion of Scripture which is our own,
when rather we ought to wish that to be our opinion
which is the opinion of Scripture.' [2]   His outlook was,

---

[1] *De Gen. ad Imperf. Litt.*, 51.   [2] *De Gen. ad Litt.*, i. 37.

in many respects, amazingly broad, and just in this degree he realised that many zealous defenders of the faith were really amongst its most insidious adversaries, partly through their ignorance, and partly through their misdirected and imprudent assertions. ' For it sometimes happens,' he says, ' that there is some question concerning the earth or the heavens or the other elements of this world, something concerning the motion and revolutions or even the size and distance of the stars, or about the undoubted eclipses of the sun and moon, or the cycles of the years and seasons, or the nature of animals, fruit-trees, stones, and other things of this sort, with regard to which even one who is not a Christian has knowledge derived from most certain reasoning or experience. But it is very disgraceful and pernicious, and of all things to be guarded against, that some unbeliever should hear a Christian who is speaking about these things as if according to the Christian Scriptures, yet talking such nonsense that, perceiving his statements, to use the phrase, to be as wide of the mark as east is from the west, he can scarcely keep from laughing. And it is not so troublesome that a mistaken individual is ridiculed, but our authors are believed, by those who are without, to have held such views, and, to the great loss of those for whose salvation we are earnestly striving, are considered ignorant, and so spurned. . . . For the degree of trouble and sorrow that these rash presumptuous individuals cause their cautious brethren cannot sufficiently be expressed.' [1]

Once again, in studying his conception of Creation, we become aware of how remarkably modern it is. In the earlier Treatise on the Book of Genesis, written with a view to countering the doctrine of the Manichaeans, he says : ' It is stated, " In the beginning, God made heaven and earth " ; not because this state of things already was in existence, but because it could be : for even " heaven " is written which was made afterwards.

[1] *De Gen. ad Litt.*, i. 39.

Just as if considering the seed of a tree we may say that
roots and trunk and branches and fruits and leaves
are there, not because they are there already, but because
they will come into existence out of it : so it was said,
" In the beginning, God made the heaven and the earth,"
as if the seed of the heaven and the earth, since up to this
point the material of heaven and earth was in confusion :
but because it was certain that from this the heaven
and the earth would be, the material itself was already
called heaven and earth.' [1] In the later Commentary,
De Genesi ad Litteram, the same point of view is adopted.
' Let us, therefore, consider the beauty of any tree you
like, in respect of its trunk, branches, leaves, fruit :
this species did not, of course, suddenly spring up of
this character and size, but in that order with which we
are familiar. For it rose from the root which the first
sprout fixed in the earth, and from this all these formed
and distinct parts grew. Further, that sprout sprang
from the seed ; in the seed, therefore, were all these to
begin with, not by a mass of bodily size, but by causal
energy and power. . . . But just as in the grain itself
were all those characters simultaneously, yet invisible,
which were in time to grow into the tree, so the world
itself is to be thought of, since God created all things
together ; thus the world itself must be supposed to have
had in itself all things that were made in it and with it,
when day was created ; not only the heaven with the
sun and the moon and the stars . . . but even those
things which the water and the land produced, potentially
and causally, before that, through the delays of the seasons,
they grew up in such manner as they are now known
to us in those works, which God is performing up till
now.' [2] ' God,' he urges, ' does not work with temporal
movements as if of His mind or body, as a man or angel
works, but by the eternal and unchangeable and stable
methods of His Word, co-eternal with Himself, and by

[1] *Lib.*, i. 11.
[2] *Lib.*, v. 44-45.

a certain fostering,[1] as I would say, alike of the co-eternal Holy Spirit.'[2] His thought of God in relation to the creative divine fiats is of 'pure intellect without any noise and diversity of tongues.'[3]

His general idea of Creation is as follows: 'Wherefore when we consider the original condition of the things created, from which works of His, God rested on the seventh day, we ought to think neither of those days as being these solar days of ours, nor of the working of God itself after the fashion in which God now works anything in time ; but rather as He has worked from whom time itself had its beginning, as He has worked all things simultaneously, bringing them also into due order, not by intervals of time but by a connection of causes, so that those things which were made simultaneously [4] might be brought to their completion by the sixfold representation of that one day. It was, therefore, not by the order of a succession of times, but by the order of a succession of causes, that there was first made the substance without form, and capable of being brought into form, both spiritual and material, from which should be made that which was to be made.'[5] 'Matter was made at first confused and formless, whence all things were made which were separate and fashioned, which I believe is called Chaos by the Greeks.'[6] St. Augustine subscribes to the beauty and order of creation : God has His own uses for all the great multitude of living things. Yet he is very frank. ' I truly confess that I do not know why mice and frogs were created, or flies or worms. I nevertheless see all things beautiful in their kind, although on account of our sins, many things seem the opposite to us : for I do not consider the body and limbs of any animal where I do not find measurements and numbers and order pertaining

---

[1] Reading *fotus*.
[2] *De Gen. ad Litt.*, i. 36.
[3] *De Genesi contra Munich.*, i. 15.
[4] *I.e.* in the mind of God.
[5] *De Gen. ad Litt.*, v. 12, 13.
[6] *De Genesi contra Manich.*, i. 9.

to the unity of harmony.' [1] We have attempted to
present these views of St. Augustine because they show
very aptly the strength and the weakness of the Christian
position of those days. The Early Church Fathers inherited the Jewish conception that the Old Testament
was the literal Word of God. ' God said '—the phrase
was taken literally ; it did not need discussion ; it was
taken for granted. Yet already we begin to find, as in
Basil and Augustine, a tendency to protest against such
absolute literalness.[2] The natural tendency of childhood in race and individual alike, particularly before the
possibility of the development of alternative explanation, is to take things literally.

The divorce of magic from the science of the day is
practically complete in the case of St. Augustine.[3] Like
most of the Fathers, he distinguishes even between magic
and astrology. To the former, its exponents and devotees,
he is consistently hostile, for magic has its origin in the
activities of demons who entice men in various ways to
become their instruments. ' Unless (the devils) first
instructed men, it were impossible to know what each of
them desires, what they shrink from, by what name
they should be invoked or constrained to be present.
Hence the origin of magic and magicians. . . . Very
many things that occur, therefore, are their doing ; and
these deeds of theirs we ought all the more carefully to
shun as we acknowledge them to be very surprising.' [4]
Of the reality of magical practice he has no doubt, particularly in face of the Scriptural records of the doings
of the magicians at Pharaoh's court, the Witch of Endor,
and the Magi and ' the Star in the East.' Powerful
as these wonder-workers are, and even to be feared,
nevertheless this world is God's world, and the demons

[1] *De Genesi contra Manich.*, i. 26.
[2] Cf. *De Genesi contra Manich.*, i. 26.
[3] Cf. Lynn Thorndike, *A History of Magic and Experimental Science*,
i. 509 ff.
[4] *De Civitate Dei*, xxi. 6 (Dods' trans.).

are subject to His will. In one passage,[1] however, as noted by Professor Thorndike, St. Augustine directly associates magic and science. ' In the *Confessions*, after speaking of sensual pleasure, he also censures " the vain and curious desire of investigation " through the senses, which is " palliated under the name of knowledge and science." ' This is apt to lead one not only into scrutinising secrets of Nature which are beyond one and which it does one no good to know, and which men want to know just for the sake of knowledge, but also into ' searching through magic arts into the confines of perverse science.' In dealing with astrology, in which he had earlier been a believer, St. Augustine cannot be said to be particularly successful. That fatalistic pseudo-science still retained its direct maternal relation to astronomy, and was, as we have seen,[2] very closely connected with primitive cosmology,—which may indeed have been a causal element in the comparative lack of Early Christian interest in that study, apart from the teaching of Genesis. St. Augustine attempted to limit the influence of the stars to human lives and then assert the ability of man to transcend all such influence by reason of his free will, but says nothing that would meet the main contention of astrology, viz. that of the influence of the stars upon the world of Nature in general, and indeed to some extent he admits it. He refers also to the possibility of predicting the positions of stars and the practical value in so doing, *e.g.* in fixing the date of Easter :[3] yet such ability helps in no respect in the interpretation of Scripture. But further, controversy began to develop, not so much from the side of science as from that of science and philosophy combined, as represented in the activities of Islam and the Arabian philosophers. From Bagdad to Cordova, in particular during the ninth and tenth centuries, science and philosophy were reverenced in Muhammadan circles,

---

[1] *Op. cit.* i. 511. The reference is to *Confessions*, x. 35.
[2] *Antea*, p. 19.   [3] Cf. *De Doctrina Christiana*, ii. 29.

as only they had been in the days of ancient Greece.
It is not improbable that as these writings and investigations become more fully known, the superiority of some
of the presentation of their leading principles to some
of the work of the Christian apologists of the time will
have to be recognised.

CHAPTER VI

'THE DARK TERRESTRIAL BALL'

THE story of the succeeding centuries is in part the story of man's disillusionment with regard to the belief that the earth was the centre of the universe, and that all things upon it were created solely to subserve his interests. Yet it is also the story of man's real discovery of the earth, the beginnings of his understanding of the Universe, and the dawning of an idea that the earth has not perhaps been so much made for man as that he has been created for the Universe. It is the story of the Middle Age, that may be said to cover the period from A.D. 450-1450, roughly a thousand years, of which those from 1100-1400 represent the fullest development of the mediaeval order. Howbeit many of the older views died hard, and it is remarkable to find even to-day, preserved in English versions of the Bible, both Authorised and Revised, a relic of one of these beliefs in the form of Addison's sonorous lines :

> 'What though in solemn silence all
> Move round the dark terrestrial ball ? '[1]

With the nominal Christianising of the Roman Empire in the fourth century, a sort of blight settled down for a time upon the world of thought. In great part this was the result of the social disorder following on the destructive activities of the irrupting barbarian hordes. But further, the understanding of what Christianity was, and the Christianising of public life, had really made very little

[1] The lines are from the fifth verse of his poem beginning 'The spacious firmament on high,' printed as Hymn II. at the end of certain editions of the English Bible.

headway. To those under a firm but mistaken conviction that the end of the world and the Last Judgment were imminent—if far fewer in numbers since the close of the second century—it seemed sheer waste of time to occupy themselves with the attempts of the human mind to understand that world : the times demanded absorption in much more serious pursuits. Again, the looseness of thought and life that so often accompanied association with Greek learning had stiffened the isolating attitude of official Christianity. In 529 the Emperor Justinian, who was a patron of learning, closed the schools of Athens because of their Neoplatonic and anti-Christian tendencies, while that at Alexandria had practically come to an end with the murder of Hypatia (A.D. 415). The torch of learning thenceforth passed for a space into the hands of Hindu and Arab;[1] and although it is still difficult to estimate exactly, owing to the comparative lack of material in translation, how much of solid contribution to learning was made particularly during the tenth century, which marked the zenith of Moorish culture in Spain, yet it would seem that the Muhammadan civilisation of these days was, both on its intellectual and its practical sides, superior to that of Europe in the Middle Age. So far from being merely an exotic, evanescent dilettantism, that in its literary aspect never got very much beyond indifferent renderings of the works of the classical writers, Islam, with less of immediate conviction at its heart, was tolerant of science as contemporary official Christianity could not be.

The specific influence of Christianity upon scientific thought at this time may be seen in connection with geography. According to Beazley, 'it was with the conversion of Constantine that Christian travel, in pilgrimage, really began.'[2] Now, pilgrimage is in some

---

[1] Alexandria was taken by the Arabs in A.D. 640.
[2] *The Dawn of Modern Geography*, i. 10. The enterprising voyages of the pagan Northmen (Vikings) during the period from the fifth to the eleventh century necessarily fall outside our purview.

ways a distinctive feature of Christianity—in Islam it was mere imitation—reminiscent of the old Jewish custom of 'going up to Jerusalem,' even if the evidence seems to show that the earliest pilgrims 'went out to see' certain living miracles of austerity just as much as sacred sites, as indeed might well have been observed at the Troitzky Monastery near Moscow, and other places, in pre-war Russia. But just in proportion to the strength of the devotional impulse under which men undertook long journeys by sea and land under very hard conditions, was their outlook limited. They were seldom interested in anything beyond their immediate business, and passed with unseeing eyes and incurious minds through strange lands and unfamiliar peoples, intent only upon their goal. There was nothing progressive about these pilgrimages—no enterprise or initiative beyond the primary impulse ; they followed the same routes for centuries, and gradually hospices were raised along the way. As a matter of fact, we have an interesting commentary on them by an eye-witness, Gregory of Nyssa, who was sent from Cappadocia in the latter part of the fourth century on a tour of inspection of the Churches in Arabia, and took occasion to go to Jerusalem in order to confer with the Church leaders there. He travelled by post conveyance with special facilities granted by the Emperor Theodosius, ' so that we had to endure none of those inconveniences which in the case of others we have noticed ; our waggon was, in fact, as good as a church or monastery to us, for all of us were singing psalms and fasting in the Lord during the whole journey.'[1] He was impressed by the difficulty that men and women had in preserving modesty under the ordinary conditions of travel, and ' as the inns and hostelries and cities of the East present many examples of licence and of indifference to vice, how will it be possible for one passing through such smoke to escape without smarting eyes ? ' Further,

[1] *De Euntibus Hierosolyma.* See 'Nicene and Post-Nicene Fathers,' vol. v.; *Gregory of Nyssa,* pp. 382-383.

Jerusalem, when you got there, was a most unsafe city. ' Rascality, adultery, theft, idolatry, poisoning, quarrel- ling, murder, are rife ; and the last kind of evil is so excessively prevalent, that nowhere in the world are people so ready to kill each other as there.' In fact, all he got by way of profit as the result of his visit was ' that we came to know by being able to compare them, that our own places are far holier than those abroad. Where- fore, O ye who fear the Lord, praise Him in the places where ye now are. Change of place does not effect any drawing nearer unto God, but wherever thou mayest be, God will come to thee, if the chambers of thy soul be found of such a sort that He can dwell in thee and walk in thee. But if thou keepest thine inner man full of wicked thoughts, even if thou wast on the Mount of Olives, even if thou stoodest on the memorial-rock of the Resur- rection, thou wilt be as far away from receiving Christ into thyself, as one who has not even begun to confess Him.' It is a very striking letter, both from the religious point of view, and also as showing the unreasonableness of expecting any serious geographical work under such conditions and governing ideas.

This seems to imply that some other impulse—that of material and commercial gain, or the extension of political power, or the sheer love of adventure—had to come into operation, at any rate at first,[1] before men were willing to start out and explore the surface of the earth, whose farther seas in the popular imagination were enveloped in darkness, its distant lands inhabited by strange monsters. Nevertheless, it was the Church behind all these pilgrimages that had alone withstood the invasions of the barbarians, mediating between the Rome that she had already spiritually overcome and the hordes that later overran the city of Romulus and Remus, and in turn slowly imparting to these same

---

[1] At a later stage ' a deep longing to extend the realms of Christianity ' was, according to A. D. White (*op. cit.* i. 113), amongst the motives that influenced the minds of certain great explorers.

invaders the Graeco-Roman culture of antiquity, modified as the result of transmission through the minds of the great Christian thinkers. This ecclesiastical organisation with its wealth of tradition, its system of canon law, and its widespread medium of culture and communication in the Latin tongue, steadfastly standing and able to trace its history from Early Christian days, represented authority, and was as a refuge for men during long centuries, when they looked around them in vain for aught else that offered security either for this world or for the next. And just in that degree the mass of men were well content to give her their whole-hearted submission, and accept her guidance and instruction.

The mere fact that so much emphasis is laid upon the establishment of schools by Charlemagne in A.D. 787 in connection with the abbeys and monasteries in his Central European realm—those institutions where, as also in the case of the Celtic Church in Ireland, and in Northumbria, the fires of learning still burned—serves to indicate how little possibility there was of conflict between science and theology in these earlier centuries of the Middle Age, sometimes designated 'the Dark Ages.' Yet all higher life begins in the dark, and the energies and raw material that went to the Renaissance of the fifteenth and sixteenth centuries were in process of primary, invisible elaboration throughout the preceding ones. Contributory elements in different ways were the mentally expansive experiences of the Crusades (1090-1290) involving the re-discovery of much of the Near East; the development of Scholasticism, which, if often suggesting little more than insistent and pedantic logomachy, yet culminated in the great and impressive systems of Albert Magnus (1193-1276) and Thomas Aquinas (1227-74), which in turn were reflected in the poetry of Dante (1265-1321) ; the manifolding and distributory effects upon knowledge — for of actual increase there was little — of the founding of famous universities such as Paris, Bologna, Oxford, and Cambridge in the eleventh and twelfth centuries ; and finally the recovery of the half-forgotten treasures of Greek wisdom—Aristotle in particular—through the refracting medium of Arabic translations, that came especially by way of the Moors in Spain. Of the names that stand out, pre-eminent for freedom and originality of thought and even of experiment amongst the more questioning assenters to the ecclesiastical dogmatic demands of his time, is that of Roger Bacon (1214-1294 ?), although a sounder comparative study of his claims [1] shows him to have been a brilliant scholar representative of the best—as also, for that matter, of the darker—features of his age, rather than a solitary genius who was far in advance of it.

But now there came the period of maritime exploration, with Prince Henry the Navigator, of Portugal, as the leading figure previous to those wonderful forty years which began with the rounding of the Cape of Good Hope by Bartholomew Diaz in 1486. 'Those persons,' Aristotle had written, 'who connect the region in the neighbourhood of the Pillars of Hercules (Gibraltar) with that towards India, and who assert that in this way the ocean is one, do not assert things very improbable.' [2] Influenced by this prognostication and other considerations,[3] Columbus sailed west in order to try to reach Cathay and India by the most direct sea route, reaching his destination on 11th October 1492, yet dying fourteen years later in the belief that the land he had discovered was Asia, whereas it was a New World. Ferdinand Magellan, likewise, strong in the belief that 'the Indies' could be reached by sailing to the west, if only he could find a strait or passage through the American continent, determined to put his faith to the test. He sailed from Seville on 10th August 1519, and although he met his death in the Ladrones, his ship

---

[1] *E.g.* Prof. Lynn Thorndike, *A History of Magic and Experimental Science*, vol. ii. chap. lxi.
[2] *De Caelo*, ii. chap. 14.   Cf. *De Mundo*, 392 ᵇ, 393 ᵇ.
[3] Cf. A. D. White, *op. cit.* i. 112, 113.

was brought to anchor by his lieutenant once again near Seville, after three years of unparalleled hardship, on 7th September 1522, having circumnavigated the globe. Thus the fact of the earth's sphericity, which had been generally accepted by the leaders of thought from the eighth century onwards,[1] was absolutely demonstrated. The idea of the Antipodes, against which St. Augustine had striven so vigorously on the basis of the fact that the ' sound ' of the preachers of the gospel ' went out into all the earth, and their words into the ends of the inhabited earth,' [2] and that therefore since these heralds had not been to the Antipodes, the Antipodes did not exist, was felt increasingly to be reasonable, in spite of the influence of the ban put upon it by Pope Zacharias in the eighth century.[3] Jerusalem, which, because the inspired prophet had spoken of her in the name of the Lord to the people of his time as set ' in the midst of the nations, and countries are round about her,' [4] was fondly believed, even by Dante [5] and many of his religious contemporaries, to be literally at the centre of the earth, had thereafter to be located rather at the centre of their affections.

Meantime the tension between the exponents of science and of theology was definitely growing. The new knowledge was pouring in. For a time the ecclesiastical authorities made some attempt to assimilate it, for it was characteristic of the scholastic mind earnestly to desire to maintain a rational theology that should harmonise science and revelation. And as Professor de Burgh observes, Islam and Judaism, having much in common with Christianity, found themselves faced with much the same situation at this time.[6] But the limits of flexibility and adaptability of the Christian

---

[1] Although, of course, already proved long before. Cf. p. 23, *antea*.
[2] Rom. 10 [18].
[3] A. D. White, *op. cit.* i. 105-106.
[4] Ezek. 5 [5]; cf. 38 [12].
[5] *The Inferno*, xxxiv. 112-115.
[6] W. G. de Burgh, *The Legacy of the Ancient World*, p. 370.

presuppositions of the Middle Age were very quickly reached, and when the point came beyond which they could not go together, the only alternative was opposition, which deepened and intensified.

With the dawn of the sixteenth century there came in a sense a revelation of new heavens, as well as of a new earth. Realising the greater value of the Pythagorean as compared with the Ptolemaic ideas when applied in explanation of the diurnal and annual motions of the heavenly bodies, Nicolaus Copernicus (1473-1543) set himself deliberately to work out and test, so far as he could, a scheme of planetary and stellar movement based on the fundamental assumption of the earth's rotation on its axis and an orbital motion round the sun. Holding to the old Greek idea of uniform circular motion, he had consequently to continue to make use of epicycles, although the greater accuracy of his general point of view reduced their number, as compared with Ptolemy's, from seventy-nine to thirty-four. Already in 1507 he had finished his famous work *De Revolutionibus Orbium Celestium*, but kept it by him, although he published a brief popular account in 1530. The complete work was only published at Nüremberg in 1543 through the interest of an enthusiastic disciple, Rheticus, and the writer's evident fear of condemnation by the Church caused him to express his views in an apologetic and tentative manner, much, indeed, as Buffon did two centuries later with an eye on the Sorbonne. Thus in the Dedication to Pope Paul III. there occurs this passage : ' I found first, indeed, in Cicero, that Hicetas perceived that the Earth moved ; and afterward in Plutarch I found that some others were of this opinion, whose words I have seen fit to quote here, that they may be accessible to all :

' " Some maintain that the Earth is stationary, but Philolaus the Pythagorean says that it revolves in a circle about the fire of the ecliptic, like the sun and moon. Heraklides of Pontus and Ekphantus the Pythagorean make the Earth move, not changing its position, however, confined in its falling and rising around its own centre in the manner of a wheel."

'Taking this as a starting-point, I began to consider the mobility of the Earth ; and although the idea seemed absurd, yet because I knew that the liberty had been granted to others before me to postulate all sorts of little circles for explaining the phenomena of the stars, I thought I also might easily be permitted to try whether by postulating some motion of the Earth, more reliable conclusions could be reached regarding the revolution of the heavenly bodies, than those of my predecessors.' [1]

He associates with the production of his work two practical reasons—the disagreements and uncertainties resulting from ' the traditional mathematical methods of calculating the motions of the celestial bodies,' [2] and his expectation that his labours would help in the difficult and unsettled matter of the revision of the Ecclesiastical Calendar. In the opinion of those competent to judge, Copernicus' achievement did not lie in the sphere of accurate observational work : indeed, his imposing and profoundly analytic structure was reared upon a comparatively slender basis of fact ; but for those who were willing to understand, it was apparent that henceforth no other explanation was possible. Yet it was hooded truth, for Copernicus did not dare to throw back his cowl and openly challenge the spirit of the age, which still found in the literal acceptance of the Scriptural word alone, the sum of truth concerning God and His world. His work was placed on the Index in 1616, while a decree of the Sacred Congregation of the Index solemnly announced that ' the doctrine of the double motion of the earth about its axis and about the sun is false, and entirely contrary to Holy Scripture.' [3] This condemnation was

[1] Quoted in W. T. Sedgwick and H. W. Tyler, *A Short History of Science*, pp. 409, 410.

[2] Dedication of *The Revolutions of the Heavenly Bodies*.

[3] Quoted in A. D. White, *op. cit.* i. 138, where the whole history is related in detail, pp. 130-166.

approved and confirmed by a papal bull signed by Pope
Alexander VII. in 1664, nor was the treatise removed from
the Index until as late as the year 1835. Nevertheless,
there is no doubt that even in spite of the grave errors
incorporated in his system, as *e.g.* that the planetary
and stellar orbits were circular, Copernicus changed the
outlook on the heavens and re-established the heliocentric
theory.[1]

There now followed a steady accumulation of events
and circumstances that as outcome not merely peopled
the heavens with stars in numbers overwhelming to the
naked-eye observers, but also disclosed a reign of law
stupendous in its sublimity and unlimited in its range.
To these in chief measure contributed the new standard
of accuracy set up by Tycho Brahe (1546-1601), the
resolving deductive genius of Kepler (1571-1630)—like
Copernicus, more of a mathematician than an observer—
that after patient calculations, conducted over well-
nigh a quarter of a century, was able to confine within
three short sentences the fundamental principles of
planetary motion; and lastly, the sweeping, penetrating
vision of Galileo (1564-1642) resulting from the newly
invented telescope. By its means the satellites of
Jupiter, the mountains of the moon, the phases of Venus,
the rings of Saturn, and several other astronomical
discoveries of first importance in establishing the
Copernican contentions, were intimated to an, at first,
largely incredulous public—discoveries that incidentally
both shook and shocked the ecclesiastical composure,
whose world still was as it had been in the beginning,
and looked very much as if it would be the same till the
end. In 1609, Kepler, who believed that each planet
was the seat of an intelligent principle, published his

---

[1] C. R. Beazley, *op. cit.* i. 276 *n.*, states that the Heliocentric
School of antiquity ' received much greater support than is often
supposed (*e.g.* Seneca will not pronounce against it, *Nat. Quaest.*, vii. 2),
and was at least known to Aristotle and Ptolemy ; but, on the whole,
was regarded as impossible, even by educated opinion.'

book *On the Motions of the Planet Mars*,[1] in which he intimated his first and second laws. These he had reached as the result of his failure to reconcile the movements of that planet with the hitherto accepted hypotheses of eccentrics and epicycles. The orbit, he found, is an ellipse, not a circle, with the sun in one of the foci, and the straight line joining the planet to the sun sweeps over equal areas in equal intervals of time. In a later work, issued in 1619, and entitled *An Epitome of the Copernican System*, he enunciated his third law to the effect that the squares of the times of revolution of planets about the sun are proportional to the cubes of their mean distances from the sun. This law was shown to hold in the case of Jupiter and his satellites, but acceptance of it was not general till Newton supplied the key. Of the four men, Galileo Galilei alone regarded the presentation of his truth as a crusade; peculiarly modern-minded, he fought a great fight single-handed. In 1632 he presented his views in the not uncommon contemporary form of a *Dialogue on the two Chief Systems of the World, the Ptolemaic and the Copernican*, in the course of which he says, ' I can listen only with the greatest repugnance when the quality of unchangeability is held up as something pre-eminent and complete in contrast to variability. I hold the earth for most distinguished exactly on account of the transformations which take place upon it,' [2]—a very far-seeing remark. If, as seems undeniable, even this strong personality was in the end cowed into a betrayal of what he knew to be the truth, no one at any rate of this generation will be found with stones of scientific self-righteousness in their hands to fling at him.

More wistful than all the great investigators and researchers stands the gaunt figure of Giordano Bruno (*c.* 1548-1600), who very early published a speculative

---

[1] The exact title was *Astronomia nova αἰτιολογητός, seu Physica coelestis tradita commentariis de motibus stellae Martis.*

[2] Quoted in Sedgwick and Tyler, *op. cit.* p. 225.

work on *The Infinity of the Universe and of Worlds*. Yet
his work was not entirely theoretical. His preoccupation with the new star that suddenly appeared in the
constellation Cassiopeia, during November 1572, and
to which Tycho Brahe paid so much attention, led him to
collect all the observations he could find about it for the
use of future astronomers. His interest in the plurality of
worlds refused to let him be limited by Scripture in what
he was ready to believe about the stars, and he did not
hesitate to maintain that it was no part of the purpose
of Scripture to teach man natural science; its truths
were moral truths.[1] From these considerations he rose
to an elaborated panentheistic view of things that in
broad outline is acceptable to many minds even at the
present day. But every system that seemed to detract
from the uniqueness of the earth, and accordingly en-
dangered the Church's scheme of salvation, was intolerable
to the ecclesiastical mind, and Bruno, scorning to recant,
was burned at the stake for loyalty to truth as he had
learned it.

A long period of observation of the apparent motions
of the heavenly bodies had now been succeeded by a
period of discovery of their real motions, and of the laws
of planetary motion. But it was Newton who inaugurated
yet another era by supplying the causal key to the whole
by the discovery of the principle of gravitation. The
transition to the Newtonian period followed upon the
marked development of dynamics with which the names
of Leonardo da Vinci, sculptor, painter, architect, and
engineer (1452-1519), of Stevinus of Bruges (1548-1620),
whose merits apparently still await adequate recognition,
and especially of Galileo, are associated. For the last-

---

[1] ' Aber jedermann kann klar und deutlich erkennen, dass die
heiligen Schriften nicht Beweise und Spekulationen über naturwis-
senschaftliche Dinge bringen wollen, als handle es sich um Philosophie ;
sie wenden sich nicht an unseren Verstand, sondern an unser Gemüt
und unser Gewissen ; durch Gebote regeln sie die praktische Sittlich-
keit ' (*Aschermittwochsmahl*, ' Vierter Dialog ').

named, by his statement of the three fundamental Laws of Motion in that work of his old age, *Conversations and Mathematical Demonstrations on two New Branches of Science*—that is to say, Dynamics and Statics—published in 1638, prepared the way for the publication of Newton's *Principia* in 1687. Throughout this treatise Galileo holds closely to experiment, drawing therefrom his results. He expressed great confidence in the future development of his ideas. 'The theorems set forth in this brief discussion will, when they come into the hands of other investigators, continually lead to wonderful new knowledge. It is conceivable that in such a manner a worthy treatment may be gradually extended to all the realms of Nature.'[1] This prediction was fulfilled within half a century, when, by the application of the laws of dynamics to the heavenly bodies, Newton accounted for all their movements, and found the active cause in the force of gravity.

Man's chief glory is not in what he is, so much as in what it lies within his power to become. Yet it is obvious that to a crudely anthropocentric world whose interest was so largely in the past, the Copernican view, implying the democratisation of an earth thus dislodged from its central position and suggesting the possibility that in other systems than our own might likewise be found homes of the 'sons of God,' seemed to entail a loss of prestige and uniqueness which was far-reaching in its theological and practical aspects. On the other hand, not merely is it true that in a very literal way the thoughts of men 'are widened with the process of the suns,'[2] but that they are also thereby rendered more of a unity. There is a sense, as the result of the work of Einstein, in which it is just as true to say that the sun goes round the earth, as that the earth goes round the sun. The measurements of the positions of the stars are the same on Copernicus' views as on Einstein's. Indeed, this would also be the

---

[1] Quoted in Sedgwick and Tyler, *op. cit.* p. 249.
[2] Alfred Tennyson, *Locksley Hall*.

case on Tycho Brahe's outlook as on that of Copernicus,[1] so that in strict logic we are not entitled to press the one view more than the other. But each of these successive views gives a more compact scheme of the universe than its predecessor. It was an enormous simplification to think that the earth was rotating, rather than the stars. If my watch disagrees with all the clocks in the city, it does not necessarily prove that my watch is wrong, although the theory of probability would be deeply involved, but it is simpler to assume that the others are right. There is, as a matter of fact, nothing absolute in science, although the followers of Einstein assume this of the velocity of light. The great merit of Copernicus' view just was that it put the earth on a parallel or equality with the other planets—treated it in the same way. Originally there did not seem to be very much in the analogy ; now we know that there is a great deal.

It is difficult to realise how every inch of ground in the reclamation of the corners of the field of knowledge, pre-empted as a whole by the Church, had to be fought for by the young sciences, or how the right to investigate had to be won in face of what seemed to be overwhelming odds. The challenge to the tyranny of tradition, the insistence on observation, experiment, and reason in place of the mere blind acceptance of mysteries, were hard to maintain against the vested authority of a Church which claimed to hold the power of the keys. It all seemed to encroach so seriously on the divine prerogative and activities as these were conceived by the Church in terms of its understanding of the Scriptures ; so Kepler's *Epitome*, for example, was immediately put upon the Index. If the world was thus an arena of the exercise of immutable law, neither God nor priest could intervene

---

[1] ' Sensible, however, of the weakness of the Ptolemaic theory, he (*i.e.* Tycho Brahe) devised an ingenious compromise in which the planets revolved about the sun in their respective periods, and the entire heavens about the earth daily, all of which is not mathematically different from the Copernican theory ' (W. T. Sedgwick and H. W. Tyler, *op. cit.* p. 209).

to stay the pestilence or cause increase in the herds :
God and the priests simply cancelled one another out.
Very desperate were some of the early expedients adopted
in order to make any headway at all. Thus we read [1]
that the condition of admission into the Accademia del
Cimento, which was founded at Florence in 1657, was
'an abjuration of all faith, and a resolution to inquire
into the truth.' It numbered Torricelli (1608-1647),
the inventor of the barometer, amongst its members, yet
after ten years of activity it was suppressed at the instance
of the Papal Government. Similarly the Royal Society
of London, incorporated in 1662, was accused of an
intention of 'destroying the established religion, of
injuring the universities, and of upsetting ancient and
solid learning.' [2] The introduction of the Gregorian
Calendar in England in 1752—nearly one hundred and
seventy years after its adoption on the Continent—
through the activity of the Royal Society, was the cause
of a remarkable religious outbreak on the part of those
who got the impression that in some way they had been
robbed of eleven days of their lives.

On the other hand, the liberating aspect of some of
the discoveries of these immortal heroes deserves to be
noticed. Thus to many minds in an age that believed
that comets were composed of the ascended sins and
wickedness of mankind in gaseous form, ignited by the
wrath of God, and doomed to return to earth again
causing pestilence and other calamities, or were of the
nature of fire-balls flung by the hand of an angry Deity,
it was something of a relief to be able to understand, with
Tycho's aid, how very far off the comet of 1577 actually
was, as also something of its real character. So also
was it with regard to the common and terrifying interpretations of meteors and eclipses, which were readily
associated with such passages in Scripture as Joel 2 [30] or

---

[1] J. W. Draper, *History of the Conflict between Religion and Science*,
p. 300.
[2] Quoted in Draper, *op. cit.* p. 307.

Luke 21 [25]. The emancipation from fear that has steadily followed in the wake of science is a partial illumination and verification of that supreme word, ' And ye shall know the truth, and the truth shall make you free.' [1]

In endeavouring to isolate some of the factors that led to the tension between the exponents of natural science and theology in the past, we have had occasion to note the bondage to the letter of Scripture that prevented the Church from doing justice to that progressive understanding of the world that was being reached through scientific investigation. To this must be added that claim of inerrancy or infallibility on the part of the Roman Church in the interpretation of Scripture and the enunciation of truth, that, as persisted in to-day, can only cause a smile on the part of any man resolved to retain his mind as his own.[2] It is only fair, however, to add that in the Middle Age this type of assumption was not restricted to the Church. Thus Malebranche in his *Recherche de la Vérité* [3] speaks of philosophers and cultured people who practically believed in the infallibility of Aristotle, and were more interested in what he had to say upon a question like the immortality of the soul than in the actual point as to whether the soul was immortal or not. He quotes Averroës as saying of Aristotle's doctrine that it ' est SUMMA VERITAS, quoniam ejus intellectus fuit finis humani intellectus.' The writings of Aristotle provided a complete system of knowledge, so dear to the mediaeval mind, while his ' tendency to seek for the principles of natural philosophy by considering the meaning of the words ordinarily used to describe the phenomena of nature, which to us is his great defect,

[1] John 8 [32].
[2] The doctrine of the infallibility of the Pope, sanctioned by Thomas Aquinas, was actually promulgated by Pius IX. at an Ecumenical Council, as comparatively recently as July 1870.
[3] *Op. cit.* livre deuxième, deuxième partie, chaps. v. and vi. I am indebted to Prof. W. P. Paterson for the reference, and for some direc tion at this point. Cf. also Dante, *Convivio*, iv. 6.

appealed strongly to the mediaeval mind, and, unfortunately, finally helped to retard the development of science in the days of Copernicus and Galileo.' [1] There was a long period when any scientific dogma that went contrary to Aristotle's teaching simply could not be true. The representatives of science and of philosophy, that is to say, were likewise in ' the gall of bitterness and the bond of ' the letter. So that there is no particular reason to inveigh against the Roman theologians any more than against the men of science or the philosophers of the Middle Age on the ground of being the subjects of foregone conclusions. Especially is this the case when we take into consideration the degree in which, from a very early stage in history, education in law and science, in addition to religion, had been in the hands of the priesthood, who really represented in these days the mind of the world, and were on the whole remarkably hospitable to whatever there was in the way of science or philosophy, as well as being, in some instances, the instigators of research.

It might, however, have been supposed that, as the result of the revolutionary and emancipating influences of the Reformation (1517), the newer teachings of natural science about the earth and its place in the Universe would have received more friendly consideration within the ranks of Protestantism. Unfortunately, in some respects, just when it seemed as if there was an opportunity of getting away from that rigid adherence to the letter of Scripture that had proved so disastrous on occasions in the past, the whole character of the Reformation, while securing that Scripture was the sole and sufficient guide for the Christian believer, in that measure riveted afresh upon the edifice of the new Church the dogmatic superstructure that had been raised upon the Pentateuchal narratives. Yet in its own way the development followed very intelligible lines.

[1] J. L. E. Dreyer, *History of Planetary Systems from Thales to Kepler*, p. 122.

In connection with the literature of the great religions, it is usually possible to discriminate different stages. There is, first, the period of origin, with the great creative minds, like the prophets in Israel, which is followed by an age of commenting scribes and interpreting lawyers. The same situation holds in a lesser degree in philosophy, where the appearance of an Aristotle, Kant, or Hegel is succeeded by an Aristotelian, Kantian, or Hegelian school, devoted to exposition and commentary. The authority of the master is set up as if he were infallible, aided by the natural tendency to magnify an authority. For, after all, the mass of men want things emphasised. 'St. Peter has spoken; this you must believe' is a more impressive way with the crowd than merely to say, 'This is a thing that finds me.' The Roman Catholic position had been, 'This is true because it is found in Scripture, as interpreted by an infallible Church,' which the Protestant countered by saying, 'There is no infallible Church, but there is this infallible Book.' It was the strongest direct reply at the moment to the Roman pretensions, and dogma tended to harden in the immediate post-Reformation times because of polemical exigencies. Throughout the Middle Age the Scriptures had been regarded as ultimate authority. 'A clear Scriptural word is decisive' was, in effect, the view of the ecclesiastical world of that era, but then it carefully selected the authoritative utterances. And this selective treatment likewise characterised the leaders of Protestantism. Said John Calvin, 'Here are the Scriptures ; they represent different stages of thought.' There were for him, assuredly, central verities—for example, justification by faith and the sovereignty of God—which he believed to be true, but then he interpreted the rest of Scripture in the light of them. With his legal training, he tended to look upon the Bible as a book of statutes ; and great and far-reaching as his accomplishments were, he undoubtedly tied the Protestant Church to a bold doctrine of verbal inspiration. There was no Protestant of these Reformation days who did not believe that Scripture was the word of God, but they also, as the Fathers of the Middle Age had done, selected their passages, and employed spiritual or dogmatic or allegorical interpretation as suited their purpose. Protestantism, that is to say, was still very largely a movement within the rigidly given and fixed content of Scripture, although it gave the right of private interpretation. To-day, with a scientific attitude towards Scripture itself, we realise that the attitude about an infallible Book can no longer be maintained, at any rate in its old form, and with this realisation the tension between natural science and theology immediately begins to slacken off. For after all it was not the Bible *qua* Bible, but the things that Luther discovered in it—the sublimity and saving power of its essential doctrine—that found and held him. The Bible constituted the defence rather than the ground of his faith.

Protestantism, then, did not bring any immediate relief from the old tendency, strong as in the days of Tertullian and St. Augustine, to measure up all science and philosophy against the relevant statements of Scripture, and of Genesis in particular. To Luther, Copernicus was 'that fool and knave,' 'an upstart astrologer,' [1] just as in judgment upon Aristotle, who had become so much to the Roman theologians, he had spoken of him as 'that ridiculous and injurious blasphemer,' whose 'propositions are so absurd that an ass or a stone would cry out at them,' 'that Greek buffoon, who like a spectre has befooled the church,' 'that cursed (*verdammte*), arrogant, rascally heathen,' 'truly a devil, a horrid calumniator, a wicked sycophant, a prince of darkness, a real Apollyon, a beast, a most horrid impostor on mankind, one in whom there is scarcely any philosophy,

---

[1] Cf. *Tischreden* in Walsch edition of Luther's *Works*, 1743, xxii. 2260; quoted in A. D. White, *op. cit.* i. 126.

a public and professed liar, a goat, a complete epicure, this twice execrable Aristotle,'[1] although not one of this battery of epithets had any justification. The divorce of official Christianity from the science[2] and philosophy of the day resulted in even harsher measures against any assertion of freedom of thought, as Calvin's share in the burning of Michael Servetus, a distinguished Spanish anatomist (1509-1553), whose anti-Trinitarian writings proved distasteful to him and the Inquisition alike, testifies. The stain of the Inquisition as a whole is indeed ineradicable, while the idea of prohibition expressed through the Index Expurgatorius is a standing insult to reason itself. Yet even these are but incidents in that century-long, debasing and degrading hold of Latin Christianity upon Europe from the sixth to the sixteenth century, when, with many notable exceptions of disinterested piety and self-sacrificing life, the papal system created a deadening atmosphere ' both as regards physical well-being and intellectual culture,'[3] in which it could maintain itself, primarily in its own sordid interests of temporal power and material estate.

There is one final matter—the delicate question of the age of the earth—the controversies in connection with which, arising out of the differences between the teachings of science and ecclesiastical chronology, are still with some a living memory. At times we fail to realise how comparatively recent the greatest conflicts have been, and that the process of adjustment is certain to continue so long as man remains a learner. Some issues indeed are decided, and others have been outgrown, but new

[1] Preserved Smith, *The Life and Letters of Luther*, pp. 26, 84; J. W. Draper, *op. cit.* p. 215.

[2] Draper considers this began when she ' compelled Origen, at that time (A.D. 231) its chief representative and supporter in the Church, to abandon his charge in Alexandria, and retire to Caesarea,' *op. cit.* p. 215.

[3] J. W. Draper, *op. cit.* p. 285. The whole chapter on ' Latin Christianity in Relation to Modern Civilisation ' may still be read as supplying a largely accurate account of Europe from the sixth to the sixteenth century under Rome.

ones loom continually on the horizon. The authority of the Patristic chronology, if not indeed the institutional authority of the Church, has ceased to be 'a live option,' and most thinking men accept some evolutionary conception as applied to man's nature both physical and spiritual. But to-day questions are raised as to whether religion may not be self-induced illusion, and whether it is permissible to believe in progress, while the readjustment in Christian theology that must follow on the recognition of the vastly extended antiquity of man, and the marked extension of more or less documented human history, is hardly even grasped as yet. There is little—some would say nothing—that will not have to be done all over again in the presentation of Christian truth, from the foundation upwards, in the light of the continually growing revelation of God in His world, but this will ever preserve at its core its final and unchanging elements.

It is instructive fact that although the human race has been in existence for at least 400,000 years, Europe had no proper chronology before A.D. 527, when Dionysius Exiguus, a Roman abbot, fixed the present Christian style of reckoning.[1] Events previous to A.D. 1 were calculated out on the bases of the Scriptural data, although it was realised that in fixing such an event as e.g. the Deluge, different results came out according as different premises were adopted. There was a general consensus up to about the middle of the nineteenth century that the creation of the world could not have taken place more than four to six thousand years before the birth of Christ, according as statements in the Hebrew text or the Septuagint rendering of the Old Testament were taken as the basis of calculation. The literal interpretation of other events related in the early chapters of Genesis had also led to much speculation, e.g. as to the primitive speech of man, and the causes of the marked reduction in longevity subsequent to the Deluge. On the other hand, there was no doubt as to the universality

[1] J. W. Draper, op. cit. p. 184.

of that catastrophe, or the original perfection in intelligence and morality of the individual, Adam. Christian Theology, as thus developed, could have met neither the idea of a great antiquity for man, which would seem as if God had reserved the supreme expression of His mercy simply for those upon whom the ends of the ages had come, nor the conception of the first man as a being other than of the degree of mental and moral development presented to us, let us say, in Milton's *Paradise Lost*, since that would have left unintelligible the doctrine of the Fall and ' the plan of salvation.'

With the question of the age of the earth the situation is very different. Geology is, comparatively speaking, one of the youngest of the sciences, and yet its testimony is corporately and uniformly indicative of an age for our planet that is inconceivably great. In 1917 Professor Schuchert [1] had estimated 800 million years for the geological eras subsequent to the initial Cosmic Era, which was itself, in Dana's opinion, not shorter than the sum of the succeeding ones. These 800 million years Schuchert divided in the following proportions: Archaeozoic, 25 per cent.; Proterozoic, 30 per cent.; Palaeozoic, 28 per cent.; Mesozoic, 12 per cent.; Cainozoic, 5 per cent. The discovery of radio-activity, and methods of estimation based with confidence upon the perfectly determinable average quantities of radium and uranium contained in the most ordinary rocks, enabled Lord Rayleigh, as the result of long investigations conducted by Professor Joly and himself, to conclude that they indicated 'a moderate multiple of 1000 million years as the possible and probable duration of the earth's crust as suitable for the habitation of living beings, and that no other considerations from the side of physics or astronomy afford any definite presumption against this estimate.' [2] We may smile or we may reflect;

[1] Cf. *The Evolution of the Earth and its Inhabitants*, edited by R. S. Lull, p. 69.

[2] *Report of British Association for the Advancement of Science*, 1921, p. 414. 'The age of the earth is therefore probably between $1\cdot3 \times 10^9$ and 8×10^9 years' (Dr. Harold Jeffreys, *The Earth*, p. 78).

but he who has realised the immensity of time has not merely gained one of the highest rewards of natural science, but is prepared to understand with the apostolic writer ' that one day is with the Lord as a thousand years, and a thousand years as one day.' [1]

[1] 2 Pet. 3 [8]; cf. Ps. 90 [4].

CHAPTER VII

THE CONCEPTION OF NATURAL LAW

No theoretical result of that exploration of the world which men call Science has been more fruitful than the conception of Natural Law. Yet this idea also was fiercely resisted by theologians from the beginning as something undesirable and subversive, and it is still looked at askance in some quarters as an implied challenge to the divine omnipotence.

The astronomer observes, as the Babylonians did four thousand years ago, that one evening he can see the moon for a few minutes as a thin arch of light low down on the western horizon, and that on successive evenings the arch broadens and is visible for ever longer periods, until as a full circle of light it shines the whole night through. Thereafter it as steadily shrinks in size till it again becomes a thin arch seen for a few moments in the eastern sky before sunrise. Then for two or three days and nights there is no sign of it at all. He further observes—and in this science his rôle throughout is that of the observer, for he can initiate no experiments—that these phases recur with periodic regularity, which, as a whole, have been called moneths or months: behaviour, that is, of the mona, or moon, or more exactly the time of one revolution of the moon around the earth. Again, the chemist takes white (*i.e.* ordinary) phosphorus (atomic weight 16·8), and heats it in the presence of its own vapour to a temperature of about 240 degrees, when it changes into an allotropic variety known as red or

144

amorphous phosphorus (atomic weight 14·7). The zoologist touches the protozoon *Stentor* gently with his dissecting needle, and immediately the creature contracts, and will do so in response to repeated provocations of this character. In all these cases there seems to be a result, or response, or behaviour which is repeated under the same conditions and about which it is possible to make predictions, although in an ever-lessening degree as the investigator comes to deal with higher forms in the scale of life.

According to Eucken,[1] the expression ' law of nature ' was originally used by the Greeks ' with reference, not to the external world, but to human nature itself,' and denoted the unwritten law, established in traditional usage and custom, as contrasted with the written law. Plato, indeed, in the *Timaeus*,[2] speaks once of results arising from ' violation of the laws of Nature,' and Aristotle likewise in a single instance makes use of the same term,[3] but the word more commonly used in this connection was ἀνάγκαι, *i.e.* the necessities of Nature—natural wants or desires. The conception of natural law was probably first applied by the Greeks in astronomy and medicine, and passed into general usage in the Middle Age through Roman writers. As yet, however, the term conveyed no idea beyond that of a certain regularity of events—the ordinary established mode of divine action, from the point of view of the Church Fathers—which might, however, quite well be interfered with, or departed from, on occasion, and was thus not inconsistent with the conception of miracle. From the time of Descartes, however, a more precise signification was attached to the expression; and with the development of scientific analysis and consequent endeavour to explain a phenomenon by its elements, the expressions of the simplest forms of motion of these elements became the

---

[1] *E.R.E.*, ' Law,' vii. 805.
[2] Jowett's trans., iii. 506.
[3] *De Caelo*, 263 A, 10 ff.

K

basis of natural philosophy. Knowledge of these formulae or laws gave man power to predict and to control, until in the state of knowledge towards the end of last century, these laws seemed in turn to control man in his thinking and his whole relationship to Nature. It is only comparatively recently, and particularly as the result of the stimulus to thought in the pronouncements of Einstein, that once again a readjustment is being made that carries with it a truer understanding of the scope and character of natural law.

The precision referred to above came from the gradual introduction of mathematics in the statement of laws, from the time of Kepler's three laws of planetary motion onwards, but the term is often applied to relations where no quantitative basis has been established, *e.g.* the Biogenetic Law of Haeckel.[1] Many a proffered solution in terms of law is, however, nothing more than the statement of a problem, and by a peculiar confusion of thought, natural laws are even sometimes identified with the forces of whose behaviour they are simply the formal expression. A natural law is merely a *résumé* of behaviour or activity, whether in the animate or the inanimate world. But just because it is an observed rule of phenomena, the natural law compels us to seek explanations, as a state of chaos never would. The Universe on which we look out to-day is a dynamic Universe, in contrast with the static Multiverse that occupied the attention of previous generations. That is to say, we are aware fundamentally of motion, of energy, of power of doing work. There is activity or behaviour in all things, and the so-called Laws of Nature are symbolical conceptual statements of the method of that behaviour in its objective and perceptual regularity. None the less they represent only singly selected and abstracted aspects ; no one law can ever fully

---

[1] 'Ontogeny is the short and rapid recapitulation of phylogeny, conditioned by the physiological functions of heredity (reproduction) and adaptation (nutrition).' *General Morphology*, ii. p. 300.

describe an event or piece of behaviour, for the event is always much too complex.[1] On the other hand, the reduction and simplification that have to be carried out in the case of any series of events before it is possible to lay bare the terms of a particular relation within that series is usually so extreme, that there is always room for a large margin of error in any subsequent general account of the series as a whole that includes the law thus isolated; in fact, the greater the degree of simplification, the greater the range of possible empirical inaccuracy in respect of that whole.

So long as natural law is realised to be what it actually is, and no more, science advances. On the other hand, that progress may be hindered for the time being when such laws are worked up into a philosophy and extended into regions other than those that supplied the data on the strength of which they were originally reached. An extreme example of this tendency is the declaration, as old as the Pythagoreans, that all scientific knowledge is capable of mathematical statement—'All things are numbers,' Pythagoras had said—and the corollary, sometimes appended, or implied, that any knowledge that cannot thus be expressed is not of real value. To be countable or numerable is a fundamental characteristic of objective things, and in the absence of all characteristics other than similarity and dissimilarity would be markedly a law, indeed the law, of things. So generally fundamental, indeed, is this characteristic that Professor A. N. Whitehead asserts that 'all science as it grows towards perfection becomes mathematical in its ideas.'[2] Such a statement, however, while on its formal side true of all things physical, seems meaningless when applied to the realm of personality, of mind and qualitative distinctions;

---

[1] Thus, 'in the simplified proof which is given of Boyle-Mariotte's law in the kinetic theory of gases it is assumed that all the molecules have the same velocity, that all collisions are central, and that the molecules can only move parallel to the three edges of a cube, and so on' (C. E. Guye, *Physico-chemical Evolution*, p. 39 n.).

[2] A. N. Whitehead, *An Introduction to Mathematics*, p. 14.

here is no measurable extension. While it is undeniable fact that mathematics has an empirical element in it and is applicable to Reality, yet mathematical laws are in a certain measure a creation of the mind. Indeed, the prior problem is far from determined, and requires investigation as to how far, as a matter of fact, mathematics does, or even can, give us a thorough-going account of Reality. From the human point of view mathematical laws imply something new ; there is nothing of the exclusively *a priori* or *a posteriori* about them,[1] and if we are to get anywhere at all, we have to assume that there must be the possibility of some correspondence between the actual laws of things and the human capacity of understanding them. The characters and dispositions and properties attaching to natural process must be amenable to intelligence, must be intelligible. Yet while we may find a tendency to order, to classification and even to activity in things, we cannot say *a priori* how far activity and actuality are the product of intelligence. That is to say, we can only learn empirically how far mathematical laws suggested to our minds, and yet in a sense created by them, are coextensive with Reality.

In addition to their abstractness, however, there are other respects in which the laws of nature, as formulated, afford less aid than we are apt to suppose towards any ultimate understanding of Reality, even if they correctly express aspects of its activity as understood up to any particular date in time. The extraordinary precision which they suggest blinds us to the fact that they can never be more than approximations. No principle is better established on an experimental basis than that of the Conservation of Matter, yet if the mass of a body is, according to the newer knowledge, proportional to its total energy, some modification of the older principle is required, and that of the Conservation of Energy becomes more fundamental. To what a slight extent

[1] E. Boutroux, *Natural Law in Science and Philosophy*, p. 40.

Reality is embraced by the scheme of natural law may be readily realised by any consideration of the limitation of those senses that aid in providing the substratum of fact, and of the character of the mental picture that we base upon the information thus supplied. For apart from sentient beings, the Universe is a realm of eternal silence and black darkness through whose ethereal consistency surge myriad waves of differing vibrational amplification and length, and these sentient beings can respond and enter into relation with but an infinitesimal proportion of the continually impinging stimuli that constitute the known ranges of vision, sound, and tactile capacity. Were our senses developed or quick enough to perceive electronic motions, space would never be void to us. There *is* no such thing as space empty ; it is simply a relative expression. The emptiness of space is relative to our interest and to the nature of the activity we exercise.

Again there is nothing to suggest that the world is self-sufficient, and there are some considerations that indicate the contrary. Reality—the Universe as we know it—appears as an increasingly complex manifestation, of which we come to know and understand aspects only, and that by abstraction from the physical and organic phenomena that exist in Nature. The complexity is both an actual development in the Universe itself, and something that becomes progressively known to us as we advance in knowledge. And when we meet with mechanical principles like the Conservation of Energy, we must always remember that we cannot isolate them from one another in Reality as if they were separate entities, and that all our knowledge of them is of the nature of inductions on a comparatively small range of experimental work. All that we are entitled to affirm is that in Reality, in the Universe, there is a mode of being and behaviour, *e.g.* the regular constant dependence between two magnitudes, which suggests the idea of mechanical law. Yet no proof is forthcoming that the support of mechanical phenomena is itself mechanical; it cannot be shown that the World-Ground is mechanical, and mechanism certainly cannot explain itself. Accordingly, any belief in the absolute immutability of natural law really transcends experience, and it may very easily be as much a retarding as a helpful attitude to assume dogmatically that the unknown is governed only by the same laws as the known. We do not *know* whether such laws as have been already formulated are fundamental and primal, or merely resultants. They may be the scaffolding, but it does not follow that the relations represented by them have not developed and may not be, even now, undergoing modification with secular slowness. They condition the building; the different elements condition one another—indeed, must do so, if the world is the unity which we believe it to be. But if the ascertained laws of Nature are not thus independent of other laws that may be concealed from us in Nature, and of which they may just as well be the consequence as the cause, we are in no position to maintain that their immutability is absolute. It may very well be that the absolute fixity that we attribute to them is relative and contingent only. If they are at all representative or expressive of phases of a developing process, it seems theoretically possible that there may be development in the relations themselves—that, in short, the laws of Nature are not, and cannot in the circumstances of the case be, absolutely rigid in themselves. Not merely may more complex relationships be in process of development during the aeons, involving modification in those statements of them known as laws, but new ones also may come to light and into being, for it is difficult to see how progress can be secured *within* a system of fixed laws alone. The laws of Nature represent at any selected time the manageable relations of things as registered on the basis of experience at that time, and within limits the phenomena of Nature comply. But that the relation has always been of that particular degree or type, and is so now in the case of corresponding situations throughout the Universe as a whole, is something that we do not know, and that can only be maintained on the basis of a tremendous act of faith.

It may appear too challenging a proposition thus to suggest that had we the means at our disposal, and a historical record of exact science of sufficient length, we should find changes to be necessary in those statements of relations which we call laws, not merely because of the circumstance that advancing knowledge brings with it more exact approximation to fact, but because in this developing process there had come about very gradual secular changes in some of the actual relationships themselves. Laws, it will be said, are mental judgments, and they are either true or false. Truth does not develop. All that could happen is that with development in process certain laws might cease to hold. There is a substance H and another substance O, and whenever these unite in the proportions of two atoms of H to one of O, we get another substance H_2O, always and everywhere verifiably recognisable as water.

Now, it seems a hard saying that for man, at any rate, truth does not develop ; in so far as true thought is thought representative of the actual nature of Reality, it must so develop. There is certainly a body of fact which may be said to grow in the sense that additions are all the time being made to it, and as a result of those additions there is development in the whole in the sense that any conspectus of it takes a slightly different form with the advance of the ages. Further, it is by their coherence with this objective body of truth already ascertained that the merits of later factual candidates for incorporation are judged as worthy or unworthy, *i.e.* true or false. With the advance in the understanding of the world, an older law would not so much cease to hold, and in that sense go out of existence, so to speak, as be subsumed in some fuller statement. And if we know that, in the interval separating the Azoic phase of our planet's history from to-day, the ocean has grown colder and more saline, that its reaction has changed from faintly acid to faintly alkaline, that, in short, the whole ensemble of conditions of temperature and atmosphere were greatly different then from what they are to-day, it becomes legitimate to inquire whether under this slow secular developmental process the properties of elements, and that which we understand by the terms chemical affinity or electricity, or indeed physico-chemical laws as a whole, may not themselves have become very slightly modified in the course of the aeons. It has been stated, on expert authority, that ' the lunar tables of the *Nautical Almanac* for 1923 had to be entirely refigured just before the volume went to press ; and the solar eclipse of the autumn before was fifteen seconds off schedule.' [1] The reason in the first instance was not, apparently, any error in calculation, but simply the fact that even to-day the theory of the moon's motion is still so far from being complete ' that the predicted declinations and right ascensions have to be adjusted from time to time ' to match the place where the luminary actually is in the sky. All scientific knowledge at any time is mere approximation, and with more accurate methods of measurement, and a growing understanding of the Universe, it is not disturbing that earlier statements of relations should be found to be inexact. In this particular case it is most probable that the recent work of Professor E. W. Brown [2] and the tables founded upon it ' will keep the moon right for about two hundred years,' by which time probably a fresh treatment will have been devised and further improvements have become necessary. Yet it is conceivable that this is not the whole explanation of such

[1] E. T. Brewster, *The Understanding of Religion*, p. 74. The solar eclipse of 24th January 1925 was three to four seconds behind time.

[2] I am indebted to Sir O. Lodge for drawing my attention to this work, and to Prof. Sampson for the following references : *Monthly Notices of R.A.S.*, ' On the Degree of Accuracy of the Lunar Theory,' lxiv. 109, lxv. 104, and lxvii. 300.

inexactnesses. For example, it is well known that the earth's magnetic field is very slowly changing. Columbus discovered the line of no variation and believed that it was a fixed geographical line or boundary between the Eastern and the Western Hemispheres.[1] Pope Alexander VI. even adopted the line as the perpetual boundary between the possessions of Spain and Portugal in his arbitration bull of May 1493. Subsequently, however, it was found that the line was moving eastward, and in 1662 it actually coincided with the meridian of London. Here we are even more in the field of the unknown, but it is not impossible that in addition we are dealing with a changing relation that is due to some developmental cause. So, too, Dr. L. A. Bauer, in an important communication upon the problem of terrestrial magnetism,[2] makes these arresting statements : ' The difficulties to be met in the formation of any adequate theory of the origin of the earth's magnetism are in part mathematical, in part geometrical, because of the sphericity of the earth-magnet, but they arise chiefly from the physical conditions involved. No matter what theory is proposed, somewhere a hypothesis must be introduced implying new properties of matter or physical conditions below and above the earth's surface, regarding which we have at present either no knowledge whatsoever or but the faintest glimpse. The same remarks apply to that other great problem of cosmical physics—the origin of the earth's electricity. It has accordingly been suggested that terrestrial magnetism and atmospheric electricity may reveal to us hitherto unknown properties of matter ; for the properties which the rotating earth and the rotating sun may possess, because of their masses, sizes, and angular velocities, may fail of detection with the experimental conditions

---

[1] J. W. Draper, *History of the Conflict between Religion and Science*, p. 162.
[2] 'Some Physical Aspects of a Recent Analysis of the Earth's Magnetic Field,' *Science*, vol. lviii. No. 1494 (17th August 1923).

possible in the laboratory.' After showing that the strength of the magnetic fields of the earth, atmosphere, and sun may be expressed approximately by the product of a physical factor, ' f,' into the angular rotation, ' ω,' the square of the radius, ' r,' and the density, D, of the body, he remarks that ' the physical factor, " f," may imply new physical properties or changes in the usual laws of electro-dynamics, which may possibly be found to hold throughout our universe.' He then proceeds to inquire what changes inside or outside the earth can be at work effecting the proven and startling annual diminution in the earth's intensity of magnetisation, and having traced them to the universal physical factor ' f,' inquires, ' Are the new physical properties, or the changes in well-known physical laws, implied in " f," subject to rather rapid changes, and if so, why ? ' The somewhat technical answer given to this question depends in part upon the possibilities involved in a change of ' about one half of a millionth part in gravity, and this is a quantity which may readily escape detection with our present gravity appliances unless observations with requisite accuracy are made continuously for a number of years at certain standard stations, so as to obtain the accumulative effect.'

A law of nature is, then, only strictly true in the particular conditions in which it has been established, and all consideration of the subject of natural law confirms its wholly provisional character. A statistical regularity deduced from a very restricted range of observation supplies the principal ground for present-day general acceptance of the absolute fixity of procedure. The new may be the hitherto undiscovered—a relation or entity in existence previous to its actual discovery—but it may also be that which was previously undiscoverable because it had not yet been developed, and this development may conceivably be the result of development in the relations themselves. The astronomer continually notes changes in the heavens, *e.g.* in the brilliancy and arrangement of the stars, which may even suggest the idea of variability in the laws of Nature themselves. The development in the present laws would be then dominated or determined by the law of their variation. Further, not merely is it most probable that there are aspects of process which seem to us immovable and rigid, simply because we have no appliances sufficiently delicate to detect and register the change, but the period of comparatively exact scientific knowledge is so brief—some two centuries—compared with the processes of Nature, that it presents us as yet with little chance of hitting upon data by which to investigate developmental changes and intrinsic differences in relationship and properties which would *ex hypothesi* only be discernible over secular periods of hundreds of thousands, or maybe millions, of years. Particularly difficult also would it be to observe and register such developments, if the mind of man itself is likewise undergoing some concomitant intrinsic, yet infinitesimal, developmental change during the aeons. The alternative view—to state it extremely—is that of a rigidly immutable system of things, with which we come to have a growingly intimate and accurate acquaintance, but which is all there, so to speak, independently of whether we come to know it or not, and unchanged throughout the ages in its essential character. For some minds, however, this must be increasingly the more incredible of the two hypotheses.

But more positively in this connection, renewed investigation [1] into the character and validity of Natural Law has served to emphasise the precariousness of much that has commonly passed under that name. ' The nerve-shattering effect of the Theory of Relativity on many physicists,' says A. D. Ritchie with a certain piquant exaggeration, ' is due to its compelling them to drag their mythologies out into the light of day ; and

[1] Cf. *e.g.* J. M. Keynes, *A Treatise on Probability*; C. D. Broad, *Scientific Thought*; A. D. Ritchie, *Scientific Method*.

very quaint some of them look too. It would be an interesting task to examine carefully any ordinary text-book of Physics or Chemistry and try to unearth all the myths to be found embedded there—the experiments that nobody has done or could do, the sophistries that support theories, and the sheer dogmatic assertion un-supported by even a pretence of evidence. There is much there as fantastic as primitive folk-lore, though not so picturesque.' [1] It is not too much to say that the Principle of Relativity, providing not so much a profounder view of physical reality as a new direction and a new mode of interpreting phenomena, has re-volutionised the concepts of physics. As a matter of fact, the laws of Nature do not lie on the surface of things. She does not wear her heart upon her sleeve, but is coy to the last degree of secrecy and reserve, continually rejecting suitors, and demanding superlative devotion of all. So that tentative thing, a natural law, is little more than a general statement that certain relations tend to hold under certain conditions. It is, indeed, simply a fallacy to suppose that a belief based on mere succession or sequence has intrinsic validity ; the degree of probability even is disappointingly low.[2] There is strictly neither logical nor experiential justification to state any law of Nature in other than a hypothetical form, e.g. to the effect that under such and such conditions such and such results tend to recur. Strive how we may, we cannot get certainty out of ignorance, and have in the end to be content with an act of faith—a working belief in the Uniformity of Nature—which is, however, always engaged in tentatively, and with that open mind which will insist on immediate modification of any provisional statement of law, or even complete surrender of it, should sufficient cause be shown. With deductive reasoning even less progress can be made, for by itself it is powerless to tell

[1] *Scientific Method*, p. 157.
[2] Cf. J. M. Keynes (*op. cit.* chap. xxx., especially p. 374 ff.) for the argument.

us about things, being confined to dealing with the
relations of propositions developed out of given premises,
the truth of which, as also the conclusions drawn from
them, are empirical generalisations.[1] But in any case,
as we have seen, experience can give us little more than
first approximations to truth, and the philosophy or
metaphysics of science is never *exactly* representative
of Reality. For example, the conditions of measurement
in the four-dimensional universe of space-time are the
choice of a system of reference or frame of space-time,
and no such frame can be absolute.

In the case of the living organism, again, we at once
find a teleological element that has proven, at any rate
as yet, insusceptible of mechanical explanations. Here,
as in a purely physical situation, action and reaction are
in a sense equal, but the reaction is definitely directed
towards the preservation of the individual. It takes
the form of closer adaptation to the environment. In
the motions of the inorganic, considered strictly apart,
there is no hint or sense of an individual or self such
as can propose an end to itself, and work and devise
means of bringing it about. the motions are not controlled and directed from any point or centre in the
inorganic itself. In the case of the organism there is a
certain wholeness, or individuality, an apparent purposiveness and an internal finality ; it makes use, by
assimilation, of elements in its environment to maintain
its own subsistence and welfare. Assuredly, wherever
motion is in evidence—and that is coextensive with the
Universe as we know it, for we have no conception of
matter that is not moving—there must be a mechanical
aspect in question. But it cannot be shown that it is
more than an aspect—that it constitutes the whole science
of the real. Indeed, applied mechanics is a matter of
experience ; and as that experience is limited, all its
results can only be of the nature of approximations.
Mechanism bulks so largely in thought and seems so

[1] A. D. Ritchie, *op. cit.* p. 87.

distinct from life mainly because of the difficulty that the human mind has in grasping Reality in its unity ; as Bergson indicated, the intellect is moulded on matter. Possibly, also, the dominance of mechanism may be due in part to the fact that astronomy, which is at once a model and the criterion of much of our exactness, is the oldest of the sciences, and that physics and physiology developed long before psychology.

It is often supposed that a certain inevitableness attends the working of mechanical law as demonstrated in any phase of Nature, but this rests upon a confusion of the ideas of necessity and determinism. Necessity, which is based on actuality, gives us the impression that the nature of things is immutable, and that laws are the relations that result from this state of affairs. ' When,' however, in T. H. Huxley's words, ' as commonly happens, we change *will* into *must*,[1] we introduce an idea of necessity which most assuredly does not lie in the observed facts, and has no warranty that I can discover elsewhere . . . the notion of necessity is something illegitimately thrust into the perfectly legitimate conception of law.'[2] Determinism, on the other hand, expresses the sum total of conditions which are requisite for the exact production of a phenomenon with all its modes of being,[3] conditions, however, which become more restricted in the case of biological problems, because of their growing complexity —thus making statistical methods less and less serviceable so far as prediction with regard to the individual is concerned[4]—and the more definite emergence of a teleological relation in the facts. The ideas are distinct,

---

[1] *I.e.* in the statement of any law of Nature.
[2] *Lay Sermons, Addresses and Reviews*, p. 124.
[3] E. Boutroux, *op. cit.* p. 90.
[4] This is just as true of the history of peoples. There is an interesting and revealing footnote on p. 75 of R. R. Marett's *The Threshold of Religion*. ' A distinguished anthropologist writes to me that, if anthropology be not subject to hard-and-fast laws, the subject would not seem to him ' worth touching with a barge-pole.' But my own opinion is that the less the man of science (who usually is no philosopher) has to do with a metaphysical postulate such as that of determinism, the better.'

and science at any rate cannot blend them. The laws of Nature are always purely experimental; we can only find out in this way, for example, that the gravitational stress is exerted inversely as the square, and not as the cube, of the distance between two particles. But, further, Professor C. E. Guye has shown that with the recent advances in physico-chemical theory based on the investigations of Gibbs and Boltzmann, Carnot's principle[1] has assumed ' a new and unexpected significance,' with the result that the seeming determinism in physico-chemical evolution is now seen to be of the nature of a larger ' statistical determinism, in which the apparently inevitable exactness is only due to the law of large numbers. In fact, this determinism permits the occurrence of other very rare possibilities, or fluctuations, particularly when the law of large numbers is no longer entirely satisfied. For this reason, the question of absolute determinism is transferred into the domain of the individual actions, between molecules, atoms, or electrons, which still evade our direct experimental investigations almost completely.'[2] Even if there is no justification for supposing that all laws experimentally established are statistical laws subject to rare fluctuations that invalidate their absoluteness, yet the discovery that any, or even a single, law is of this character[3] must produce a profound modification in our understanding of the world-process. For ' it is possible to suppose that a fluctuation of large amplitude is able, theoretically at least, to make the system return to an anterior state, or even to its initial state ; thus making the entropy decrease, not only by quantities inaccessible to experi-

[1] The reference is to the Carnot-Clausius principle or second law of thermodynamics, which states that the entropy or unavailability of the energy in the universe tends towards a maximum.

[2] *Physico-Chemical Evolution*, p. ix, to which work reference should be made for detailed evidence of such fluctuation.

[3] ' It would indeed appear that in the Brownian movement there is an experimental proof of the actual existence of fluctuations ' (C. E. Guye, *op. cit.* p. 83).

ment, but making it proceed altogether in the reverse direction.' [1]   Particularly in connection with the organic, Professor Guye is led to the conclusion that ' Carnot's principle, considered as a statistical principle, must disappear when it is sought to apply it to more and more heterogeneous media, such as very probably constitute living matter, as the law of large numbers on which it rests then ceases to be applicable.' [2]   In the case of living matter, fluctuations which may be masked by the great numbers of molecules in substances, e.g. two gases, undergoing a purely physico-chemical reaction, may be of greater effective importance in a minimal unit of organic matter, so heterogeneous in its pure structure compared with any inorganic compound, and probably containing within identical measures far fewer molecules than purely inorganic substance.   In other words, the laws of organic evolution ' are no longer necessarily exact statistical laws as are those of our physical chemistry,' [3] and conceal within them something more fundamental and individual.

If, then, with the Pythagoreans we believe that everything due to the actualities of space and time is quantitative, we naturally tend to think that everything is necessarily determined.   Is this, however, as Boutroux asks,[4] a truly constitutive principle or merely a regulating principle and guiding idea ?   Does Science actually prove that the basis of everything is exclusively quantitative, or is this only her working assumption ?   Science assuredly deals with the measurable, but she can show no warrant for calling the unmeasurable unreal, and in any case Nature herself does not show this dichotomy. We cannot separate quality and quantity in Reality. If in his treatment of life the biologist gets nothing out but measurable physico-chemical results, that is only because with physico-chemical methods it is difficult to see what other results he could obtain, and constitutes no proof that there is nothing in life that is not physico-

---

[1] Guye, op. cit. p. 87.　　　　[2] Op. cit. p. xi.
[3] Op. cit. p. 145.　　　　[4] E. Boutroux, op. cit. p. 207.

chemical. He has found no direct measurable general relation between the psychical and the physical, and even if it were so, there is no reason why the former should depend upon the latter rather than the latter upon the former.

Science, as including all the natural sciences, is in truth knowledge of the abstract. The number of postulates increases as we work up from physics to psychology, and mathematics in this respect becomes increasingly useless ; nobody proposes to deal in foot-pounds of hatred or love, however much the physical concomitants of the emotions may be amenable to calculation. Even in the case of the inorganic sciences, man as investigator has been mainly interested in what he can measure, and has largely chosen to neglect the rest. But the more we understand Reality, the more we must observe and infer, rather than depend alone upon quantitative analysis, for the latter method is too abstract for dealing exhaustively, say, with the concrete living organism.

The conception of natural law gives us our basis of understanding the world, as also in great measure the World-Ground. In the aspect of uniformity it represents for us the idea of self-consistency, almost what a Scriptural writer described as a ' faithful, i.e. trustworthy, Creator.' [1] Without that similarity, or measure of regularity and dependableness, we could have had neither science nor theology, and experience would have meant nothing. It is only in a largely settled order of things that spirits could develop in the knowledge and love of a God. The existence of these conditions, therefore, suggests the existence of God, although they do not and cannot prove it. But that world is also infinitely full of surprises, and questions continually arise that prevent us from resting content with conceptions based on the laws of Nature as ascertained up to 31st December 1925 as our final statement. In themselves they sometimes show

[1] 1 Pet. 4 [19].

L

strange anomalies, even in the more or less abstract science of Numbers. ' If we take numbers in order 1, 2, 3 . . . we see that there are some, such as 3, 5, 7, 11, which cannot be divided by any number smaller than themselves ;   these   are   called   prime   numbers ;   the number of such primes which are less than a given number is a matter of very considerable importance, and Gauss, many years ago, gave, without any rigorous proof, a rule about it.   The rule was tested by actual trial for numbers up to a thousand millions, and, as it was found to be true over that immense range, it was accepted as universally correct in spite of the absence of a satis-factory proof.   Quite recently, however, Mr. Littlewood, one of our Fellows, has shown that, in spite of this over-whelming evidence in its favour, the result is not general, but the numbers for which it breaks down are so enormous that it would be quite beyond the powers of human endurance to detect its failure by actual trial.   I may say, in passing, that, enormous as these numbers are, they are mere nothings compared with what we have to deal with in many branches of Physics.   Here, then, we have a result which has satisfied, and apparently always will satisfy, any direct test that can be applied to it, and yet it is not generally true ;   there seems to me to be some-thing of a tragedy, perhaps the suspicion of a sermon, in this investigation, which is in a paper of a highly technical character, quite unintelligible to any one who was not an expert mathematician.' [1]   Nor are such anomalies con-fined to theoretical fields.   In the case of the bombard-ment of the nucleus of an atom by a positively charged helium atom, the ordinary law of electric repulsion and attraction—the law of inverse squares—proves insufficient at a point whose nearness to that nucleus has been calcu-lated to be between $\frac{1}{10}$th and $\frac{1}{100,000}$th of the diameter of the atom itself.   There is, then, no need for man to imagine

[1] Anniversary Address by Sir J. J. Thomson, O.M., President of the Royal Society, *Proc. Royal Soc. of London*, xciv. 187.   I am indebted to Prof. H. Stanley Allen for the reference.

himself, still less make himself, the prisoner of law. Indeed, the more thoroughly mechanism, where it exists, is understood, the more clearly do we see that, so far from limiting and confining us, it really is a means at our disposal for acting on things and gaining power over them. So far from checking our freedom, it really makes it efficacious.

Finally, the evolutionary process, whose ingredients are of the character which we have been considering, shows itself throughout as exhibiting fulness of wisdom and power, and likewise apparent purposiveness. At any rate, the present *dénouement* is the climactic creation of beings who are able both to understand and in growing measure to co-operate with that purpose as it is disclosed. And although the basis of the process has been the inorganic with its almost entirely rigid, fundamentally though not absolutely immutable, relationships that have given rise to the conception of uniformities, yet through it and out of this basis, being also itself an expression of Infinite Energy and Mind, there has developed, by a later organic phase of gradual dominance of mind and growing freedom, spiritual beings who can realise the place of law, the uses of mechanism, a worthy conception of miracle,[1] and the fundamentally spiritual character of the whole.

[1] See in this connection H. E. Fosdick, *The Modern Use of the Bible*, chap. v. ; F. R. Tennant, *Miracle and its Philosophical Presuppositions*.

CHAPTER VIII

THE COMING OF EVOLUTION

EVOLUTION, as a philosophical suggestion, is very old, almost as old as thought itself, and the story of the evolution of the theory of evolution, which is a fact and not a mere repetition of words, forms a most fascinating study in the gradual development of truth.[1] On the other hand, the shrewdest of ancient guesses after truth, the most attractive of unverified hypotheses, is comparatively valueless when set alongside a modern sound-based induction. Evolution as demonstrated fact is little more than a hundred years old, or, more exactly, it is only within that period that Evolution has commanded general acceptance by those qualified to express an opinion, as an induction from a continuously growing number of facts, and proven itself to be the principal contribution of biology to human welfare and progress. Nevertheless, no sharper conflict ever took place than just at this point.

It seems probable that with the growing appreciation of the relatedness of the inorganic and organic realms, the very direct influence exerted by the earlier recognition of developmental process in the case of the earth itself in helping to establish developmental views of the origin of species, will be increasingly realised. The natural tendencies that keep the studies of geology and of zoology to a great extent apart, prevent the full force of this influence being duly appreciated even to-day. There

[1] Cf. *e.g.* H. F. Osborn, *From the Greeks to Darwin*; J. W. Judd, *The Coming of Evolution.*

was no lack of generous admission of the fact by Charles Darwin himself. ' I always feel,' he wrote, ' as if my books came half out of Lyell's brain, and that I never acknowledge this sufficiently ; nor do I know how I can without saying so in so many words—for I have always thought that the great merit of the *Principles* was that it altered the whole tone of one's mind, and therefore that, when seeing a thing never seen by Lyell, one yet saw it partially through his eyes.' [1] Huxley likewise expressed himself to the following effect : ' I have recently read afresh the first edition of the *Principles of Geology*, and when I consider that this remarkable book had been nearly thirty years in everybody's hands [in 1859], and that it brings home to any reader of ordinary intelligence a great principle and a great fact — the principle that the past must be explained by the present, unless good cause be shown to the contrary ; and the fact that, so far as our knowledge of the past history of life on our globe goes, no such cause can be shown—I cannot but believe that Lyell, for others, as for myself, was the chief agent in smoothing the road for Darwin.' [2] It is permissible to imagine, especially on the strength of his own statements, that had Charles Darwin sailed in the *Beagle* without the first volume of the *Principles of Geology*, acquired by him on the advice of Professor Henslow, or failed to receive the second volume at Monte Video during the voyage, the results of his field work on the Pampas in the interior of South America would have been at any rate less immediately fruitful. Further, in view of the close and enduring friendship which sprang up between Darwin and Lyell after the return of the former from his long voyage, it is important to remember that Lyell had quite early become convinced [3] that the truth of evolution applied both to the organic

[1] *More Letters of Charles Darwin*, ii. 117.   Cf. also *The Origin of Species*, p. 415 ; *Life of Charles Darwin*, p. 33.
[2] *Huxley's Life and Letters*, ii. 190 ; cf. also *Collected Essays*, v. 101.
[3] *Life and Letters of Sir Charles Lyell*, i. 467 ; cf. also ii. 212, 365.

and to the inorganic realm, although it was long before he accepted the Darwinian explanation in terms of Natural Selection.

In fact, not merely had study of Lyell's book ' altered the whole tone ' of many minds, but the conflict between Natural Science and Theology had already actually begun in connection with the study of points raised by his application of evolutionary principles in the domain of the inorganic, and it is in the interesting pages of the *Principles of Geology* [1] itself that some earlier threatenings of the coming storm are set on record. Evolutionary principles had an even harder initial struggle for acceptance in the realm of the inorganic than they later had in the organic kingdom. Dealing with the controversy as to the real nature of fossil organic remains,[2] Sir Charles Lyell, after a reference to a treatise on the fossils of Calabria published by a Sicilian in 1670, in which the writer, while recognising the organic character of fossil shells, yet regarded them ' as the effects and proofs of the Mosaic deluge,' continues : ' the theologians who now entered the field in Italy, Germany, France, and England were innumerable ; and henceforward, they who refused to subscribe to the position, that all marine organic remains were proofs of the Mosaic deluge, were exposed to the imputation of disbelieving the whole of the sacred writings. . . . An additional period of a century and a half was now destined to be consumed in exploding the hypothesis, that organised fossils had all been buried in the solid strata by Noah's flood. Never did a theoretical fallacy, in any branch of science, interfere more seriously with accurate observation and the systematic classification of facts. . . . In short, a sketch of the progress of geology from the close of the seventeenth to the end of the eighteenth century is the history of a constant and violent struggle of new opinions against

[1] Vol. i. was published in January 1830 ; vol. ii., which dealt with matters bearing on organic evolution, in January 1832 ; vol. iii. in May 1833. [2] *Op. cit.* i. 33 ff.

doctrines sanctioned by the implicit faith of many generations, and supposed to rest on scriptural authority.'[1] According to Lyell, ' Quirini was the first writer who ventured to maintain that the universality of the Mosaic cataclysm ought not to be insisted upon.'[2] Ideas forming supposedly irrefragable elements in the theological construction of this time were the recent origin, the gradual running down, and the final destruction by fire of the terrestrial system, and even those writers, like Robert Hooke,[3] Ray,[4] Woodward,[5] Burnet,[6] and Whiston,[7] who attempted to harmonise the newer discoveries with the teachings of Scripture, kept within well-defined limits.

It is an interesting circumstance, which has recurred more than once, that the name linked with a real advance in sound natural explanation by reference to secondary causes, as apparently opposed to that of a primary and sufficient Cause which by a single creative act produced the world that we know, is that of a Churchman, to wit, Cirillo Generelli, a Carmelite friar. About the middle of the eighteenth century, at a meeting of the Academy of Science in Cremona, he gave an exposition of the views of Moro, a fellow-countryman, who had published a work in 1740 *On the Marine Bodies which are found in the Mountains*, and declared that it was now possible to explain the existence of

---

[1] *Op. cit.* i. 37, 38. [2] *Op. cit.* i. 38.

[3] His writings on these subjects appeared posthumously in 1705. To such methods, including that of anonymity, were some writers reduced, fearing the spirit of their age.

[4] *Miscellaneous Discourses concerning the Dissolution and Changes of the World*, 1692.

[5] *Consequences of the Deluge*, 1695.

[6] *The Sacred Theory of the Earth; containing an Account of the Original of the Earth, and of all the general Changes which it hath already undergone, or is to undergo, till the Consummation of all things.* Published in Latin, 1684.

[7] *A New Theory of the Earth ; wherein the Creation of the World in Six days, the Universal Deluge, and the General Conflagration, as laid down in the Holy Scriptures, are shown to be perfectly agreeable to Reason and Philosophy,* 1696.

marine fossils in mountainous regions ' without violence, without fictions, without hypothesis, without miracles.' [1] On the other hand, Buffon published his *Natural History* in the same year (1749), and two years later received an official letter from the Sorbonne or Faculty of Theology in Paris, informing him that fourteen propositions in his works ' were reprehensible, and contrary to the creed of the Church.' Amongst the principles expounded by him was one to the effect that ' the present mountains and valleys of the earth are due to secondary causes, and that the same causes will in turn destroy all the continents, hills, and valleys, and reproduce others like them.' [2] Invited to furnish an explanation or recantation of his doctrine, Buffon was forced to include a statement in his next work, which commenced : ' I declare that I had no intention to contradict the text of Scripture ; that I believe most firmly all therein related about the Creation, both as to order of time and matter of fact ; I abandon everything in my book respecting the formation of the earth, and, generally, all which may be contrary to the narration of Moses.' [3]

It is only when we realise the power that could be, and was, exerted on the expression of scientific opinion by the Church throughout the course of eighteen centuries, that it is possible to estimate the extent of the change wrought by the writings of Charles Darwin. The mere statement by the Uniformitarian Hutton, that in the economy of the world, as the result of his physical investigations, he could ' find no vestige of a beginning—no prospect of an end,' [4] seemed to a still literalist generation to erase the finger-marks of the Creative Hand, and, by the substitution of the doctrine that all past changes on the surface of the earth had been brought about by the slow operation of existing causes, opened up a vista

[1] Quoted in Lyell, *op. cit.* i. 54.
[2] *Ibid., op. cit.* i. 58.
[3] *Hist. Nat.*, tom. v. éd. de l'Imp. Royale (Paris, 1769).
[4] *Theory of the Earth*, i. 200.

of geological time that corresponded to the realms of space, disclosed by the genius of Newton.[1] It was an unsettling outlook, and seemed designed to support certain other tendencies of the period towards the undermining of the foundations of the Christian faith. The general attitude of disturbed orthodoxy towards the activities of the geologists at this time is well reflected in the lines by the poet Cowper :

> 'Some drill and bore
> The solid earth, and from the strata there
> Extract a register, by which we learn,
> That he who made it, and reveal'd its date
> To Moses, was mistaken in its age.'[2]

One inevitable result of the foreshortened time-scale was that in order to account for the evident geological phenomena, action in the past on an intensely magnified degree compared with that of the present, had to be posited. The understanding of the world, based on a literal reading of Scripture as revealed truth, in fact demanded a catastrophic view of agency. Biblical record and teaching are largely presented in a catastrophic and apocalyptic setting ; and this as applied in particular to the sudden beginning and end of the world seemed to fit in with, and be reinforced by, the apparent evidence for a series of intervening cataclysmic revolutions on the earth's surface, during each of which all the existing forms of life were destroyed. It was further supposed that some time after each cataclysm the surface of the earth was again stocked with a new fauna and flora, which were, however, in many respects curiously like their predecessors. And so the catastrophic explanation came to be regarded with an added significance as *orthodox* science, while evolutionary uniformitarianism savoured of heterodoxy, and for many a long day the time demands of the evolutionary geologist were resisted in the name

---

[1] C. Lyell, *op. cit.* i. pp. 76, 77.

[2] *The Task*, book iii. ll. 150-154. The reference is to the Usherian date of 4004 B.C. for the Creation of the World.

of physics and theology alike. Nature, that is to say, was interpreted by Scripture : it was a mistaken method. To-day we realise that there is much that is developmental, and uniformitarian almost, in the Scriptural view of things, and particularly in the teaching of Jesus. It might be said that we ought, therefore, to interpret Scripture by our modern understanding of Nature, but that also would be a mistaken method. For there is no such dichotomy in Reality as these suggestions would imply. The world that we inhabit is one world. Accordingly, just as the doctrine of the fixity of the earth had been replaced by the idea of its rapid movement through space, so the conception of the surface of the earth as unaltered since the first creative days was gradually being superseded by the doctrine that it had always been in process of undergoing slow but continual change. There remained only to transfer the same idea from the inorganic to the organic—to substitute for the conception of a static, changeless world the idea of a dynamic realm in broadly continuous transformation—and this was the work of Darwin.

We have stated that the idea of Evolution in varying degrees of definiteness had fleetingly entered the human mind from a very early stage, and study of the immediate predecessors of Charles Darwin would show an increasing persistence in the attractiveness of the conception. In the Historical Sketch introduced into later editions of *The Origin of Species*, Darwin referred to some thirty-four writers who were sympathetic to the idea of the modification of species. The list in the text does not directly include the name of Johann Wolfgang Goethe ; [1] yet it is a remarkable fact that at different stages in the development of evolutionary thought, men have appeared who had no very special claim to be considered men of

[1] There is, however, a quotation on p. xxix from the French botanist Lecoq to the effect that ' On voit que nos recherches sur la fixité ou la variation de l'espèce, nous conduisent directement aux idées émises par deux hommes justement célèbres, Geoffroy Saint-Hilaire et Goethe ' ; as also a reference in a footnote on p. xx.

science on the grounds of scientific research, but who by
the intuitive powers of their minds, reflecting on the
data mainly provided by others, have been able to make
suggestive contributions of considerable value. Amongst
such may be included Goethe, Herbert Spencer, and
Samuel Butler. With Goethe the idea of the unity of
plan in vertebrate structure came to more definite and
scientific expression than at any previous time, while his
work in support of his views on the metamorphosis of
plants,[1] and even his rather fantastic vertebrate theory
of the skull [2] which flashed into his mind as he was con-
templating a dried sheep's skull in the Jewish cemetery
at Venice, all helped to some extent in making some minds
hospitable to the view that species might have developed
from other species by modification. But, further, there
was nothing static about Goethe's poetic spirit, and it was
only natural that his interest, as E. S. Russell has indicated, lay ' not in *Gestalt* or fixed form, but in *Bildung*
or form change.' [3] The former was but a momentary
phase of the latter, whose inner secret of activity could
never be discovered by any mere process of technical
analysis, such as that to which he himself elsewhere
refers :

> ' Wer will was Lebendigs erkennen und beschreiben,
>   Sucht erst den Geist heraus zu treiben,
>   Dann hat er die Teile in seiner Hand,
>   Fehlt, leider ! nur das geistige Band.' [4]

Living things, to Goethe's mind, strive ' to manifest

---

[1] In essence this amounted to the statement that the stem-leaves,
sepals, petals, and stamens of a flowering plant are all modifications for
different purposes of a single typical plant appendage.

[2] On the analogy of the metameric repetition and modification of
parts in some lower forms, *e.g.* centipedes or ringed worms, Goethe
supposed that the skull might be composed of a number of serially
modified vertebrae.

[3] *Form and Function*, p. 49.

[4] *Faust*, part i., 1582-1585. ' He who wishes to understand and
describe a living thing first tries to drive the living spirit out of it.
Then he has the parts in his hand, excepting only, alas ! the living
bond.'

an idea.   They are Nature's works of art—and so, incidentally, they require an artist to interpret them.' [1] He knew, as Browning proved to a later generation, that to the poet as to the artist the sense of the whole comes first ; to the man of science it comes last, and sometimes never at all.

Of the individuals definitely mentioned in the text of Darwin's Historical Sketch, easily the most interesting is Jean Baptiste Chevalier de Lamarck (1744-1829), whose profoundly psychological conception of life and evolution really makes him the unconscious founder of psycho-biology, and whose views, in part, in a modified form are slowly winning a renewed measure of acceptance in biological circles to-day.   The recognition of the fact that all organisms strive to adapt themselves to their environment, and, from the Protozoa upwards, not merely can learn by experience, but may even transmit modified results of that experience to the next generation, [2] is bound sooner or later to affect the whole interpretation of evolution, following as it does on the disproof of some of the older contentions, or rather assumptions. [3]   It is a great tribute to Charles Darwin's candour of mind that in retrospect he came to realise, and frankly admitted, his underestimate of a main Lamarckian position in those early days when his mind was filled, as was Weismann's later, with the idea of the ' all-sufficiency ' of Natural Selection. [4]   In these same pages Darwin further showed that even in that attempted explanation of the method of Evolution to which he and

[1] E. S. Russell, *op. cit.* p. 50.

[2] Cf. E. W. MacBride, *An Introduction to the Study of Heredity.*

[3] *E.g.* the proof supplied by ' pure line ' investigation of the incorrectness of the assumption that small variations are continually occurring in every conceivable direction, and that these particular variations are always inherited.

[4] ' In my opinion the greatest error which I have committed has been not allowing sufficient weight to the direct action of the environment, *i.e.* food, climate, etc., independently of natural selection ' (*Life and Letters*, iii. 159) ; A. Weismann, ' The All-sufficiency of Natural Selection,' *Contemporary Review*, September 1893.

A. R. Wallace gave the name of Natural Selection, there had been definite anticipation. The number of such cases of anticipation slowly increases ; [1] nevertheless the fact remains that Charles Darwin was the first who really made people believe in Evolution on the basis of irrefutable data which he had himself collected through twenty long years. He had begun to wonder why it was that the fossil remains of great sloths and armadillos dug up by him on the Pampas were so strangely reminiscent of the present fauna. Had each new creation succeeding some Cuvierian [2] catastrophe been a mere general facsimile of the previous creation, or was there some more direct connection between the two ? Under his treatment the conception of Evolution became in the end a power, for he was the first to realise the idea vividly in its fulness. Hitherto, in most of the minds that had glimpsed it, Evolution was something vague.

It is a little difficult for the present generation to realise the sensation caused by the projection of *The Origin of Species* into the intellectual and religious atmosphere of the year 1859 (24th November) both at home and abroad. The first edition was exhausted on the day of publication. Weismann is especially interesting in describing the situation in Germany : 'It is impossible to estimate the effect of Darwin's book on *The Origin of Species*, published in English in 1858,[3] in Germany in 1859, unless we fully realise how completely the biologists of that time had turned away from general problems. I can only say that we, who were then the younger men, studying in the fifties, had no idea that a theory of evolution had ever been put forward, for no

---

[1] Cf. *e.g.* the claims made on behalf of J. C. Prichard by Prof. Poulton, *Essays on Evolution*, chap. vi. ; also Wollaston, *On the Variation of Species* (1856) ; and Godron, *De L'Espèce et des Races dans les Êtres Organisés* (1859).

[2] Georges Cuvier (1769-1832), the great French comparative anatomist and founder of the science of palaeontology, supported the hypothesis of sudden catastrophes, followed by immigration from regions outside the area of disturbance.

[3] This is a mistake. See above.

one spoke of it to us, and it was never mentioned in a lecture. It seemed as if all the teachers in our universities had drunk of the waters of Lethe, and had utterly forgotten that such a theory had ever been discussed, or as if they were ashamed of these philosophical flights on the part of natural science, and wished to guard their students from similar deviations. The over-speculation of the " Natur-philosophie " had left in their minds a deep antipathy to all far-reaching deductions, and, in their legitimate striving after purely inductive investigation, they forgot that the mere gathering of facts is not enough, that the drawing of conclusions is an essential part of the induction, and that a mass of bare facts, however enormous, does not constitute a science. . . . It is therefore not to be wondered that Darwin's book fell like a bolt from the blue ; it was eagerly devoured, and while it excited in the minds of the younger students delight and enthusiasm, it aroused among the older naturalists anything from cool aversion to violent opposition. The world was as though thunderstruck, as we can readily see from the preface with which the excellent zoologist of Heidelberg, Bronn, introduced his translation of Darwin's book, where he asks this question among others, " How will it be with you, dear reader, after you have read this book ? " and so forth.' [1]

Nor was it otherwise in Great Britain. So strong was the general acquiescence in the view of Special Creation and the fixity of species in the first half of last century, that the only book [2] published in Great Britain between the years 1809 and 1858 that offered a thoroughgoing exposition of evolutionary views came out in 1844 anonymously, and fellow-citizens of the supposed author who had read it, discussed it in whispers after dinner as they might tell about some *risqué* French novel.

[1] August Weismann, *The Evolution Theory*, i. 28.
[2] *Vestiges of the Natural History of Creation*, by Robert Chambers (1802-1871), author and joint original partner of the Edinburgh publishing house of W. R. Chambers.

Even the tenth edition was still unclaimed, and the secret of its authorship was only disclosed in a contributed introduction to the twelfth edition which came out thirteen years after the author's death. The state of opinion in the scientific world may be gathered from an excerpt from *An Introduction to Zoology*, published by Philip Henry Gosse in 1844, even if there were some few botanists and zoologists who were questioning in their own minds how far the received views were really supportable. ' Each order was distributed into subordinate groups, called Genera, and each genus into Species. As this last term is often somewhat vaguely used, it may not be useless to define its acceptation. It is used to signify those distinct forms which are believed to have proceeded direct from the creating hand of God, and on which was impressed a certain individuality, destined to pass down through all succeeding generations, without loss and without confusion. Thus the Horse and the Ass, the Tiger and the Leopard, the Goose and the Duck, though closely allied in form, are believed to have descended from no common parentage, however remote, but to have been primary forms of the original creation. It is often difficult in practice to determine the difference or identity of species ; as we know of no fixed principle on which to found our decisions, except the great law of nature, by which specific individuality is preserved—that the progeny of mixed species shall not be fertile *inter se*.' [1] This statement differs little from the famous dictum in which Linnaeus a century previously had practically stereotyped the conception of a species.[2]

[1] *Op. cit.* p. xv.
[2] ' Species tot sunt, quot diversas formas ab initio produxit Infinitum Ens ; quae deinde formae secundum generationis inditas leges produxere plures, at sibi semper similes, ut Species nunc nobis non sint plures, quam quae fuere ab initio ' (*Genera Plantarum*, p. ii, quoted from 2nd edition 1742 ; 1st edition 1737). It is interesting to note the variations in the edition of 1791 edited by Haenke : ' Species tot sunt, quot diversas et constantes formas in hoc globo produxit Infinitum Ens ; quae formae secundum generationis inditas leges producunt plures, sibi similes, quam quae fuere.'

The species was the pre-Darwinian unit of classification. That is to say, had Linnaeus been asked, What is a species ? he would have answered with rare piety and a certain indirectness, 'There are exactly as many different species to-day as there were different forms created in the beginning by the Infinite Being.' But what did Linnaeus know of species ? In his day they were sharply defined, and not over-numerous. In the tenth edition of his *Systema Naturae* (1758) he classified some four thousand species of animals in all ; by 1895 some 250,000 species of insects alone had been described, and Dr. Sharp estimated at that date that ' this is probably only about one-tenth of those that really exist.' [1] To-day the number of known species of insects approaches half a million.[2] So that for Linnaeus, with his modest herbarium and his little cabinets of stuffed birds and desiccated fish skins, the question of the origin of species was very different in form from that which it takes for the modern naturalist, with his recognition of the prodigality of the kinds of life on the globe, and his growing sense of their unity. Species as known to Linnaeus corresponded to the various ' kinds ' after which Holy Writ affirmed God to have created the world of life. Varieties were cross-fertile ; with species was introduced cross-sterility —the divine barrier set for the preservation of organic order. The sole difference between Linnaeus and Gosse is that the latter appears to have known of a possible alternative explanation—and deliberately rejected it.

The attitude in the religious world may be illustrated by the remarks addressed to Canon J. M. Wilson by his father, a country clergyman, to whom young Wilson, then a master at Rugby, had taken a copy of Darwin's

[1] *The Cambridge Natural History*, v. 171.
[2] ' I have recently had occasion to consult the authorities of the British Museum as to the number of known species. They estimate that mammals number 10,000 ; birds 16,000 ; reptiles and amphibia 9000 ; fish 20,000 ; mollusca 60,000 ; crustacea 12,000—probably an under-estimate—whilst the number of insects is now put at 470,000 ' (Sir A. E. Shipley, *Life*, p. 104).

book as a Christmas gift in 1859, one month after its
publication. ' I cannot conceive,' said the older gentle-
man to his son, ' how a book can be written on the subject.
We know all there is to be known about it.   God created
plants and animals and man out of the ground.' [1]   In
many minds outside the ranks of scientific workers, the
conception of Creation still found its easiest expression
in terms of Milton's seventeenth-century imagery :

> ' The Earth obey'd, and straight
> Op'ning her fertile womb, teem'd at a birth
> Innumerous living creatures, perfect forms,
> Limb'd and full grown : out of the ground up rose
> As from his lair the wild beast where he wonns
> In forest wild, in thicket, brake, or den ;
> Among the trees in pairs they rose, they walk'd :
> The cattle in the fields and meadows green ;
> Those rare and solitary, these in flocks
> Pasturing at once, and in broad herds upsprung.
> The grassy clods now calv'd ; now half appear'd
> The tawny lion, pawing to get free
> His hinder parts, then springs as broke from bonds,
> And rampant shakes his brinded mane.' [2]

It is always difficult for one generation to appreciate
the standpoint of another, just because knowledge is a
developing, growing thing, and it is impossible to divest
the mind of the subsequent gains and the moulding
effected under their influence.   An individual mind may
slip back to a lower level of activity, but a healthy
mind can never exactly reproduce in itself the conditions
of the past, just because of the development that has
resulted from its health.   So to a generation that finds
it even more ' difficult in practice to determine the
difference or identity of species ' than did Philip Henry
Gosse—so difficult, indeed, that one distinguished investigator, Sir E. Ray Lankester, has expressed himself
as ' inclined to think that we should discard the word

---

[1] *Evolution and the Christian Faith*, by Canon J. M. Wilson, p. 10.
[2] *Paradise Lost*, vii. 453-466.

species not merely momentarily but altogether ' [1]—
the whole Early Victorian setting of the problem tends
to become as fantastic and difficult to assume as some
of the material forms of physical clothing of that period :
nor has the difficulty been lessened by the discovery that
cross-sterility between some species is by no means absolute
but rather of the nature of a variable characteristic, whilst
the power of hybrids to reproduce varies from zero to
complete and lasting fertility. Part of the delay in clinching the demonstration lay in the fact that it was always
possible for the defender of the older point of view to
change his position. The pre-Darwinian conception of a
species implied the absence of intermediate links, and its
inherent apartness and immutability. Now even when
intermediate forms were found, as occasionally happened,
e.g. by the careful examination of areas connecting the
widely separated regions occupied by well-marked species,
or were demonstrated in such a complete series as the
Planorbis shells from the Tertiary fresh-water deposits
of Steinheim, so thoroughly studied by Hilgendorf in
1866 and again by Hyatt in 1880, it was still possible
for the non-transformist to save the situation for a time.
If confronted with a form intermediate between two
others up to that time considered specifically distinct,
he simply replied, ' Pardon me, I have been in error ;
what I believed to be separate species are evidently
merely varieties of a single species, and you have found
an interesting intermediate variety.' Sometimes belief
was maintained in less circular ways. In his *Autobiography*, Nathaniel Southgate Shaler, humanist and
sometime Professor of Geology at Harvard, relates how
he ' used to debate the Darwinian hypothesis privately '
with Stimpson, a pupil of the conservative and orthodox
Louis Agassiz, ' for to be caught at it was as it is for the
faithful to be detected in a careful study of a heresy. . . .
The logic of these [special creationist] views bothered
Stimpson less than it did me, because he was a man of

[1] Prof. E. B. Poulton, *Essays in Evolution*, p. 62.

facts and not fancies. He was puzzled by transitional varieties between many of the species of molluscs he was studying, especially those occurring among the fresh-water gasteropods. On one occasion I saw him throw one of these vexatious shapes on the floor, after he had studied it for a long time, put his heel upon it and grind it to powder, remarking, " That 's the proper way to serve a damned transitional form." ' [1] There was no other way. Not otherwise could he have kept his neat regimented series of discontinuous types, each of which had descended without modification from some ancestral pair created by the Divine Hand in the beginning, and perfectly adapted to the special environment in which it was found.

It is no part of this study to follow the more recent and ever-growingly complex developments in the theory of Evolution. Never perhaps capable of absolute de-monstration, being rather of the nature of an induction from an ever-widening range of facts which nothing has supervened to contradict, the doctrine of descent has at no time been more surely grounded. Yet the question of causation and method was never more uncertain than to-day. For some investigators, the Darwinian age seems already very far away. ' We go to Darwin,' says William Bateson, ' for his incomparable collection of facts. We would fain emulate his scholar-ship, his width and his power of exposition, but to us he speaks no more with philosophical authority. We read his scheme of Evolution as we would that of Lucretius or of Lamarck, delighting in their simplicity and their courage. The practical and experimental study of Variation and Heredity has not merely opened a new field ; it has given a new point of view and new standards of criticism.' [2] As a matter of fact, *The Origin of Species* was published in 1859, when Gregor Mendel, the Prälat of the Königskloster at Brünn, had already commenced

[1] *Op. cit.* pp. 128, 129.
[2] Pres. Address, *Brit. Assoc. Report*, 1914, p. 10.

his eight years' series of experiments in the cloister garden on peas and other forms, the results of which, given to a local society in 1865 and published the following year, were to prove somewhat unfavourable to Darwinism as distinguished from Evolution. ' Mendelian experiment has established the existence of definite unit characters which do not appear to be subject to change. This result is opposed to the Darwinian idea of the gradual accumulation of minute differences, under the influence of Natural Selection.' [1] Bateson in turn, ten years after the occasion of his British Association Presidential Address, speaks with less assurance about the value of Mendelism, of which he has been so brilliant a practical exponent, as an ultimate explanation of Evolution. ' In dim outline evolution is evident enough. From the facts it is a conclusion which inevitably follows. But that particular and essential bit of the theory of evolution which is concerned with the origin and nature of *species* remains utterly mysterious.' [2]

The situation is further complicated by the slow re-entrance of the Neo-Lamarckian factors, subject to some modification, into a position where they count as they never have done during the decades of Weismannian dominance.[3] It has been too freely assumed that because the results, for example, of experimental mutilation of plants or animals, conducted over a comparatively short period, are not inherited, therefore that which the plant or animal does, as it were, for itself in reaction to the environmental conditions over a long series of generations cannot affect in any way fundamental characteristics of the species. It is not merely the Darwinian, but the Weismannian and Mendelian attempts at explanation, that have delighted succeeding generations of workers by ' their simplicity and their courage.' They have all

---

[1] D. H. Scott, *Extinct Plants and Problems of Evolution*, p. 10.

[2] ' Evolutionary Faith and Modern Doubt,' *Nature*, cix. 553.

[3] For a good account of the present situation, cf. *Evolution in the Light of Modern Knowledge*, chaps. iv., v., and vi.

proved to be necessary and helpful contributions. The only mistake has been when any worker imagined that any one of these or corresponding explanations was sufficient and complete in itself.[1] The problem is much more complex than any of the earlier workers supposed, but this does not mean that it is ultimately insoluble.

To-day, then, no scientific wanderer in the Indian or African jungle expects to come across a lion pawing the ground ' to get free his hinder parts,' for he knows that lions do not come into the world in that sort of way ; and, on the contrary, is decidedly interested in possibilities in the ' tigons,' or tiger-lioness hybrids, recently born in the private park of the Jam Sahib of Nawanagar. The fixity of species has gone, not in the sense that all species are cross-fertile, but that some are not cross-sterile. There is a certain loosening in the rigidity of the conception : it is not necessarily that all existing species are now regarded as mutable, although they are assuredly the more or less modified descendants of previously existing species, but that they are not all immutable.[2] The idea naturally follows that the origin of species has differed in no wise from the origin of classes or varieties or individuals. After all, it is the individuals that are real, rather than the species, which is but a group of them.

Now, in whatever way species came into existence, it must have been none the less a method of creation. The real question then is, What was the method ? Has it been a method of slow development from within, under direct environmental influence, or of offhand fashioning from without ? Has life come into being as an activity, dependent on some energetic source of which it is a peculiar expression, or was it something originally disconnected with anything previous to it, and that was called into being

---

[1] *E.g.* de Vries : ' I intend to give a review of the facts obtained from plants which go to prove the assertion, that species and varieties have originated by mutation, and are, at present, not known to originate in any other way ' (*Species and Varieties*, p. 9).

[2] For detailed examples, reference should be made to some text-book, *e.g.* Arthur Dendy, *Outlines of Evolutionary Biology.*

suddenly in myriads of more or less highly developed as well as lower forms ? Whatever be the answer, the fact of Infinite Creative Energy remains, Energy which, when we consider the organic series as a whole, gives the impression of working purposively—as if, that is to say, it had an end in view. The contrast as stated is rather that between the picture conveyed in Milton's rich and vivid imagery, and such a simple and more sober statement as that with which Darwin concluded his evolutionary account of the origin of species : ' There is grandeur in this view of life, with its several powers, having been originally breathed by the Creator into a few forms or into one ; and that, whilst this planet has gone cycling on according to the fixed law of gravity, from so simple a beginning endless forms most beautiful and most wonderful have been, and are being evolved.' [1] There can be no doubt as to which of the two accounts corresponds in a general way more closely to fact as we know it, nor which of them is the loftier and more worthy conception of Creation. For the mind that becomes aware of a transcendent creative activity continuously at work in the world process—transcendent in the sense that it is never exhausted by its activity, and gives the impression of representing something a great deal more than any definite expression of itself in time and space— has a manifestly truer and more comforting assurance of things than one that believes in a far-off discontinuous God who intervenes only at critical moments, or in no God at all.

' There are reverent minds,' read Henry Drummond from the proofs of *The Ascent of Man* to three friends as they sat together in a field under a hedge in Low Glen Cloy in the Island of Arran one day near Eastertide of 1894, ' who ceaselessly scan the fields of Nature and the books of Science in search of gaps—gaps which they will fill up with God. As if God lived in gaps ? ' [2] Then,

---

[1] *The Origin of Species*, p. 669.
[2] The passage will be found on p. 426 of *The Ascent of Man*.

looking up for a moment, he added, as if by way of explanation, ' There was a foolish man who wrote a book to show that God existed only in the gaps.' Whereupon one of his listeners remarked, ' But why take notice of him ? All that he said will have been forgotten.' To which the answer came, ' Mrs. Whyte, *I* was that man.' [1] The sense of security and of the achievement of truth in the later position had made him almost impatient with what now seemed to be the paltriness of his previous experience, and his presentation of it.

The coming of evolution has thus meant the recognition of continuous becoming, in which process there has been the ' emergence ' at successively higher levels of distinctive and more complex characters. In its widest aspect, it compels us to look on the whole process, inorganic and organic, as one—a climactic process issuing in man, and the subject of a teleology embracing the whole. For it is a process that apparently has a specific direction, and it is maintained in that direction by the activity of some Infinite Source of Energy. And if, as a result of the examination of all alternative explanations of the world process, we are still left with man, a genetic product of that process, inducing and controlling slight changes in its energy-distribution for definite ends in virtue of the activity of his consciousness, the theistic view of a Supreme Ground or Consciousness working out a great idea, dimly cognisable by the human mind, seems to supply the most fruitful, theoretically and practically, of all interpretations.

Finally, in this connection it must be borne in mind that men are progressively understanding both Scripture and the world better, as also themselves. They realise, for example, that the Jews were mistaken in their ideas

[1] The reference is, of course, to his earlier work, *Natural Law in the Spiritual World*, from the distinctive position in the Introduction to which book Drummond subsequently travelled far. Drafts of a series of new Prefaces illustrating this development of thought—which were, however, never used--will be found in *Henry Drummond* (Famous Scots Series), pp. 122-137.

of a time-limit to inspiration, just as they also had no sound reason for their ' exaggerated estimate of the Law as compared with the Prophets and the Psalms,' and were apparently quite ' wrong in their views of the date and authorship of the books of the Old Testament.' [1] They are humiliated as they recall days when, in nominally Christian States, ignorance, hatred, and violence united in acts of abandoned cruelty to countless numbers of men and women, on the basis of such isolated words as ' Thou shalt not suffer a witch to live,' [2] and ' Compel them to come in.' [3]   Even for John Wesley ' the giving up witchcraft' was ' in effect giving up the Bible.' [4]   Yet such liberation from error, accompanied by further entering into understanding of the world process as it is revealed to men in their reverent and humble scientific pursuit of truth, has only deepened the feeling in many minds of the infinite wonder of it all. For them the most reasonable and only ultimately satisfying explanation is that the Infinite Power being also Love, created man through a process which meant for him the possibility of attaining freedom, and that likewise in that process God has drawn near and growingly revealed Himself to man.   It would further appear that of all races the Hebrews showed themselves peculiarly responsi ˇe to, and receptive of, this revelation, while the register of their experience as a people, and in particular of their choicest souls, as it is contained in their Scriptures, has proven itself indeed to be the word of God, under the illumination of that Spirit which leads continuously into all truth.

[1] Dr. J. Skinner, in Peake's *Commentary on the Bible*, p. 40.
[2] Ex. 22 [18].
[3] Luke 14 [23].
[4] *The Journal of the Rev. John Wesley*, Curnock's Edition, v. 265. Cf. also : ' The infidels have hooted witchcraft out of the world; and the complaisant Christians, in large numbers, have joined with them in the cry ' (*ibid.* p. 375).

CHAPTER IX

OF HUMAN ORIGINS

If Pope was right in his contention that 'the proper study of mankind is man,'[1] there is no age in which that study has been prosecuted more assiduously than the present. And the study is peculiarly intensive; for each decade since that year[2] when the searchlight of Darwin's genius illuminated the pathway through and past the Garden of Eden to the jungle still farther to the east, has yielded a wealth of factual result that not merely adds impressively to the antiquity, but to the dignity of man. It is a thought at once arresting and solemnising that when the artistic Magdalenian reindeer hunters of Aquitaine were depicting action in animals on the walls of caves and rock shelters in so spirited and life-like a manner that experts do not find the equal of their work again in this respect in Europe till the eighteenth century, contemporaneous with them in Asia were civilisations that in every other regard were far in advance of theirs. If man is literally the heir of all the ages, we are only at the commencement of realising how immense and extended is that inheritance in its strictly human constituents alone.

In the light of these rapidly broadening discoveries, it becomes increasingly interesting to consider comparatively the various ideas entertained with regard to the past history and origin of man by the outstanding peoples of antiquity. They stood much closer to these

[1] *Essay on Man*, ii. 2.
[2] *The Descent of Man* was published on 24th February 1871.

origins than do we, yet in default of modern methods and background they knew relatively much less; just as to-day any higher-grade schoolboy may have a conspectus, and in some respects more accurate knowledge, say, of the Roman classical period, than any of the great writers who helped to make that era probably had. Conspicuous in this, as in so many other respects, were the Greeks, who, hampered by no mistaken conceptions about revelation, were able, through such minds as had the instinct or the interest, to collect the available data, even if, with little power, at any rate in the case of the earlier writers, to distinguish between rumour and observed fact, they filled in through the imagination the gaps and links left in their presentations.

Of these earliest writers Homer and Hesiod were outstanding as authorities on the early history of mankind; and if to-day it is realised that ' the Homeric poems are, in the main, the expression of a highly organised and advanced society,' [1] it stimulates us to pay all the more attention to the occasional light thrown in these pages on the social life of other peoples,[2] known only by hearsay, who were already recognised as being primitive compared with the Greek civilisation of that time. With the progress of geography as a science, and the contacts brought about as the result of the expansion of Greek trade, first-hand knowledge of contemporary barbarian peoples grew rapidly. Such a collection of data may be found in the works of Herodotus, who has been called 'The Father of Anthropology,' but he had no clear principle of comparative co-ordination or explanation. Further, the Hesiodean belief in a Golden Age from which man had degenerated, proved as difficult to dislodge as did later its Hebraic counterpart; and the fact, glimpsed first by Xenophanes and Aeschylus, that the savage represented a more primitive state of society out of which even Greece herself had emerged, called for ever stronger

---

[1] E. E. Sikes, *The Anthropology of the Greeks*, p. 2.
[2] *E.g.* the Abii, and largely mythical Cyclopes.

support in order to meet successfully the challenge of the older view. The relatedness of man and the lower creation was a familiar Greek conception : many analogies are drawn between human and animal life, *e.g.* in Plato's *Republic*.

On the origin of man many views were held, very diverse in their character. For Hesiod, gods and men alike sprang from the union of Earth and Heaven ; trees, stones and even ants all figure in different myths as the material out of which Zeus created men. Most widespread of all, perhaps, was the Promethean myth, paralleled in Babylonian, Hebrew, Egyptian, and much savage lore, in which man was created from clay : it is not fixed, however, in Greek or Roman literature before the end of the fifth century B.C. Probably the two leading types of theory represent views originally held by two different races,[1] the original Pelasgi claiming descent from the Earth, whilst the later Achaean invaders came in with their chieftains, whose heroic ancestors were the sons of the gods. The two types of belief persisted as the result of the admixture of conquerors and conquered. With the development of thought, the theory of divine origin became serviceable by reason of its ethical value, and was incorporated in the Stoic system. It helped also to make easy the transition to the claim of divine attributes or origin for individuals so unlike one another as Empedocles and Alexander the Great. The later guesses of the Ionian philosophers as to the origin of man differed from the speculations of the epic poets in this, that the former definitely submitted their fancies to the arbitrament of reason, and sought to justify their pronouncements by argument. So that variant of Anaximander's teaching which envisages the development of man from an encapsuled fish-like stage, was framed to meet a difficulty in the application of the current theory of his day regarding the origin of life, to the human species : while Empedocles, on his particular

[1] E. E. Sikes, *op. cit.* p. 30.

views, showed reason for emphasising the relation of man to other living things.

Indeed, the ideas of these two philosophers bear restatement not merely in themselves as typical of the best that their age produced, but also in view of their faint adumbration of later positions. Thus with regard to Anaximander's beliefs there are the following statements : [1]

(1) ' Anaximander says that the first animals came into existence in a moist medium, covered with thorny husks, and as their age increased they climbed out on to drier ground, that the husk then burst, and the animal then lived a little longer.'

(2) ' He says further that at the beginning man sprang from animals of a different species, because whereas the other animals soon find food by their own efforts, man, and man alone, needs a long period of nursing.[2] Wherefore at the beginning, being what he is, he could not have survived.'

(3) ' He proves that men originally came into being in fishes, and being nurtured like dogfish,[3] and becoming able to shift for themselves, they were then cast out, and got hold of the earth.'

(4) ' (Anaximander says) that living things sprang from moisture, vaporised by the sun (?).'

With regard to the opinions of Empedocles, the most definite pronouncement is as follows : [4]

' Empedocles says that the first animals and plants that came into being were anything but complete, their parts being merely yoked together, not growing together. The second (lot) [5] looked like statues, for their parts grew together into one. The third generation (*i.e.* race or creation) consisted of hermaphrodite forms. But the

---

[1] The text followed is that in Ritter and Preller,[9] par. 22, and for the translation I am indebted to Prof. H. J. Rose.

[2] Something more than the period of suckling is intended.

[3] Reading $\gamma\alpha\lambda\epsilon o i$ = scyllium.

[4] Ritter and Preller,[9] par. 173.

[5] Not thought of as descended from the first.

fourth race were not produced like from like, but by the action of one another,[1] because in some individuals the pressure of food (on the intestines) and in others the beauty of the females set up irritation of the seminal motion. The species of all living things are differentiated by their specific composition.'

In a peculiar degree the Greek scientific and philosophical outlook was anthropocentric, and the number of the names of their great physicians and anatomists exceeds that of their biologists. The most extreme form of this attitude, perhaps, is to be found in the *Timaeus*,[2] where various classes of animal life are represented as created out of different types of imperfect or degenerate men.

The Creation Narratives of Genesis, on the other hand, evince a markedly different conception of man. In both accounts [3] the supremacy of man over all the rest of creation is clearly asserted, the First Narrative indicating this by its story of a graded ascending order of creation which culminates in man, the Second Narrative beginning its recital with the creation of man first of all living things. In the First Narrative man is made in God's image, just as ' Adam begat a son in his own likeness, after his image.' [4] While the conception of the divine image in the First Narrative undoubtedly has special reference to man's spiritual capacity, the anthropomorphism of the passage just as surely expressed in original intention the primitive belief of the Hebrews with respect to the human physical form. Man was made in the image of God, and so he is peculiarly worthy to be the friend of that God [5] who is represented in the Second Narrative as taking a special interest in his welfare from the beginning. For it is only on the

---

[1] He means that with the fourth race or creation, asexual reproduction ceased, and biparental reproduction began.

[2] Jowett's trans., iii. 514, 515.

[3] Gen. 1 1–2 4a ; 2 4b–3 24.

[4] Gen. 5 3 ; cf. 5 1.

[5] Ex. 33 11 ; 2 Chron. 20 7 ; Is. 41 8 ; James 2 23.

basis of such a personal relationship between God and one who is made in His image, that these Old Testament writers consider the approach of man to God and the revelation of God to man as possible.[1] The form of the conception of the creation of man as detailed in the Narratives of Genesis is found with certain modifications amongst the traditions of peoples other than the Hebrews,[2] yet the content is different. Whilst Babylonian and Greek alike thought of the gods as like themselves and with little claim upon them, the Hebrew conception of God as a supreme ethical personality implied a challenge to the creature made in His image to lead a moral God-like life.[3] That man has a destiny in relation to God was never taught in any pagan myth. At the same time, Scripture recognises a relationship or kinship of man with the lower creation to the extent that both are made of the dust of the earth,[4] and in one case the writer speaks as if the relationship implied no distinctive difference or superiority on the part of man.[5]

With literal acceptance of these Narratives and elaboration of the story of the Fall, which was the starting-point of their whole system of theology, some of the Church Fathers yet ventured on observations that have a strangely modern ring about them. A single instance must suffice, taken from Lactantius' treatise entitled *On the Anger of God*;[6] chapter vii. discourses Of man, and the brute animals, and religion. In the course of it he asks : ' Does not the position of the body itself, and the fashion of the countenance, declare that we are not on a level with the dumb creation ? Their nature is prostrated to the ground and to their pasture, and has nothing in common with the heaven, which they do not look upon. But man, with his erect position, with his elevated countenance

---

[1] Prof. A. R. Gordon, *The Early Traditions of Genesis*, p. 146.
[2] Cf. Sir J. G. Frazer, *Folk-lore in the Old Testament*, i. chap. I.
[3] Gen. 17.1 ; Micah 6 8.
[4] Gen. I 24 ; 2 7.
[5] Eccles. 3 19 ; so also in Ps. 49 12-20, of the unworthy man.
[6] Trans. Ante-Nicene Christian Library.

raised to the contemplation of the universe, compares
his features with God, and reason recognises reason.'
Even more pointedly he observes elsewhere : 'Man
does not immediately upon his birth walk upright, but
at first on all fours (quadrupes), because the nature
of his body and of this present life is common to us with
the dumb animals ; afterwards, when his strength is
confirmed, he raises himself, and his tongue is loosened
so that he speaks plainly, and he ceases to be a dumb
animal. And this argument teaches that man is born
mortal ; but he afterwards becomes immortal, when
he begins to live in conformity with the will of God,
that is, to follow justice, which is comprised in the worship
of God, since God raised man to a view of the heaven and
of Himself.' [1] His answer to the question as to why God
made man, is the following : 'As He contrived the world
for the sake of man, so He formed man Himself on His
own account, as it were a priest of a divine temple, a
spectator of His works and of heavenly objects. For
he is the only being who, since he is intelligent and capable
of reason, is able to understand God, to admire His works,
and perceive His energy and power ; for on this account
he is furnished with judgment, intelligence, and prudence.
On this account he alone, beyond the other living
creatures, has been made with an upright body and
attitude, so that he seems to have been raised up for the
contemplation of his Parent.' [2]

But now, in the name of science, a story of man's
origin has very gradually been pieced together that has
seemed to derogate from these noble conceptions of his
creation. It may safely be said that if the publication
of *The Origin of Species* on 24th November 1859 came
like a bombshell into the placidly thinking world of
English culture, the appearance of *The Descent of Man*,
on 24th February 1871, would have produced nothing
less than consternation had it not been for the patient,

---

[1] *Divine Institutes*, vii. 5.
[2] *Treatise on the Anger of God*, xiv. ; cf. also *Divine Institutes*, vii. 5.

brave preparatory work of Thomas Henry Huxley in the interval. Evolution as applied to the rest of the animal world was slowly coming to be accepted in view of the overwhelming evidence, but as applied to man it was regarded as at once treachery and blasphemy. Already, on 10th February 1860, at a Friday evening discourse ' On Species and Races, and their Origin,' [1] delivered at the Royal Institution, London, Huxley had said : ' Another, and unfortunately a large, class of persons take fright at the logical consequences of such a doctrine as that put forth by Mr. Darwin. If all species have arisen in this way, say they, Man himself must have done so ; and he and all the animated world must have had a common origin. Most assuredly. No question of it.' How high feeling ran is illustrated by the mere fact that it was possible to arrange the oft-described public debate [2] between Huxley and Samuel Wilberforce, Bishop of Oxford, at the meeting of the British Association for the Advancement of Science in that city during the summer of the same year, when the honours both in common courtesy and substantial argument lay with the former. It is true that Huxley enjoyed the rôle of ' Darwin's bull-dog,' as he called himself,[3] but there was also the deeper side to his nature, to which Lord Ernle has borne the following vivid testimony : ' Huxley was not always the gladiator. To me he was irresistibly attractive, partly perhaps because I fancied that I had caught a glimpse of his true outlook on life. When I think of his destructive criticism, I see again the arabesque with which he had adorned the side of the first page of his article on " Lux Mundi." Up the margin ran a vine-clad trellis ; on the top crowed the cock of theology, and towards him crept the fox of

[1] *Scientific Memoirs*, II. xviii. p. 388.
[2] Cf. ' Reminiscences of a Grandmother,' *Macmillan's Magazine*, October 1898 ; *Life and Letters of Thomas Henry Huxley*, i. 179-189 ; *Life of J. R. Green*, pp. 44, 45; Alfred Noyes, *The Torch-Bearers*, ii. 310 ff.
[3] *Life and Letters of T. H. Huxley*, i. 363.

science. I remember also discussing with him one of his numerous controversies — I think the Gadarene swine. With the impertinence of comparative youth, I expressed surprise at the quantity of vinegar and mustard which he mixed with the discussion of questions that to many people were matters of life or death. " My dear young man," he answered, " you are not old enough to remember when men like Lyell and Murchison were not considered fit to lick the dust off the boots of a curate. I should like to get my heel into their mouths and scr-r-unch it round." Then his mood of half-comic, half-serious ferocity passed. A wistful smile lit up his plain, rugged face, as he added : " And they never seem to reflect what a miserable position mine is—standing on a point of Nothing in an abyss of Nothing." The world saw much of the first mood, little of the latter.' [1]

The story of man's origin, still in the form of an incomplete puzzle-picture where some of the pieces are lacking, while others that are known have not as yet been correctly fitted in, has been told and retold with differing emphases by many competent and recognised authorities.[2] On few essential points is there complete agreement as yet, for the study is only in its infancy and the supply of material is scant. Enough, however, is known to make the gradual ascent of man from some common ancestry with the Primates [3] indubitably certain, even if many of the stages of this ascent are still problematical. The outline sketched by Professor G. Elliot Smith at any rate provides a tentative theory of origins. It is based on the assumption of a growing cultivation of the power of vision, and the dominance of that sense over

[1] ' Victorian Memoirs and Memories,' *Quarterly Review*, April 1923.
[2] *E.g.* Marcellin Boule, *Les Hommes Fossiles* (Eng. trans. *Fossil Men*, by Dr. J. Ritchie) ; R. A. S. Macalister, *A Text-Book of European Archaeology* ; Sir Arthur Keith, *The Antiquity of Man*; G. Elliot Smith, *The Evolution of Man* ; Henry F. Osborn, *Men of the Old Stone Age.*
[3] The name applied to the highest order of Mammals, comprising all the monkeys, from the Anthropoid Apes to the Marmosets and Lemurs.

N

the sense of smell in certain primitive mammals represented to-day by the Jumping Shrews of Africa or the Tree Shrews of the Malay Archipelago, and Tarsius, the ' Spectral Tarsier ' of Borneo, Java, and the Philippines—an offshoot from the primitive Lemurs—with corresponding development of the associated areas of the brain. ' Before the close of the Eocene Period one of the Tarsioidea acquired the power of stereoscopic vision and became transformed into a primitive monkey with a very considerable increase in the size of the brain and an enormous enhancement of the power of skilled movement and of intelligence.' [1] This very suggestive possibility will require, however, decades of work to elevate it into the region of high-grade probability. If this stage in the evolution of Primates took place, as Professor Elliot Smith supposes, ' somewhere in the neighbourhood of Central America,' it would involve the further supposition that ' representatives of all three branches, Lemurs, Tarsioids, and Monkeys, wandered across from the New World to the Old, across bridges which stretched from North America to Africa and Europe, and also from North America to Eastern Asia ' ; [2] not, however, before some Tarsioids had developed into tailed Platyrrhine monkeys whose descendants survive in the South America of to-day.   We are on less speculative ground in noting early and diminutive representatives in Egyptian Oligocene deposits both of the Old World tailed Catarrhine Monkeys—undoubtedly derived from some primitive Platyrrhine form—and of the Anthropoid Apes (*Propliopithecus*). These Anthropoid remains are found thereafter over an increasingly large area, comprising Europe, Africa, and Asia, until in the Miocene of Northern India in particular are disclosed larger forms ancestral to the modern Great Apes and showing points of contact with man.   Nevertheless, in view of the paucity even of the remains that are considered closest to man, it would be hazardous to place any one of them on the main line

[1] G. Elliot Smith, *The Evolution of Man*, p. 13.   [2] *Op. cit.* p. 13.

of that ancestry, and for the present it is probably wiser to consider them as representatives of collateral forms that split off from the direct line of human development. In short, we are left with a picture of myriads of forms, all of them at one stage or another of their racial history standing for a longer or shorter period in that narrow, crowded upward way that led to man, yet passing out of it sooner or later in specialised, and so increasingly static, adaptation to some particular aspect of the physical environment. Man alone retained that degree of primitive structure, and particularly of plasticity, in virtue of which he has shown himself the supremely adaptive and progressive animal.

Of the earliest human remains, that of the Javan *Pithecanthropus* the Erect, most probably from the bottom of the Pleistocene, and on the whole more man than ape ; *Homo heidelbergensis*, represented by a primitive lower jaw uncovered in a sandpit at the village of Mauer near Heidelberg, from beneath nearly eighty feet of Pleistocene deposit ; *Eoanthropus*, the Dawn Man from Piltdown in Sussex, England, possibly a later form than the Heidelberg man ; the various skulls and skeletons of Neanderthal man including the latest recruit from Galilee ; and the Rhodesian skull, which, if in some respects more primitive than a typical Neanderthal skull, probably represents a much later survivor— have been held on morphological data to represent distinct species, even if the surest specific test of cross-sterility is necessarily inapplicable.[1] There is, however, recognisable relationship between the Heidelberg

[1] With regard to the Taungs skull found in 1924 in a Bechuanaland (S. Africa) stratum not older than the Pleistocene, and described under the name *Australopithecus africanus*, Sir Arthur Keith has shown conclusively that it belonged to a young anthropoid ape, ' an extinct relative of the chimpanzee and gorilla but one with more man-like features than are possessed by either of these.' The discovery ' throws light on the history of anthropoid apes, but not on that of man ' (*Nature*, cxvi. 11). The fragment known as the Galilee skull, typically Neanderthal, was found by Mr. Turville-Petre in 1925 in a cave deposit near Tiberias on the western shore of the Lake of Galilee.

mandible and the Neanderthal type of lower jaw, while, on the other hand, the physical characters of *Pithecanthropus*, and perhaps of *Eoanthropus*, are such as really exceed the normal degree of specific relationship, and justify their inclusion in distinct genera of the Human Family. The single molar from the form designated *Hesperopithecus*, taken in 1922 from a Nebraskan bed of undoubted Pliocene Age, will, if the problematic conclusions favouring its resemblance to *Pithecanthropus* are later justified, constitute the first known representative of Pliocene man. It is not till we reach the Late or Upper Palaeolithic Age, covering, say, from the years 25,000 to 10,000 B.C., that we have to do with races, *e.g.* the Cro-Magnon people of Aurignacian days, that are directly ancestral to, or as definitely of the type *Homo sapiens* as any of, the human varieties of to-day. It is also noteworthy that in the oldest stratum of this Late Palaeolithic (Early Aurignacian) Age have been found two skeletons showing a number of distinctively negroid characters.

In endeavouring to differentiate the principal physical characteristic with which the advance from the man-like ape to the ape-like man was most definitely associated, we at once instinctively turn to the brain ; and here the objective data from the study of living forms, and from the endocranial casts that can be made from the skulls of extinct types, provide fairly direct indications. One outstanding feature in the series of living forms from the Jumping Shrew to Man is the noticeable growth in the relative size of the neopallium or cortical area of the brain, and even more particularly of the regions in that cortex concerned with hearing, touch, and skilled movement, but especially vision. This is accompanied at the same time by a progressive diminution of the olfactory region of the brain, and at the level of *Tarsius* there has been a change-over from a life dominated by the sense of smell to one in which sight is the directing sense, due in great part to the adoption of an arboreal life in place of an existence on the ground. *Tarsius*, although possessed of binocular vision, seems, however, to be incapable of appreciating stereoscopic effects, without which power the form, substance, and texture of objects cannot be perceived. It is only in the next higher stage of such a series, represented by the marmoset or American monkey, that a further marked development is evident, not merely in all these cortical areas to which reference has already been made, but more particularly in the pre-frontal area, which experimental investigation shows to be concerned with the process of learning to perform skilled movements. This involves, however, facility in exact convergence of the eyes, and various other complex adjustments which permit of that focussing of the image upon associated spots in the two retinae, without which concentrated attention could not be evoked. Thus the higher Primates acquired the ability ' to appreciate the form and size of objects by following their outline by means of delicate eye-movements.' [1]

This power of stereoscopic vision, stimulating curiosity and attention, reacted in turn on the tactile and pre-hensile facility of fingers and hand, and this again meant in time the attainment of still higher degrees of muscular skill, which reacted once more upon the powers of vision. Now, all this cycle of development is represented in the growing neopallium, which became increasingly an organ for the unification of the various stimuli passing in along the different sensory pathways, and for registering impressions of past experience. Thus memory, becoming more and more of a factor in behaviour, entered into the choices between impulses made under the growing power of discrimination, so modifying them. The important feature was the progressive growth of the brain, which led to the associated development along particular lines of the fore-limb and its extremities. The resulting activities involved a growing familiarity with, and fuller

[1] G. Elliot Smith, *op. cit.* p. 145.

understanding of, the various objects and aspects of the physical environment with which the organism was thus brought into ever closer contact. Such appreciation meant a growing tendency to distinguish objects, and we may then suppose that the power of uttering cries and monosyllabic exclamations expressive of emotional states, developed into the ability to make sounds representative of given objects, in other words, to name them. Long previous to this, gesture and facial expression must have been elements in the process of communication. The remarkable fact connected with the racial development, as brought out especially by Professor Elliot Smith, is that in a comparison between the brain of the gorilla and that of man ' the enormous increase in the cortical territories of the latter affects chiefly three areas, the parietal region . . . the pre-frontal region, and the inferior part of the temporal area. These are the areas that reach their full development last in the human child. They were also the most defective parts of the brains whose forms and proportions can be inferred from the moulds of the brain-cases of *Pithecanthropus* and *Eoanthropus.*' [1] Now, these are the regions that are intimately connected with the capacity for the deeper understanding of the meaning of words, sentences, and situations, for the attainment of muscular skill, and for the general appreciation of speech, respectively, although activity of the cortex as a whole is a necessary accompaniment in each case. As they developed, *Homosimius*, as our theoretical ancestral form may usefully be termed, would take on increasingly the aspect of an ape with an over-developed brain. The simian characteristics in jaw and face and limb would be retained long after the brain had reached the distinctively human level—a point of view which is confirmed even by the *Pithecanthropus*, and more especially by the *Eoanthropus*, remains. Such enhanced mental activity and skill in action must, however, have been principally devoted to the securing

[1] *Op. cit.* p. 148.

of food and the avoidance of danger. Then, as to-day, reflection based on investigation and the resulting leadership in thought and activity, were confined to the few. We may say that the passage from *Homosimius* to Man was made when a being was developed who appreciated space and time, could distinguish objects by their several characters and attributes, and was vividly aware of himself as other than the world around him. This racial transformation is briefly rehearsed in the case of every individual human life.

If the newer knowledge upon the question of human origins involved a certain measure of readjustment in theological thought, that of the antiquity of man seemed, in the first instance, even more upsetting, and we are only as yet at the beginning of appreciating the change in outlook that it really implies. On a view under which it was believed that the creation of man had taken place definitely at a precise hour on a certain day in the year 4004 B.C.—for pagan philosophy likewise had no different understanding of events so far as the time scale was concerned—and that the approaching end of the ages would come within no very great passage of time, it was natural for any one living in the Middle Age to regard the great writers of Greece and Rome and their contemporaries as ' ancients.' Pagan mythology and Jewish anthropology alike agreed in positing some primitive Edenic state of human life from which the subsequent racial history was degeneration or a fall. When, however, the evidence began to accumulate of a history that had covered hundreds of thousands of years, and of aeonian generations of life preceding the ascent of man and not altogether unconnected with it, it became apparent that, so far from being ' ancients,' the writers in question and the men of their time had, as a matter of fact, stood nearer to the childhood of the race, even if separated from us by a span of years that is barely noticeable on the scale of human history as known in its entirety to-day.[1] Such

[1] See *infra*, chap. xi.

a readjustment, which involved the conception of a slow, though not necessarily uniform, ascent, coming on the previous modification of ideas which had inevitably followed on the discovery that the earth was not the centre of the Universe, and man, therefore, not entitled to the importance that seemed his right as an implication of the geocentric outlook, compelled a fresh examination of the question, What is Man ? This reinvestigation, if it has consigned much Mediaeval Theology to the limbo of outgrown ideas, has given us a truer, more wonderful, and more inspiring answer, and, at the same time, must lead to a renewed appreciation of the truth of the declarations of Jesus concerning the nature and destiny of man.

The fact of the great antiquity of man rests, however, not merely on the basis of the actual discoveries of fossil human remains in strata whose age can be determined with comparative exactness, but on the circumstance that the modern species, *Homo sapiens*, includes three principal types—the Negro or black man (*H. aethiopicus*), the Mongolian or yellow man (*H. mongolicus*), and the white man (*H. caucasicus*), which are characterised by marked physical and even mental features. Amongst the living varieties of the human race none is more primitive than the native Australian.[1] Indeed, Professor Elliot Smith considers that this people represents perhaps the survival, with comparatively slight modifications, of the actual primitive type of the species.[2] But this would be to make them ' contemporary ancestors ' of all subsequent races ; they cannot represent more than *a* primitive type of our species. Next to the Australian in this respect comes the younger Negro Race, differing from the Australian in many characteristics, yet sharing with him the black pigmentation of the skin. The

---

[1] The native Australian is peculiarly difficult to classify, being placed, *e.g.* by A. H. Keane, *Man, Past and Present* (p. 39), in a primitive ' pre-Dravidian ' sub-division of the Caucasian group ; but this is unsatisfactory.

[2] *Op. cit.* p. 1.

next offshoot from the ancestral stock was the Mongolian Race, where the reduction in pigmentation is very considerable, but the specialisation no less marked in various particular directions. The main line is thereafter represented by a white stock showing continued reduction in pigmentation, yet with the retention of other primitive characters, which first threw off the so-called Alpine Race, and latterly is represented by the Mediterranean and Nordic Races.

As the evidence constituting the first line of support tends to suggest that the three principal types had a common ancestry, it becomes obvious, on the basis of modern rates of change, that a very considerable period of time must have elapsed since this differentiation began to take place. Older views of a polyphyletic origin of the human race are gradually being replaced by a monophyletic origin, which is generally supposed to have taken place somewhere in the region of the great Iranian plateau, from which centre primitive man could move out to those various localities where his remains have been found. This seems the most likely view at the moment, even if those anthropoid apes which on the whole are most akin to man, viz. the gorilla and chimpanzee, are found to-day in Africa—his wandering heralds. Other features that link this continent with early stages in human history are the very primitive Rhodesian fossil remains,[1] and the probability that Neanderthal man entered Europe by one of the Mediterranean land-bridges. Nevertheless, the bulk of the evidence points towards the north-eastern region of the Iranian plateau as the area within which the last stage of the great transformation was worked out. Not very far away from the westernmost slopes of this plateau were Elam and the broad tract 'between the rivers' Tigris and Euphrates, the lower reaches of which were inhabited by the Sumerians, who appear to

---

[1] *H. rhodesiensis*, found in 1921 at the Broken Hill Mine in Northern Rhodesia. For an account, reference may be made to *Man and the Attainment of Immortality*, pp. 109, 110.

have come originally from the highlands to the north-east, and, finally, Egypt—the seats of the three earliest civilisations of which we have accurate knowledge. When to these are added the Assyrians and the seafaring, mercantile Phoenicians, it becomes apparent that the focus of primitive culture was a comparatively restricted area of the earth's surface, which will in due course, as the result of future discovery, probably suffer still further contraction. Diffusion quickly added to the number of such foci.

It is certain that much of our past thinking on the origin and growth of civilisation will be recast in the light of more exact observation and fuller discovery of the records of the past. As long as the individual made all the articles of his primitive economy for himself, he was in all likelihood contented with any kind of workmanship. If the life of the community lay along some river bank, there was always room for the young members to move farther down the river, and so they tended to maintain the old practice of making every article for themselves. So long as things went easily, we may suppose, the customs of the past were followed. It was only under the increasing pressure of existence, when, with the growing size of the community, the struggle to secure food became more intense, that the inferior arrow-head maker would become discontented with his workmanship, and by his continual repairing for assistance to some more skilled maker of arrow-heads, the professional worker in flint implements came into existence. It seems as if we shall have to recognise that most new discoveries and fresh inventions have been brought in or introduced into the communities where they are found, having each of them originated in a single locality, rather than suppose that they have been separately discovered by different individuals in regions now widely apart, although the possibility of this in certain instances can never be wholly excluded.

The earliest exactly known date in human history

appears, for the moment, to be 4241 B.C., when the
Egyptians fixed their calendar. But such an achievement
in itself means centuries of previous observation and
investigation,[1] so that it is a moderate computation to
suppose 4500 B.C. as an approximate date for the time
when Egypt emerged from a pre-dynastic tribal condition, corresponding to the close of her Neolithic Age,
into what was a relatively stable or ' civilised ' condition
of local organised states. Whatever term be allotted
to the Neolithic—and it cannot well be less than 10,000-
12,000 years—the beginning of the Neolithic Age in
Egypt is found to synchronise with about the middle
of the Magdalenian, *i.e.* Late Palaeolithic, in Western
Europe. In other words, the Palaeolithic and Neolithic
of Egypt in some degree antedate the Palaeolithic and
the Neolithic of Europe. The same is true of the Copper,
Bronze, and Iron periods, so that the search for origins
moves eastward. What is true of the Egyptians holds
as markedly of the Sumerians, who were certainly
established in city states on the lower stretches of the
Tigris-Euphrates valley, in the fourth millennium B.C.,
as also of the Elamites still farther to the east,[2] whose
historical records may yet be found to antedate those of
Sumeria itself. Like the Egyptians, the Sumerians had
a fully developed Neolithic civilisation long in advance
of the corresponding cultural stage in Europe; and so
far as comparison with Egypt is concerned, if they
were behind in some respects, in others, *e.g.* the domestication of certain animals and the use of metals, they seem
to have been ahead. It is impossible to suppose that
two such civilisations grew up entirely unrelated and
independent of one another. On the contrary, it looks
as if the richest discoveries in ancient civilisation are still
to be made in the sweep of territory embracing Egypt,

[1] The same conclusion would follow from the extraordinary variety
in the types of vase that can be definitely associated with the beginning
of the Pre-dynastic Period in Egypt.

[2] Raphael Pumpelly, *Explorations in Turkestan.*

the Sumerian lands, and the Iranian plateau. Here we have still much to learn with regard to the relations of the annual floodings of the Nile and of the Tigris-Euphrates system to the development of agriculture, as also with regard to the still larger questions of migration and the transmission of cultures in general. The domestication of animals was, so far as we know, first put into operation in Asia. Thence came the dog, man's oldest friend; long after it the ox, the sheep, the pig, the camel, and, much later, the horse. Agriculture, which in some regions, at any rate, preceded the domestication of animals, was probably first practised in Mesopotamia or Egypt. In the attention which it directed to the cycle of the seasons, the shorter lunar phases, and the apparently fertilising power of water, it aided in the development of primitive science. On such a time-scale as is gradually opening out, the subsequent Semitic invasions from Arabia into Lower and Upper Mesopotamia will growingly prove to be comparatively late developments, while the Hebrew literature as a whole must even now, as we have seen, be placed at a point less than half-way down the course of exact human history. Here also, increasingly, adjustment will be required which, while it will have to surrender the no longer warrantable views as to the absolute antiquity and origins of Scripture, will yet find in it an even more significant testimony to the divine in history. For while the progress of Science yields increasingly interesting and valuable data as to the story of the slow ascent of man, she offers in herself no interpretation of the fact of the existence of man. Yet nothing that she discloses goes contrary to those profound glimpses into man's destiny and the meaning of human life that have been given to their fellows by those who have thought most worthily of man because they have lived closest to God, and especially to that estimate that was at once revealed, lived up to, and died for, by Jesus Christ.

CHAPTER X

CONCERNING THE SOUL

> At last she said, ' Sweet brothers, yesternight
> I seem'd a curious little maid again,
> As happy as when we dwelt among the woods,
> And when ye used to take me with the flood
> Up the great river in the boatman's boat.
> Only ye would not pass beyond the cape
> That has the poplar on it : there ye fixt
> Your limit, oft returning with the tide.
> . . . but this night I dream'd
> That I was all alone upon the flood,
> And then I said, " Now shall I have my will " :
> And there I woke, but still the wish remain'd.
> So let me hence that I may pass at last
> Beyond the poplar and far up the flood,
> Until I find the palace of the King.' [1]

BEYOND the poplar on the cape, the rustling of whose tremulous leaves perhaps seemed to whisper of life [2]— what indeed lies there ?   In his beautiful word-picture, the Victorian poet has expressed that insatiable, pathetically human wondering which has haunted man since those early moments when first the thought of the soul was glimpsed in his mind. For it is generally agreed on the basis of such data as were set down in Tylor's classical *Primitive Culture,* that the conception of the soul has formed an element in the cultural life of all peoples at some stage or another. As Crawley rightly remarks, ' few conceptions can show the universality and permanence, the creative power and morphological

[1] Alfred Tennyson, *Idylls of the King : Lancelot and Elaine.*
[2] In classical lore, the poplar was sacred to Zeus and to Hades, and was supposed to grow on the banks of Acheron (cf. A. B. Cook in *Folk-Lore,* xv. 297, 421).

influence, which have characterised throughout history the Idea of the Soul.'[1] It was developed in all probability partly as the result of reflection upon experience of a dream-life as vivid to primitive man as his waking life, and partly as the result of a persistent visualising in memory of the form and activities of the dead.[2] As a matter of fact, in several instances in contemporary savage life the conception of the soul corresponds in definite features to a faded and reduced facsimile of the original individual, the reduction corresponding to the smaller size which the human figure assumes when at the distance at which the body can be most conveniently envisaged as a whole by the observer. Its tenuous substantiality may then be correlated with the fact that it is a memory-image. The conceptions of modern savage tribes, however, apart from sundry indications of more primitive beliefs which may sometimes be extracted from their terminology, have no practical value in the elucidation of the truth or the illusions concerning the soul. Of the peoples of antiquity, the Semites, in a lesser degree the Egyptians, and the Greeks, contributed the ideas that had most to do in shaping thought on this great topic during the earlier centuries of human history.

Now, it is not altogether easy to set down in clear outline the Hebrew conception of the soul, partly owing to misleading translations in the Authorised and Revised Versions of the Old Testament[3]—probably due to some extent, as in corresponding instances in the New Testament,[4] to the influence of Platonic presuppositions upon the minds of the translators; partly owing to the primitive unsupportable views of the Hebrews on human

[1] A. E. Crawley, *The Idea of the Soul*, p. 1.
[2] A. E. Crawley, *op. cit.* chap. iii.
[3] Thus in Gen. 2 [19] the phrase applied to the animal world and rightly rendered 'living creature' is translated by 'living soul' in verse 7, when it is applied to man. For other O.T. examples, cf. H. Wheeler Robinson, *The Christian Doctrine of Man*, p. 16.
[4] Cf. *antea*, p. 25, *n.* 2.

anatomy and physiology which coloured their thinking upon certain aspects of the life of the soul; and partly owing to the fact that their views upon the soul, on the evidence of Scripture itself, underwent development and modification.[1] Thus they had no ideas, and so no words, relating to the existence of the brain, the nervous system, or the respiratory system; and while they referred various psychological states and activities to organs whose primary function at any rate is known to-day to be quite other, there does not seem to have been any thoroughgoing dualism of body and soul in Hebrew thought. Just because the body was alive, every part and organ in it might have its own psychical and moral side. Yet while the Hebrews had no separate word for 'body,' the distinction is clear between 'flesh' and 'spirit': [2] on the other hand, the soul still had a body of a certain kind although it was not 'flesh.'[3] The 'soul' was at first identified with the breath and also with the blood in which the breath resided; these *are* the life.[4] As such the soul 'departed' at death[5] for Sheol, whose inhabitants are collectively described as 'rephaim,' the pithless 'shades' of the dead. Just as with the Romans, later, the idea of *anima* (breath) developed into that of *animus* (soul), the conscious subject of thought and feeling and desire, so the Hebrew equivalent, which primarily indicated the breath, regarded as the symbol or medium of animal life, became a general word for *a* soul or self or personality. With regard to the Greek and Hebrew terms rendered 'soul' and 'spirit' respectively,[6] it is perhaps simplest to say that they are employed in more than one sense in relation to man,

---

[1] This development has been traced, *e.g.*, by H. Wheeler Robinson, *op. cit.* pp. 11-27. Cf. also J. O. Dykes, *The Divine Worker in Creation and Providence*, pp. 309-315, and L. B. Paton, *Spiritism and the Cult of the Dead in Antiquity*, chap. viii.

[2] Is. 31 [3].

[3] I Sam. 28 [14]; Ezek. 32 [27].

[4] Gen. 2 [7], 9 [4]; Deut. 12 [23]; Lev. 17 [11].

[5] Gen. 35 [18].

[6] *Nephesh* = ψυχή = soul; *ruach* = πνεῦμα = spirit.

and that in practically every one of these differing senses
the two terms are interchangeable, although the significance of ' spirit ' often lies in its association with the
conception of man in the higher aspects of his nature as
' open to influences from the unseen world, whether
good or evil.' [1] It is only when St. Paul is speaking
ethically, and dealing with the contrast between re-
generate and unregenerate human nature, that there
is any deviation in his usage from the general sense
of the word ' spirit.' The terms ' soul ' and ' spirit,'
that is to say, refer to differences of aspect, but not of
essence. Even if the term ' soul ' is more commonly
employed with reference to man as the subject of experience in contact with the phenomenal world, and the
term ' spirit ' with reference to his relationships to that
which is transcendental, nevertheless it is the same
individual subject that is contemplated. Apart from
a single instance,[2] where St. Paul, with no apparently
dogmatic intention, employs a phrase suggestive of a
well-known Platonic conception, and a passage in the
Epistle to the Hebrews, there is no hint in Scripture of
any tripartite division of human nature into body, soul,
and spirit, and apparently no warrant for considering
such to be its avowed teaching.

Of the Egyptians Herodotus tells us that they were
' the first to teach that the human soul is immortal,
and at the death of the body enters into some other
living thing then coming to birth ; and after passing
through all creatures of land, sea and air (which cycle
it completes in three thousand years), it enters once more
into a human body at birth.' [3] The enormous extension
of known Egyptian history has done nothing to throw
doubt upon the very sure, almost axiomatic, belief of the
Egyptian mind in what was apparently a post-mortem

[1] J. O. Dykes, *op. cit.* p. 154.
[2] I Thess. 5 [23] ; cf. Heb. 4 [12]. Of the first reference Prof. Moffatt
says, ' The collocation . . . is unusual, but, of course, quite untech-
nical.' Cf. *E.G.T.* in locis.
[3] *Historia*, ii. 123 (Loeb trans.).

development or rebirth of a soul.[1] The conception of the future life varies, possibly reflecting in some respects cultural developments in succeeding dynasties, yet assuredly conditioned by a heightened ethical standard, and a growing sense that the attainment of immortality depended more on soul quality than external agency. But the belief is as strong in the end as it was in the beginning, and in its defiance and contempt of death, and its associated idea, at any rate during the Osirian phase, of a life of bliss in the skies, furnished elements that survived its many inconsistencies. Just because life would be renewed, the Egyptians sought to preserve the body from which the vital principle had fled.

One other contribution alone calls for notice in this connection. Greek thought upon the soul, particularly as expressed in the Socratic-Platonic disquisitions, moved in the region of the eternal and the prime movement of things, and linked its origin with the gods. For Socrates it was the conscious self, ' the thing in us which is of more importance to us than anything else whatever,'[2] and which, therefore, it behoves us to try to make wise and good. The Greek contribution took the form at first of a refinement of the earlier popular conception of a tenuous mobile soul-substance that was distinct from the body proper. This underwent a gradual process of dematerialisation, as it were, until from Plotinus' view of the soul as an immaterial emanation from the Soul of the All, it was no far step to St. Augustine's adoption of the idea and further elaboration of it by the

---

[1] Prof. J. H. Breasted states that originally the soul ' came into existence really for the first time at the death of the individual. . . . After the resuscitation of the body, there was a mental restoration or reconstitution of the faculties one by one, attained especially by the process of making the deceased a " soul " (ba), in which capacity he again existed as a person, possessing all the powers that would enable him to subsist and survive in the life hereafter ' (Religion and the Future Life, edited by H. Sneath, p. 31). In strict interpretation, therefore, the Egyptians did not hold a belief in the immortality of the soul as an inherently imperishable entity.

[2] Prof. J. Burnet in The Legacy of Greece, p. 78.

denial of extension to the soul thus immaterial. Nevertheless, this soul functioned in every living and moving
part of the human body. It is important to note that the
Orphic-Platonic idea of an inherently immortal soul which
passed by way of Neoplatonism into Christian thought
during the first three centuries of this era is an essentially
natural conception grafted on to, and fused with, the
other Hebraic-Christian belief. Few of the Church
Fathers had, however, accepted the Platonic premise of
the pre-existence of the soul. From the seventeenth
century onwards this comfortable view of the soul, which
had practically reigned supreme from the time of St.
Augustine, was aggressively attacked, or subjected to
various forms of substitutionary statement in its own
defence. The growing success of mechanical explanations of phenomena inspired attempts to bring the
sequestered stirrings of the soul likewise under the same
category, while other philosophers strove to maintain
its autonomy and even its hegemony. At least four
clearly elaborated solutions were on offer—' the animistic Dualism of Descartes, the parallelistic Animism
of Leibnitz, the Identity-hypothesis of Spinoza, the
Materialism of Hobbes,' [1] supplemented later by the
idealism of Berkeley and the scepticism of Hume.

The philosophical controversies of the eighteenth
century were conducted principally with reference to the
conception of substance, material and immaterial, and
Hume accorded to the latter the same kind of treatment
that Berkeley had meted out to the former. Nevertheless, it was impossible to remain satisfied with Hume's
description of mankind as ' nothing but a bundle or
collection of different perceptions, which succeed each
other with an inconceivable rapidity, and are in a
perpetual flux and movement.' [2] After all, a bundle, in
order to constitute a bundle, has to be held or kept

[1] W. M'Dougall, *Body and Mind*, p. 59, where chaps. i.-vi. are
devoted to a historical *résumé* of the varying fortunes of Animism.

[2] *A Treatise of Human Nature*, Book i. Part iv. § 6; quoted in
M'Dougall, p. 72.

together in some sort, and in any case the futile solipsism implicit in the logical application of Hume's principles makes them no resting-place for the normal mind. Still, while Kant held the balance true between Hume and Berkeley, by maintaining the validity of Berkeley's inference from our sense-preceptions to some agent or agencies that evoke our sensations, and by denying with Hume that we can infer the nature of those agencies,[1] the really effective and damaging criticism of the old substantial standpoint came in the nineteenth century from the rapid extension of the domain of mechanistic explanation from the inorganic to every phase of the organic. For, to begin with, the thorough ransacking of the human organism, and in particular of the brain, yielded no seriously supportable punctual position of the soul, and the exact determinations following the establishment of the doctrine of the conservation of energy seemed to leave no place in the linkage of process for the intrusion and free play of a soul. At the same time it became unquestionably evident that the brain was the only organ with which any ' soul ' activities could be plausibly associated. The localisation of specific functions in definite areas of the cerebral cortex, the first instance of which was established by Broca, brought the physico-chemical processes in the region defined into closest relationship with the corre-sponding sensory, motor, or even intellectual activity. Even if the energy released in connection with any such functioning may bear no regular stateable relation to the intensity of the particular stimulus, the continued rapid progress in the physiology of the brain made it seem reasonable to suppose that eventually it would be possible to provide a complete description, in terms of physico-chemical change, of any sequence of events issuing in action, thus making any view of action and reaction between soul and body, through the medium of the brain, not merely impossible but superfluous.

[1] W. M'Dougall, *op. cit.* p. 75.

From the general point of view, the question of the soul [1] is bound up with the larger question of the ultimate character of the world process as a whole. Is it fundamentally a spiritual process—that is to say, one which, on a review of all the possible interpretations, is most reasonably and completely interpreted in terms of a means whereby beings can be, and are being, evolved, who are fit to become increasingly co-operators with a purpose of God for themselves and the Universe, both now and throughout eternity, by growing in likeness to Him through the knowledge of Himself? If, on the other hand, the view that we are dealing with a closed system of events which can be completely and successfully explained in terms of physics and chemistry alone, or of extension and motion only, is within any measurable distance of establishment, it seems improbable that sufficient value will be left for the idea of the soul to make it even worth discussion. It is necessary, therefore, in the first place to consider briefly the larger issue.

To-day it is possible to accept a view which brings the inorganic into closest relationship with the organic, and indeed considers the whole evolutionary process as essentially biocentric. [2] The duality of matter and energy has been resolved in favour of the more ultimate character of the latter, of which matter is but a particular expression or manifestation. It is further possible to arrange substances and compounds of increasing molecular complexity in related series up to a point where the next difference in grouping would be between inorganic and organic colloids, and there is some reason to believe that some such series corresponds to the actual historical development. The distinctiveness of the transition

[1] Throughout this chapter the terms ' soul,' ' spirit,' and ' self ' are used more or less interchangeably, as it is more important to emphasise that which they represent in common, than the subtle and sometimes fanciful distinctions that are drawn between them. To the same category belongs the term ' person,' where the shade of meaning is forensic, implying a sense of individual and social responsibility.

[2] L. J. Henderson, *The Fitness of the Environment*, p. 312.

at this stage appears to lie, however, not so much in further molecular complexity as in a certain, as yet indefinable, energetic relationship which expresses itself in organisation. Out of mere complexity of molecular constitution alone, the *actively* new has not been shown to emerge, although it may provide the conditions for its 'emergence'; qualitative differences seem to lie within the energetic domain, whether by a progressive condensation of energy leading to new forms of greater efficiency and intensity that may be graded,[1] or by the more definite growing control of that energy by the co-efficient of mind, which study of the objective evolutionary process discloses as there from the beginning, and always more significantly coming to light.[2]

But, further, the vulnerability of the mechanistic explanation so far as it lays claim to be a complete account of process, instead of a provedly serviceable working hypothesis with limitations, has become, if anything, more apparent with the advance of science. For not merely does it seem preposterous on reflection to imagine that a complete understanding of the world process can be reached by means of our very limited senses, even when aided by all the mechanical devices that have been invented by man, and will yet be invented, but the *tour de force* involved in attempting to explain individual or national history in terms of mechanical law alone, without any reference to thought, purpose, or feeling, becomes more evidently something of the nature of an illusion. Of the isolated event, our understanding consistently grows by aid of these methods, but not at all to the same degree in respect of the linkage or connection of the series as a whole. The idea of the soul, or of the essential spirituality of the world process, cannot then be merely dismissed as inconceivable, or

[1] J. M. Macfarlane, *The Causes and Course of Organic Evolution*, chap. iv.

[2] For a more detailed statement, reference may be made to *The Spiritual Interpretation of Nature*, chap. xi.

regarded as eliminated as the result of present-day knowledge, particularly when so many statements of physical conceptions indicate the uncertainty and difficulties attending the attempts at exact definition. The difficulty so commonly urged against interactionist views, viz. that we cannot conceive how an idea could produce a motion in the particles of the substance of the brain—a difficulty, after all, simply due to the limits of the human imagination — should not necessarily be considered a final stumbling-block. A generation that has been liberated through the newer knowledge about hormones from the bondage to Weismannian doctrine under which its predecessors lay, in great part owing to the vaunted inconceivability of any method as to how changes in the body could affect the germ-cells, should be chary of objections based upon mere inconceivability. But, indeed, the idea of a guiding influence of mind upon matter without the association of doing work or breach of the law of the conservation of energy— itself to-day called in question as an absolute statement —has become, at any rate, theoretically conceivable.[1] There is nothing known that rules out the possibility of the direct action between them, while psychical activity may itself involve actual increase of energy. How suggestion acts we do not know, yet it certainly liberates vital powers.[2] The stimulus may come from the inorganic environment, or from another mind; it may operate from the subject's own subconsciousness, or through that subconsciousness from what can only be described as the living God Himself. Mind influences energy, i.e. causes changes of energy distribution, and is affected by energy, i.e. becomes aware of such changes. If this is true of the human mind, it is at least a permissible hypo-

[1] Prof. J. H. Poynting, 'Physical Law and Life,' *H.J.*, vol. i. No. 4; W. M'Dougall, *op. cit.* p. 212.   Cf. also H. Driesch, *The Science and Philosophy of the Organism*, ii. 180.

[2] Cf., *e.g.*, 'The Phenomena of Stigmatisation,' by the Rev. Herbert Thurston, S.J. (*Proceedings of the Society for Psychical Research*, vol. xxxii., July 1921).

thesis to posit a Divine Mind which can thus control the energy distribution of a universe. The practical question, however, is, Are there any respects in which the conception of the soul is either necessary or helpful ?

It has been remarked that study of the objective evolutionary process leaves us with two ultimates in the form of Infinite Energy and Infinite Mind. With the question of the relationship of these two, or of the possibility of resolving this final dualism in terms of Mind as creative of and informing and directing the operations of Energy until they issued, in the course of ages, in the production of free moral personalities — a result unobtainable except through the tribulation of process— it is impossible for the human mind to deal, with any great satisfaction. There is, however, no moment at which fitness for some subsequent stage in a long-continued process, as well as convergence and co-operation, are not in evidence in some degree, and, throughout the development, growingly apparent. There is a sense of anticipation suggestive of an all-pervading purposiveness, as also of a definite direction, and striving towards an end. This appears in the tendency of the evolutionary process as a whole—its culmination in man with his potentialities and possibilities [1]—and also, in the case of all the forms that comprise the ascending scale of organic life, as a growing dominance of mind over body, in the ever greater control over the lines along which the expenditure of energy takes place, and in extension of the area in which the mechanistic postulates require supplementation in order to furnish a satisfactory explanation. The regulation and readjustment of embryonic development even when experimentally interfered with ; the facts connected with regeneration in the plant and animal kingdoms ;

---

[1] 'And the outcome of it all is to endow man with a simple and worthy conception of the story of creation, and to fill him with reverence for the wondrous scheme which, unrolling through the ages, without haste, without rest, has prepared the world for man's dominion and made him fit and able to occupy it ' (Prof. W. W. Watts, Pres. Address, Section C, *Brit. Assoc. Report*, 1924).

the response by 'trial and error,' and the ability to learn
by experience, which are visible in a minimal degree even
in the lowest forms of life; the continuous effort or
adaptive striving towards well-being that is of the essence
of all organic activity; the co-ordination implied in the
distinctive unitary reaction of the organism to varying
kinds of stimuli; and finally, that most definite type of
response that follows on the apprehension of *meaning*
in the character of the stimulus, *e.g.* the case of a spoken
or written communication—all involve something more
than a mere listless mechanical reaction. 'In human
behaviour,' as M'Dougall shows, 'the independence of the
reaction on the nature of the sense-stimuli becomes
complete, so that on the one hand very diverse conjunctions of sense-stimuli evoke the same reaction, and,
on the other hand, conjunctions of sense-stimuli differing
only in respect to some minute detail may evoke totally
different reactions; that, in fact, the dominant part in
the determination of the reaction is played by the meaning which the individual discovers in the sensory presentation, by the value which he attaches to this meaning, and
by the relation of this value to his settled purposes.' [1]
There is suggested, accordingly, some principle, positive, active, and in a sense transcendent, which initiates
activity and is a subject of modification as the result of
the life experience as a whole. Call it what we like,
self or soul, in its higher stages of development it
is that spiritual, primary, controlling and pervasive
ground of the physical, which we can never completely
or even directly know in our planetary space-time
existence—the spiritual entity which *is*, in its distinctive
activities and qualities. Just because of this, all description of it necessarily becomes vague, yet even to deny

---

[1] *Op. cit.* p. 271. Cf. also: 'Meaning . . . plays an essential part
in the determination of the sequence of bodily reaction on sense-
impression, and meaning has no immediate physical correlate in the
brain that could serve as its substitute and discharge its functions '
(p. 311). A similar claim is made with regard to 'the immediate
conditions of feeling-tone ' (chap. xxiii).

the self requires the existence of a self, and without it experience is unthinkable.

Much of the difficulty that attends elucidation of the problem of the soul arises from the fact that the term ' consciousness ' is ordinarily taken to represent a certain constant specificity of awareness, whereas the clearest consciousness of every human being waxes and wanes, sometimes to an almost alarming degree, within comparatively short periods of time. Further, consciousness is distributed in varying degrees in connection with the nervous system, and it is apparent that a superior quality or order of consciousness is associated, e.g., with prefrontal structure and functioning. The general growth in intensity and clearness of consciousness can be followed in the development of every infant. In the adult it is apt to be most lucid in attention, which implies concentration or focalisation of consciousness, and it has been supposed, with some reason,[1] that such activity of the mind has a definite share in bringing about a certain organisation of nervous elements in the brain into systems or paths along which nervous energy eventually flows with that ease which constitutes habit. On the other hand, as we pass down the animal scale, beginning with the higher mammals, we find ourselves dealing with a succession of forms whose lives become increasingly a series of disconnected moments, until in the case of the lowest invertebrates the very structure of the nervous system prohibits the possibility of more than a local high degree of sensitivity. More exactly and objectively, it is possible to distinguish, in descending order, less and less complex forms of neuronic arc through which the centralised nerve control passes. Typically, such an arc consists of a series of long, conducting cellular elements or neurons, connected by shorter (internuncial) neurons. The latter are usually limited to the grey matter of the central nervous system, e.g. in the association areas of the human brain or in the neuropile within the ganglion

[1] Cf. W. M'Dougall, op. cit. pp. 275-279.

of each segment in the case of the earthworm.[1] These series of neurons, highly complex in the higher animals, are linked together in a series of arcs. Five types of neuron or neuronic arc have been differentiated, beginning, from above, with the ' psycho-associational neuron ' as in man, the ' supra-segmental reflex neuron ' as in the lower mammals, the ' intersegmental reflex arc ' as in the earthworm, the ' reflex arc ' as in the jellyfish and sea-anemones, and neuroid sensitivity or irritability as in the sponges and protozoa. Yet it is not possible to make absolute distinctions, or indicate with any confidence at what precise point in the scale the simplest of ideas, still less the vaguest ideation, comes into existence. It is a simple matter of fact, distressing to many elaborated, clean-cut schemes of zoological classification, that consciousness as implying awareness or perception and memory is present, if necessarily in a minimal degree, throughout the animal kingdom, from the protozoa upwards. At the level of the lower mammals behaviour evidently ' becomes subject to a certain degree of supervisional review, guided by a primitive form of judgment.' Quite definitely, as we descend, consciousness becomes more and more diffuse and less integrated, until it passes into that general irritability or sensitivity which is characteristic of all living matter. Yet there is no form of life which does not give a ' total reaction ' to external stimuli, although the degree of individuality or wholeness is necessarily minimal in the protozoa.

Of the foregoing characteristics attendant upon the development of consciousness, none would appear to be more important in any discourse concerning the soul than the fixed popular belief in the unitary nature of consciousness. Unity of consciousness or spiritual individuality has throughout the ages been assumed to

[1] Prof. R. J. A. Berry, ' Brain and Mind,' *British Medical Journal*, No. 3303, p. 707, from which paper certain of the immediately following data have been taken.

be the indefeasible God-given perquisite of humanity.
Yet there are many facts that may give us to pause.
Even if certain well-established cases of dissociation of
personality have been suspected with good reason to be
the subjects of ' some degree of functional dissociation
among the elements of the brain,' [1] yet the abnormality
in these extreme instances is after all but a matter of
degree, for it does not take much introspection for each one
of us to become aware of the duality [2] or even the plurality
of potential selves, not merely alternating but concurrent,
within ourselves. *In*dividuality and continuity are in
process of gradual attainment, and there is no proof of
dissociation into completely developed selves.[3] Once
again, the remarkable fact that apparently alone amongst
the cell systems of the human body, the 9,280,000,000
neurons in the cerebral cortex do not increase in number
after birth, although development goes on within them,
and particularly in the number and length of the connecting branches, might seem to afford, in their relative
fixity and permanence, a physical correlate of the sense
of continuity in personality, yet, on the other hand, the
elements of a neuronic arc are structurally discontinuous.
Further, it is interesting to note how with the advance
of science some of the older positions in which Materialism
once encamped, have been gradually abandoned by the
researchers. Thus we are informed [4] that it is erroneous
to suppose that ' there is some particular part of the
cortex, such as Broca's area, which is the one and only
area concerned in speech. At the best, the occipital
end of the third frontal convolution can be little more
than the place of origin of, perhaps, the final common
effector pathway.'

But now when we regard the structure of the human

[1] W. M'Dougall, *op. cit.* p. 118.
[2] Cf. R. L. Stevenson, *Dr. Jekyll and Mr. Hyde*; St. Paul, Rom. 7 [23];
Ovid, *Metam.*, vii. 20.
[3] For a fuller discussion of these points, reference may be made to
Man and the Attainment of Immortality, chap. ix.
[4] R. J. A. Berry, *op. cit.* p. 710.

body particularly in relation to those capacities that seem to us highest, we note that eye and ear and hand— in short, the whole range of means for entering into relationship with the Environment in all its aspects—are all adapted to minister to consciousness, and to the apparatus and content of consciousness. Co-ordination of the different elements in this *rapport* takes place by means of that apparatus, which is the brain. And when we further consider the dominating rôle of consciousness in life, and superlatively in human life, it certainly seems more true to say that the brain has developed in the interests of consciousness rather than that consciousness has developed as a by-product of brain activity. Now, consciousness is exerted always towards an end—the preservation and development of the life of the conscious being; and even in those activities of the body, of which in normal conditions we are unaware, the activity is of the same type, even if the end is not immediately present to any consciousness. In other words, the whole activity of the living organism, clearly conscious or only dimly so, is purposive throughout, and becomes a whole simply in virtue of this directed co-ordination of activity. A living being is alive in the degree and range of its functioning, and to speak of its function or of the function of its constituent parts is to speak of its purpose—of mind active in it or in relation to it. The individual mind can only, with any satisfaction, be thought of as in some way related to that Mind which, in its fulness, seems to be the necessary counterpart of a sustained, broadly progressive, directed, and end-attaining process. In both alike it is this purposive activity, this functioning, that *is* creation. The means may be mechanical—it is difficult to see how, as a basis, they could be anything else; but directly associated with these energetic activities is mind —*the* 'vis creatrix' in the sense that it controls the behaviour of energy, and may even be its ultimate source.

The superlatively difficult problem of the relation of mind and body has been dealt with in great detail by many investigators, and notably by Professor M'Dougall,[1] yet in no other case does the exact solution seem so far off. A relationship is very clearly and incisively established, perhaps in no instance more strikingly than in the simple fact that in the human embryo the pre-frontal, upper parietal, and inferior temporal areas of the cortex—those associated with the highest mental functions—are the last to be developed, thus exhibiting in the individual history what is demonstrably true in the racial record : further, it is precisely these last-developed regions that are the first to be affected by the passage of time or the immoderate use of alcohol. The crucial question has always been the nature of the relationship. For Huxley, every psychosis or phase of mental process was accompanied by a specific neurosis or phase of physico-chemical neural process, but the latter was the reality of which the former was but the shadow effect. The neurosis was the phenomenon ; the psychosis but an epiphenomenon—something like the whistle given off by a steam-engine, as he put it, yet what a whistle ! This view is merely a refined Materialism, inasmuch as all causal or productive activity is limited to the brain process ; consciousness comes into being at a certain definite stage of molecular complexity, and is, therefore, simply an attribute of matter in a particular state of complexity and integration. Now, apart from some biologists and physiologists—the nature of whose work in general keeps them persistently occupied with the physico-chemical aspects of living process till it becomes almost a second nature with them to suppose that every other aspect is merely a dependent expression of the physico-chemical—this view has recommended itself to few. It can only be maintained, as M'Dougall points out, by sacrificing the law of causation to the doctrine of the conservation of energy, ' for it assumes that a physical process, say a molecular movement in the brain,

---

[1] *Op. cit.* passim ; cf. also J. Arthur Thomson, *The System of Animate Nature*, lect. vii.

causes a sensation, but does so without the cause passing over in any degree into the effect, without the cause spending itself in any degree in the production of the effect, namely, the sensation.' [1] And if the force of this criticism is technically lessened by the modern scientific tendency towards the general abandonment of the conception of causation in favour of the less embarrassing because more colourless conception of mere sequence, the strength of the original contention remains. It lies in the facts that it is impossible to lay one's finger on any particular point or stage in the advance of life after which it can be said that we have to do with consciousness for the first time; and that consciousness as we know it, both in the form of memory and that normal selective capacity to forget—which may be of not less importance —persists with continuous dynamism, and has a direct effect upon the physico-chemical processes of the brain, and so upon the organism as a whole, in different kinds of ways, as when I blush at the recollection of some ignoble act. Further, as previously remarked, the dualism of matter and energy has been resolved by modern science in favour of energy as the more ultimate, so leaving us with a process indicative of Infinite Energy in association with Mind, and therefore with no shred of fact or reason for supposing that these have originally proceeded from Matter. Yet, even more, it may be that the relation between psychical and physical is profounder and more intimate than anything that is designated by the word ' causal '—a term which in any case we are hard put to it to understand.

Of other theories of the relation of mind and body, that of Psycho-physical Parallelism, whether in the more restricted form, where brain processes alone are supposed to be accompanied in time by a strictly parallel series of psychical processes, without, however, any interaction or causal relationship, or in the broader form, in which all organic and even inorganic happening is supposed to have

[1] *Op. cit.* p. 150.

some degree of psychical concomitant, has likewise never commanded any general acceptance, largely because it raises more difficulties than it solves. The initiation, the exactness of the posited relation between the two series, its maintenance without any connection between them, together constitute a mystery greater than that which the theory was propounded to resolve. Accordingly, we seem to be left with some form of hypothesis that combines the measure of truth in the so-called Identity hypothesis and the Animistic point of view. That particular type of Identity hypothesis, sometimes spoken of as the ' two-aspect ' hypothesis, in which the psychical and physical series are regarded as two different ' modes of appearance ' of a single real process, involves, however, the very great difficulty that the term ' aspect ' is applied in connection with a situation, where the aspects have so little in common that the suggested analogy tends to be deceptive. The physical series or aspect is understood as the result of observations made through the senses, and reflection upon such observations; but the appearance or aspect which represents the psychical side is not open to inspection or study in just that kind of way : it can be apprehended only by reflective introspection. Yet it is not possible in the circumstances of the case for the same observer, nor indeed for any observer, to be aware of the two supposed aspects successively or together.

A more satisfactory presentation of the Identity hypothesis is that ordinarily known as Psychical Monism, according to which consciousness is the sole reality, and the physical world and everything in it are but the objectification of consciousness other than our own. Consciousness constitutes, it is said, the only mode of being of which we have direct and immediate knowledge, and accordingly has the highest title to be regarded as Reality, while the continuity of organic and inorganic involves the association of some degree of consciousness with every form of material existence. Now, this may be true, and some recent work suggests not merely the existence of neuroid elements in some of the Protozoa but an extension of sensitivity into the plant kingdom,[1] to a degree that had not been hitherto suspected. But even truer is the fact of the existence of definite degrees of unity of consciousness—of that increasing movement towards the development of individuals or personalities which appears to be of the essence of the evolutionary process. Such individuals are discrete entities, whose distinctness and unity are even now in process of attainment. If valid by reason of these and other considerations, such a view militates against the conception of absorption in some Absolute Consciousness, and is one of the points at which Psychical Monism, as ordinarily presented, falls far short of completeness as a statement of actuality, and has therefore been rejected entirely by some psychologists in favour of Animism.[2] Some view that represents the fact of embodied mind, that is animistic without being dualistic, and yet does not imply an expressional identification of the cerebral cortex with personal consciousness or the equating of brain change or structure with personality, would seem to be called for by the circumstances of the case. Our neatly separated and exclusive abstractions rarely correspond to anything in Reality.

The tendency to wholeness, to the holding together as a distinct entity of a multiplicity of experiences in such a way that those that are past are liable for review, and may enter consciously and unconsciously into the reaction of the individual at any moment, so modifying that reaction, constitutes the supreme characteristic of a soul or self. Its action, further, is always directed towards an end in its waking life and even in its dreams ; and certainly whether in waking or in sleeping it always has this disposition. It is this active, developing, yet relatively persistent, individual centre of consciousness

[1] And for that matter, into the mineral kingdom as well. Cf. *Response in the Living and Non-Living*, and other works by Sir J. C. Bose.
[2] *E.g.* by W. M'Dougall, *Body and Mind*, pp. 160-178.

focalised, though not necessarily localised at only one particular point in the brain—this structure of personality —whose existence constitutes the real problem. Aware of itself, it acts and feels and knows and contrives, and knows itself as such. It cannot be resolved into anything else, or explained away; it is there, and asserts itself at a certain stage of development in challenge of all attempts to ignore it. The present high degree of development towards that individuality or unity of consciousness is evidenced by its power to compare, arrange, and systematise ideas, as also by the fact that all sensations or perceptions have in the end to be referred to such a unified consciousness or incipient self. Perceptions simply do not float around in isolated unrelatedness, or made up into ' bundles,' as Hume contended, nor for that matter can any amount of compounding or amalgamating of sensations result in an act of cognition or produce an inference. The ' stream of consciousness,' most misleading of figures, ignores the vital fact of this unity, together with those conditions, stable and enduring, which make the stream what it is.

The conception of the self or soul seems further demanded by the fact that simultaneous sensory stimuli are combined psychically rather than combine sensorily, in the production of distinctive psychical effects.[1] It is also called for as the locus or agent of the initiation and maintenance of that concentration, and sustained direction of expenditure, of energy which is characteristic of human effort. Again, as Professor Pratt remarks, ' almost every work on aphasia ' indicates that ' by persistent activity of the will much of the language loss in aphasia may be regained through a laborious process of re-education.'[2] This suggests at any rate some integral and integrating self that with its power of initiative can deliberately set itself to the task of training new brain centres to take the place and do the work of those that have been de-

[1] W. M'Dougall, *op. cit.* pp. 289-293.
[2] J. B. Pratt, *Matter and Spirit*, p. 155.

stroyed. Observationally, the evidence for the soul cannot be of the strongest, because under space-time conditions the unextended must necessarily be something of an inference. The possibilities of complexity in neural process are limited, however, compared with the illimitability in the organisation of ideas, the depth of meaning and the feeling of pleasure, that attend and characterise that assertive continuous striving towards an end, wherein the existence of a human being so largely consists. We are often liable to draw erroneous conclusions by confining our attention to the past—just as in retrospect all actions seem clamped in an unavoidable linkage of deterministic causation, whereas in the actual moment of choice between alternatives we are directly aware of a freedom of which no attempted explanation in terms of false physical analogies of the preponderance of a stronger motive over a weaker one, can ever rob us. So in the present we may be immediately aware of that which is ultimate, though in no absolute sense static and unchanging, even with that lowly degree of personality that has been developed thus far, and conscious of something about us which transcends the physico-chemical,[1] even if expressing itself in and through it, organised in some measure, and with a power of memory which is something more than mere mental habit.

Man apparently is, rather than has, a soul, potentially individual and immortal; he is becoming a person. Even to-day it is possible to recognise in the human organism hints of a progressive development in connection with the relation of the soul or spirit at the various functional levels of the central nervous system in the adult. These levels have been conveniently summarised as the visceral (vegetative), the sensori-motor, and the psycho-motor.[2] At the first of these, where the degree of distribution of consciousness, e.g. throughout the alimentary

[1] Notably in its emotional and moral life.
[2] Prof. D. Fraser Harris, 'A Defence of Philosophic Neo-Vitalism,' *Scientia*, April 1924.

system, is at its lowest, the soul is not actively involved under normal conditions, although it speedily becomes aware of any disturbance in functioning. At the sensori-motor level, in Harris's words, ' there is psychical involvement, but it is not causal.' There is consciousness of stimulation attendant on the dragooned excito-motor reflex responses of the human organism,[1] but at the psycho-motor level, clear consciousness and striving are of the very essence of the emotio-motor and ideo-motor reflexes, which can either excite or inhibit activity of the part or of the whole, as *e.g.* on the receipt of good or bad news. And this becomes even more manifest in all those higher neural activities, such as volition and the power of abstract thought, that are attendant on that degree of self-realisation that constitutes our present-day incipient personality. Further, we must never forget that mind and the nervous system are not synonymous and co-extensive, and one of the great advances in medicine resulting from war conditions has lain along the line of a more extended and exact appreciation of the power of the mind over the body in health and disease. Up till then our conception of health had been mainly physical. We are only at the beginning of understanding the meaning and power of the healthy, well-balanced *Mind*.

From the standpoint of the evolutionary process, there has been a broadly progressive movement from Mind-bodies to Body-minds, where the presently embodied mind manifests itself ever more freely. The same progression holds true of a normal individual human life. But this whole movement, both racial and individual, has been the result of an ever-widening and deepening range of commerce with differing manifestations of that Environment, proximately physical, more truly sensed through gradual revelation as spiritual, which in its ultimate aspect is God. Concurrently with this, though only very gradually, conduct has been more and more governed by ideas and ideals rather than by instinct or impulse—ideas corre-

[1] *E.g.* when the eye waters, following the entrance of some irritant.

sponding to the gradual discovery of the true character
of the Universe, and ideals, both subjective and objective,
that have been conceived and manifested in the course
of the development of that Universe. Now, if there be
such a state as that described by the word Immortality,
it must be very immediately and functionally connected
with some character or way of human life. For life is
not mere persistence ; still less can immortality be so.
Revealing itself as in some way even now transcending
the space-time conditions of its manifestations—for
the soul or self persists while the molecules of neuro-
plasm of the neurons change, if not the latter themselves
—and in a sense carrying the future within itself even as
it does the past, each individual soul is to-day living in a
phase of the history of the race where eternal life in the
one case, and survival in the other, seem to be morally
conditioned. There is, that is to say, for the individual
a superlatively eventful destiny in process of realisation,
to which St. Paul referred when he spoke of those ' that
are being saved ' and those ' that are perishing.' [1] The
differentia he found to be connected with what he
described in his special terminology as ' the law of the
Spirit of life in Christ Jesus ' which made him ' free
from the law of sin and of death.' [2] Of Jesus, the man
most competent to express an opinion testified that to
Him the Spirit had been given ' without measure.' [3]
Increasingly it looks as if in an understanding acceptance of that Spirit will be found the secret of racial
survival as well as of individual immortality.

[1] 2 Cor. 2 15. Rom. 8 2. [3] John 3 34 (A.V.).

CHAPTER XI

IT is evident that the idea of progress could not well have entered the mind of man until he had become aware of himself not merely as living in a world of movement and change, but also as the possessor of such definite knowledge of the past as would enable him to frame tolerable views about the future, based on some kind of a belief in the uniformity of Nature. The idea of evolution is very old, but because of the lack of exact data covering any considerable period of time, it carried no suggestion, and certainly no conviction, of even partial sustained progress, before the middle of the nineteenth century. The knowledge concerning evolution to-day is very considerable, but the degree in which Evolution implies progress, if indeed it implies it at all, is still an open question in the opinion of many competent authorities.

The idea of progress, then, in the sense of the possibility or probability of indefinitely continued practical, intellectual, and moral advance, constituted no element in the general thought of antiquity. It hardly ever entered a Greek mind; there was nothing in their experience to suggest it. The common belief, as we have seen, was in a Golden Age of simple life—to which, it may be remarked, our growing knowledge of the conditions of the Neolithic Age gives colourable support—from which men had shown degeneration in the interval. There was no sense of the antiquity of the race, even if there was sporadic recognition of limited movements of flow within the larger ebb. On the contrary, a quite definite and distinctive

Cyclic Theory of events, noticeable in the Greek treatment of religion, philosophy, and history, practically precluded such an idea. In great measure this would appear to be a survival from primitive thought. Thus Spencer and Gillen [1] show how the savage does not easily grasp the idea of new generations following one another in infinite succession. He tends rather to think of the sum-total of life in his community as limited by a series of births and re-births. This literal conservation of the human species leads to the doctrine of metempsychosis, which was an important element in Greek religious thought. Again, for the primitive mind a specific day has something almost akin to individuality in its power for good or evil; it will recur in the following year, and demands consideration. Such a fact, together with the phases of the moon, the recurrent cycle of the seasons, the curiously far-reaching rhythms of life, vegetative and animal,[2] inevitably suggested a cycle for human life as a whole. This idea was specially developed by Plato,[3] by whom human life was viewed as moving through a cyclic upward phase of 72,000 solar years, the result of the creative impulse, after which there was a corresponding downward phase of equal duration which called for a renewal of the divine creative act to inaugurate once again a new cycle. This re-entrant conception, corresponding in part to the Greek conception of order and perfection visualised in the circle, thus provided for phases of alternate ebb and flow, at the end of which things were pretty much as they had been in the beginning. For the Greek the immutable was higher than the variable; any deviation from the order of society originally imposed could only be a step downwards. While Plato could hold his particular views along with acceptance of the

---

[1] *Native Tribes of Central Australia*, p. 265.

[2] In a chapter devoted to Rhythm in a recent book, *Life*, Sir A. E. Shipley gives interesting confirmations by modern science of traditional views of the influence of the lunar rhythm upon some forms of terrestial life.

[3] *Statesman* (Jowett trans.), iv. 467, and *Republic*, Book VIII.

idea of an original Golden Age, the latter conception was
gradually surrendered by rationalists like Xenophanes
and Aeschylus. Further, if the Greek was able to per-
suade himself, as apparently Aristotle did, that he was
living towards the end of a cycle in which almost everything was known that could be known,[1] it was not so
difficult to believe that there had been a slow ascent
within that particular cycle. None the less, it was only
a cycle with its inevitable catastrophic end. Perhaps
also the sharp and ever-present distinction between
Greek and barbarian tended in very many cases to restrict
the Greek outlook, for in the period of Greek decline this
permitted of no saving hope as a result of the inter-
fusion of races.[2] A race, like a species, was a fixed thing;
and just in so far as civilisation was identified with the
Greek race, with the decay of the latter would come the
passing of the former.

In a general way the same held true of the representatives of Roman culture, who had taken over the
Cyclical Theory from the Greeks. Thus Marcus Aurelius
in his *Meditations* again and again makes reference to this
idea, reflecting in his comments the reaction of his mind
to it. ' Nature treads in a circle, and has much the same
face through the whole course of eternity. And therefore
it signifies not at all whether a man stands gazing here
an hundred, or two hundred, or an infinity of years ;
for all that he gets by it is only to see the same sights
so much the oftener. . . . The periodic movements of
the universe are the same up and down from age to age.
. . . In forty years' time a tolerable genius for sense and
enquiry may acquaint himself with all that is past and
all that is to come by reason of the uniformity of things.' [3]
Seneca, as Professor Bury has shown,[4] might believe in

---

[1] *Pol.* ii. 5, 126a 2 ; vii. 10, 1329b 25 ; quoted in E. E. Sikes, *The
Anthropology of the Greeks*, p. 43.

[2] E. E. Sikes, *op. cit.* p. 46.

[3] *Op. cit.* ii. 14 ; ix. 28 ; xi. 1 (Collier's trans.).

[4] *The Idea of Progress*, p. 14. The references are to *Naturales
Quaestiones*, vii. 25 and 31, and *Epist.* 64.

the growth of knowledge, but was too convinced of the corruption of the human race to be able to imagine progress in connection with it. Lucretius, who with the Epicureans rejected the doctrine of a Golden Age in the past and a phase of subsequent degeneration, came nearer the idea than any one else. ' Ships and tillage, walls laws arms roads dress and all such like things, all the prizes, all the elegances too of life without exception, poems pictures and the chiselling of fine-wrought statues, all these things practice together with the acquired knowledge of the untiring mind taught men by slow degrees as they advanced on the way step by step.[1] Thus time by degrees brings each several thing forth before men's eyes and reason raises it up into the borders of light ; for things must be brought to light one after the other and in due order in the different arts, until these have reached their highest point of development.' [2] But even for these thinkers, sooner or later there would be a catastrophe ; [3] there is no suggestion of evolution as continuous, orderly and broadly progressive change sustained into an indefinite future. And with this general outlook is correlated the profound pessimism of the thinkers of antiquity—a pessimism that characterises even one of the Old Testament writings.[4] They lived in a world of a fixed order which was as intransgressible on its human as on its purely inorganic aspects. The transcending of that fixed order was too audacious a thought to have occurred in connection with man ; he could not in this way become godlike. The limitation of their thought and knowledge made them concentrate on the present, relieved by no outlook on the future. Man had to discover a very great deal before he could formulate the idea of progress.

We have already seen how the Middle Age was domi-

[1] *Pedetemtim progredientis.*
[2] *De Rerum Natura* (Munro trans.), v. 1448-1457.
[3] *Op. cit.* v. 95.
[4] The reference is to Qoheleth or The Book of Ecclesiastes. The writer sees no sign of a purpose, and so no progress, in life.

nated by the teaching of St. Augustine. The forces of
that world to come which gave such meaning to the
present were so strongly felt that even yet in many minds
little far-reaching interest was taken in the present, or
man's terrestrial destiny. If the idea of an expanding
church upon earth was slowly taking shape, nevertheless
nothing had any real importance save as it prepared the
souls of men for the life hereafter : hence the comparative
stagnation in thought and social activity. Mortality
as compassed by famine and epidemics, by wars, malaria,
and a high infantile death-rate, was a gloomy and awesome prospect, and an uncompromising doctrine of
original sin foreclosed any possibility of moral advance.
The future life alone was in any degree illuminated by
Christianity ; for it men lived, or rather endured, believing
that it contained compensation for their meantime passage
through a vale of tears. Any day might be the Last Day;
and if not felt to be so imminent as in the Early Church,
it would come sooner rather than later, for men were
now living in the last days. As soon as the elect were
gathered in, the Day of Wrath would break. History
was a series of divinely ordered and providentially
enacted events ; there was no idea of natural development. Yet, as Professor Bury has remarked,[1] while
maintaining the idea of human degeneration from a
previous estate of moral excellence, Christian mediaeval
theology abandoned the Cyclic Theory. For the first
time a meaning was given to history—to the history of
the earth and its inhabitants as a unique purposive
phenomenon in time and space.

The opening decades of the Renaissance were characterised by that rediscovery of the classical writers which for
a time led to the re-enthronement of some of their outstanding ideas. Thus it is really at once Machiavellian
and ' ancient ' to believe with some modern politicians
in the immutability of human nature, to assert that change
from the past must be essentially of the nature of corrup-

[1] *Op. cit.* p. 22.

tion or degeneration, and that legislators with 'first-class brains,' regardless of character, are an absolute necessity for the sound organisation of society, to dispense with whose services or depart from whose conceptions is both folly and ingratitude on the part of the proletariat. So soon, however, as that sapping of the positions of antiquity which began in the sixteenth century was carried out and finally pressed home in the seventeenth, the way was open towards belief in progress. The emancipation and rehabilitation of the natural man in relation to ecclesiastical authority was followed by 'the vindication of this world as possessing a value for man independent of its relations to any supramundane sphere.'[1] Of writers in the sixteenth century who were themselves in the line of progress, Professor Bury refers [2] to the French historian Jean Bodin, who rejected the theory of the degeneration of man from a Golden Age 'of virtue and felicity,' recognised a general progress in the past, although almost entirely in terms of the growth in human knowledge, and held that the history of man together with that of the rest of the Universe constituted a divinely planned whole. He believed his own age—the age of the invention of the mariner's compass, of printing, and of gunpowder—to be as great as any in the past in respect of science and the arts, and he had a certain conception of the solidarity of the human race in common interests, and of history as dependent on the will of man. His compatriot Louis Le Roy, who was inclined to a cyclical view of things, showed a strange yet recurring confidence of his and other times that man had reached the practical limit of all that there was to be known, at any rate in certain departments of knowledge. 'We can affirm that the whole world is now known, and all the races of man '[3]

---

[1] J. B. Bury, *op. cit.* p. 34.
[2] *Op. cit.* chap. i.
[3] *De la Vicissitude ou Variété des Choses en l'Univers*, 1577; quoted in Bury, *op. cit.* p. 45. Le Roy's remark, untrue at the time, is probably correct to-day so far as races are concerned. Cf. A. C. Haddon, *Races of Man.*

—a remark that reads peculiarly even in days that report the discovery of a new variety in the Itogapuks of the Amazon valley,[1] or a large segregated group of Indian albinos in the Darien district of Panama. His general conclusion, based on ' the memory of the past,' was that things were again approaching an end that would mean a reversion to a primitive chaos, although even this eventuality ultimately depended upon the Divine Will.

It is by comparison with views such as the above that it becomes possible to understand how complete was the break with the past in the thought of the seventeenth century upon this idea of Progress. When Francis Bacon declared that ' antiquity was the youth time of the world,' and ought to be considered and criticised as such, while we were the true ancients, he introduced a new element into the mental atmosphere of his day ; at the same time he found it impossible to accept much of what was distinctively modern, *e.g.* the heliocentric system. Likewise in his realisation that the pursuit of knowledge is only properly conducted with a view to its application to the amelioration of the conditions of human life here and now, he prevented that atmosphere from becoming too speculatively thin, and made it of more practical assistance to society. Unlike Le Roy, he realised that knowledge progresses, and thought that ' if the errors of the past are understood and avoided there is every hope of steady progress in the modern age.' [2] Yet tending to imagine, as the results of the signal successes of the new knowledge, that it would only require the work of a few generations to wrest all the secrets of Nature from her, and firm in his conviction that his generation really belonged to the old age of humanity, he did not foresee that indefinite advance in the future in which the conception of progress so largely consists.

[1] Cf. *Among Wild Tribes of the Amazon*, by C. W. Domville-Fife. For the 'White Indians,' cf. *Man*, Nov. 1924.

[2] Bury, *op. cit.* p. 56.

In the Cartesian affirmation of the supremacy of reason, the challenge to authority and tradition was more aggressively renewed ; in that of the invariability of Nature, the contemporary conception of Providence seemed to be ruled out. Accompanying these characteristic tendencies in the liberating thought of the seventeenth century was sometimes to be noticed the feeling, engendered by the growing sense of superiority to the past and satisfaction with the achievements of the times of Louis XIV. (1638-1715), that the world, so far from being in a state of degeneration, was well-nigh as perfect as a world could be. The violent contemporary controversy as to the comparative merits, literary, artistic, and scientific, of the Ancients and Moderns implied the conclusion, in so far as the cause of the Moderns as being at any rate on an equality with the Ancients was favoured, that Nature's resources were not becoming impaired, and might continue so. Again, however, the old error was repeated, and Charles Perrault, the protagonist of the Moderns, insisted, ' Our age has, in some sort, arrived at the summit of perfection. And since for some years the rate of the progress is much slower and appears almost insensible—as the days seem to cease lengthening when the solstice is near—it is pleasant to think that probably there are not many things for which we need envy future generations.' [1] There was still no outlook into a future exhibiting continued advance as the past had done.

The generality of cultured minds in the seventeenth century, however, only gradually came to realise that the century in which they lived could be shown to provide advance on the past in science, literature, art, and morality. The doctrine of the degeneration of man seemed like dying hard, and indeed never became extinct ; there were few who did not feel that the end of the world was within measurable distance. Further, the advantages of such practical instruments as the mariner's compass were

[1] *Parallèle des Anciens et des Modernes* (1688-1696) ; quoted in Bury, *op. cit.* p. 87.

slow in winning general recognition as compared with
the appreciation of literary and philosophical work. A
new type of mind almost had to be created, and the
establishment of the Royal Society in London (1660)
and the Academy of Sciences in Paris (1666) did much
to make physical science both popular and fashionable.
Once again men became so engrossed in the expected
' quick results ' of the present that they had no time to
peer much into the future. Moreover, Descartes did
much to tighten up the connecting links of thought ;
reasoning was never quite so loose after him as it had
been before him. On the other hand, there were many
conditions that hindered progress—barbarian invasions,
continual wars, bad government, and prejudices, *e.g.*
against dissection.

According to Bury [1] it was Fontenelle, another Modern
protagonist and singularly open-minded writer, who, in
his *Digression on the Ancients and Moderns*, first clearly
gave real value and completeness to the theory of the
progress of knowledge ' by including the indefinite future.'
He deliberately rejected Bacon's misleading metaphor
of old age as applied to the present phase. ' Man will
have no old age ; his intellect will never degenerate ; and
the " sound views of intellectual men in successive generations will continually add up." ' [2] To his mind progress
was also ' necessary and certain.' Yet while applicable to
knowledge, Fontenelle's views did not hold of Nature or
society, which were alike immutable in their character.
Man would always be the same kind of a creature.

Undoubtedly it was the discoveries in physical science
that more than anything else aided men in accepting
a general doctrine of Progress. Between the years
1690 and 1730, the idea of an indefinite progress of enlightenment slowly made its way in French intellectual
circles, until in 1737 the Abbé de Saint-Pierre made a
distinct advance upon Fontenelle by giving actual figures
in his *Observations on the Continuous Progress of Universal*

---

[1] *Op. cit.* chap. **v**. [2] Bury, *op. cit.* p. 109.

Reason, not merely representing his conception of the duration of the past history of the race, but opening for the first time a ' vista of an immensely long progressive life in front of humanity.' [1] For him civilisation was only in its infancy ; the best minds of his day marked an advance upon Plato and Aristotle ; there were no irremovable obstacles to the possibility of organised persistent human progress. In all this he showed himself something of a precursor of the Encyclopædists [2] (1751-1765), who, though subjecting traditional beliefs to remorseless criticism, and carrying on a vigorous campaign against authority and superstition, yet believed more or less convincedly in the perfectibility of man, and made various positive constructive proposals towards this end. Under the intense consciousness of the enlightenment of their own age, they examined all conceivably relevant circumstances, as, *e.g.,* the influence of climate and geography upon civilisation. There was a clear realisation of the determining importance of the environmental cultural atmosphere—so often misleadingly spoken of as the ' social inheritance ' or ' heritage,'—as compared with the physical tendencies in the case of the normal human being.[3] In the glow of their enthusiasm, all human races were included in the possibilities being opened up along their vista of Progress, and, further, no people was doomed to perpetual racial inferiority—positions both of which are again gaining a large measure of scientific assent,[4] and to which the official Christianity of these days was not alive, although they are essentially Christian truths.

[1] Bury, *op. cit.* p. 137.
[2] This term is applied to a group of French rationalistic writers led by Diderot and d'Alembert, all of whom did work in connection with an extensive *Encyclopædia.*
[3] Many observers of the German people during the half-century or so preceding the Great War had noticed the slow evaporation of their once typical *gemüthlichkeit* under the desiccating blight of the spirit of Prussianism.
[4] Cf. Franz Boas, *The Mind of Primitive Man* ; A. A. Goldenweiser, *Early Civilisation.*

At the same time, there were variants in this reading of history amongst the rationalists themselves. Rousseau, for example, told of Arcadian days succeeding the original 'state of nature' than which no subsequent period of human history had at any rate been happier. Man's faculty of self-improvement had really been his undoing, because in turn it had involved the development of the self which tended to set itself against society. But all such special argumentation had little chance in face of the hopes inspired by the events of 1789. The idea that the French Revolution was but the beginning of a movement of world-renovation [1] naturally strengthened the belief in human perfectibility. Condorcet, in his *Sketch of a Historical Picture of the Progress of the Human Mind*,[2] showed once again that recognition of the progress of knowledge 'had created the idea of Social Progress and remained its foundation.' [3] Accordingly, it was only natural that he should take the idea of the advance of knowledge in the past as the clue wherewith to attempt to estimate its direction in the future : of such continued, if slow, progress, limited only by the duration of our planet, he was quite certain, although he reached no law expressive of it. In Great Britain, Adam Smith's doctrine that free commercial intercourse, unhampered by government policies, tended more than anything else to the 'wealth of nations,' was of indirect assistance to the theory of Progress in its suggestion of economic racial solidarity. The German philosophers Kant, Fichte, Hegel, and Schelling did much to raise the idea of progressive development to the level almost of a category of thought. ' The idea of progress, development,' said Guizot,[4] ' seems to me to be the funda-

---

[1] The general resemblances between the French and the recent Russian Revolution are more or less obvious, but it yet remains to be narrated how deliberately, and in some respects ludicrously, the later movement was based in its initial stages upon the earlier.

[2] Published 1795.

[3] Bury, *op. cit.* p. 209.

[4] *Histoire de la Civilisation en Europe*, 1828.

mental idea contained in the word *civilisation*,' and, adds
Professor Bury, ' there we have the most important
positive idea of eighteenth-century speculation, standing
forth detached and independent, no longer bound to a
system.' [1] In fact, throughout the eighteenth century
it was a sort of dogma ; men believed in an inevitable
law of progress. Scientific invention, geographical exploration, the development of commerce, intercommunica-
tion on a world scale, the general increase in knowledge,
new social hopes, all tended to consolidate opinion in this
direction.

With the beginning of the nineteenth century came
further support; but as it advanced, men also began to
question and test the theory. There was indeed a well-
marked trend in the French thought of the Restoration
period towards the conception of history as a progressive
movement, influenced perhaps in part by the conceptions
of development and continuity that were being put
forward by the early evolutionary writers. What now
required to be done was to discover the Law of Progress
in civilisation. Saint-Simon accordingly maintained that
' epochs of organisation or construction and epochs of
criticism or revolution succeed each other alternately.' [2]
The Middle Age was a constructive period, followed
by a critical, revolutionary period which had now come
to an end.[3] He was even prepared to predict, and say,
that in the fresh epoch of organisation now being inaugurated, a new religion based upon physics would
supersede Christianity and Deism. He stood for Social-
ism, and placed the Golden Age in the future. So also
with Auguste Comte's famous system, which, as Professor
Bury shows,[4] was anticipated in its main feature by
Turgot, and of which the idea of progress was the very
soul. The famous ' law of the three stages ' through
which in its development every branch of knowledge is
supposed to pass—the theological, corresponding to the

[1] *Op. cit.* p. 274.   [2] Bury, *op. cit.* p. 284.
[3] He died in 1825.   [4] *Op. cit.* pp. 157, 292.

stage when the mind fancifies or invents, the metaphysical or philosophical, when it abstracts, and the positive or purely scientific, when it submits itself to substantiated fact—may be illustrated, for example, in the case of cosmogony, but really gets a bad start from the simple fact that there was a pre-animistic stage in man's development previous to this supposedly infantile theological way of looking at things which is posited as the first stage of all.[1] When directly applied to history, as in its definite statement that the theological stage came to an end about A.D. 1400, and that the second stage was drawing to a close even as Comte did his work in preparation for the ushering in of the third or positive stage, the system only shows a semblance of working. Its lame performance, further, is only possible under conditions which rule it out as a scheme of universal history, e.g. in the restriction of it to Europe, in ignoring the fact that all sciences can never be at the same stage of development at the same time, and so on. Its fundamental unsoundness is seen in the complete failure of its author whenever he attempted to predict upon the basis of it. Unlike his predecessors of the eighteenth century, he did not envisage progress as progressing indefinitely in the future, although it would be maintained continuously ; his system, as Professor Bury insists, was ultimately a closed system,[2] and in its full development under the urge of purely intellectual ideas it would mean the disappearance of liberty. All socialistic schemes, in the degree in which they ignore the fact that freedom of initiative and the greatest possible measure of individual liberty constitute ' the condition of ensuring the maximum

[1] According to Comte, Fetishism was the dominant expression of religion in the first stage of this theological period, followed in turn by Polytheism and Monotheism. But Fetishism, as implying the recognition of an individual self, who with the aid of his private fetish can set himself, if he so desires, in opposition to the aims of the community as a whole, so far from being the first, manifestly represents a comparatively late stage in the religious development of man. Cf. antea, p. 6.
[2] Op. cit. p. 304.

of energy and effectiveness in improving our environment, and therefore the condition of attaining public felicity,' [1] are essentially tyrannical and unprogressive.

It is peculiarly important to have some understanding of the very gradual way in which the idea of progress has become clear in human history.[2]   The comparatively recent date at which it seized upon the mind of man suggests that this delayed revelation corresponds to fundamental truth, but much yet remains to be learned. The three principal factors that have contributed to the belief in progress have undoubtedly been natural science, political history, and Christianity.   Yet in the name of each doubts have been freely expressed, and some recent events, in particular the Great War, have been supposed to settle the issue negatively in no uncertain fashion.

It is a question which can only be decided by taking a broad, or, one should rather say, a long-distance view of things.   In this way many seeming arguments against progress come to wear pretty thin, the greater the distance over which their texture is stretched.   Thus it is a commonplace procedure in this connection to make a roll-call of the great names in the Classic Age of Greece, and challenge the citing of any similar group in subsequent history who may be deemed their peers, not to speak of being their superiors.   But a challenge of this character, even if it could be sustained—for the environment of these days was much less complex than is that of modern civilised man—is really meaningless when set in the perspective of all the facts.   The eight-and-fifty generations separating us to-day [3] from the commencement of the Christian era, when supplemented by another

[1] *Op. cit.* p. 306.
[2] The best recent work in this connection is Prof. J. B. Bury's *The Idea of Progress : an Inquiry into its Origin and Growth.*   Cf. also R. Flint, *Historical Philosophy in France and French Belgium and Switzerland* ; Benjamin Kidd, *Social Evolution* ; W. R. Inge, *Outspoken Essays*, second series, pp. 158-183 ; H. E. Fosdick, *Christianity and Progress.*
[3] On the rough basis of three generations to a century.

twelve to take us back into the heart of those two wonderful Attic centuries from 530 to 330 B.C., make a span of seventy generations lying between us and the men who first looked on the Athena and Zeus of Pheidias, or listened to the words of Pericles, or marvelled at the plays of Sophocles. Yet these seventy generations correspond to a very brief period in the long history of mankind. Assuming, with great moderation, that that history has covered some 400,000 years, we find that these last twenty-four centuries would be the equivalent of eight and a half minutes in a day of twenty-four hours. So that except on a minute scale where, in turn, the difference between these Attic days and the present would be so small as to mean little or nothing in comparison with the whole, these seventy generations are more correctly regarded as a unit in themselves, to be compared to their great advantage with very many previous units of corresponding size. And further, it has to be borne in mind, as several writers have pointed out,[1] that Athens, being in those days the intellectual and social capital of the world, attracted ambitious and able men from the whole Mediterranean area. Good immigration played its part along with the good native stock in making Athens what it was.

As a matter of fact, it is impossible for the evolutionary biologist to deny the fact of progress, over the whole, although it is also necessary to ask him to state exactly what he means by the term.[2] He is able to arrange the regimented forms of present-day animal life [3] in an ascending series, and believes that this classification is possible simply because it corresponds in a general way to the order of the emergence of the various types. With the aid of the brilliant studies of Professor L. J.

[1] *E.g.* E. G. Conklin, *Heredity and Environment in the Development of Men*, p. 293.
[2] For a good account from this point of view, reference may be made to Prof. Julian Huxley, *Essays of a Biologist*, pp. 3-63.
[3] The same can, of course, be done in the case of the plant world; cf. D. H. Scott, *Extinct Plants and Problems of Evolution*.

Henderson,[1] he further believes that he can give a purposive account of those earliest stages in terrestrial development which culminated in the preparation of a unique environment in which, under the permissive temperature, colloidal, and other conditions, life, probably at first molecular, yet always inherently an energy manifestation, in the fulness of time drew into being. It is not easy to believe in the utter ultimate futility of a process that covered hundreds of millions of years in reaching the stage at which life became possible, particularly in view of the fact that the process nowhere else puts us to lasting intellectual confusion. 'The whole evolutionary process,' in Professor Henderson's words, 'both cosmic and organic, is one, and the biologist may now rightly regard the universe in its very essence as biocentric.'[2] The immense thicknesses of the Archæozoic strata suggest how slow were the initial stages in the development of life—with what heavy steps life passed from the molecular stage by way of the unicellular, to the multicellular. Still, if, as seems probable, it took practically the whole of the Archæozoic Era for life definitely to consolidate itself upon a unicellular basis, at the end of that period there was progress in the sense that life was able to do what in its previous simpler condition it had been unable to do ; it was now capable of a slightly wider range of commerce with the environment, and of a slightly greater control over energy. Next followed a distinct series of delimitable steps, commencing with the colonial protozoan forms, whose aggregation and consequent increase in size aided in the first results of co-operation, e.g. greater rapidity of motion and security from predatory protozoa, and came to involve an incipient division of labour on the part of the constituent cells, which in turn meant growing capacity for, and efficiency in, the doing of work. Thereafter,

---

[1] *The Fitness of the Environment* (1913), and *The Order of Nature* (1917).
[2] *The Fitness of the Environment*, p. 312.

above the sponges, and the group of the Cœlenterata (comprising the sea-anemones, jelly-fish, corals, and other forms) whose bodies are alike built up of two layers of cells, come all the higher forms, where the body is composed of three primary layers, the third layer or mesoderm being split off from the inner of the other two. Yet in this upward succession of worms, molluscs, and insects, of fish, amphibians, and reptiles, birds and mammals, there appear not merely increasing complexity of bodily structure, but deepened and broadened commerce with different aspects of the enveloping and stimulating environment. This progress does not necessarily mean better adaptation to environment, although it may mean adaptation to a better environment. Probably no creatures are so well adapted to their environment as certain parasites, which show almost perfection of adaptation. It would be difficult to say that man is better adapted to his environment than the trypanosome in his blood that carries him off. What we do find is that the modifications of the ground-plan of structure so early laid down consist sometimes of increase in size within the groups, sometimes in extension of the duration of life, and generally of increase in efficiency of functioning of the parts. The gradual ascent, that is to say, expresses itself, amongst other characters, in improvement in the structure of the various organs and parts of the body, and in their material adjustment and subordination to the needs of the whole. It may be the result in part of a summation of germinal factors ; there is nothing to support the idea that it is due to an elimination of such factors or the unpacking of some original complex. It is a movement towards increasing fulness and more abundance of life. All this development is registered in a sense in the growing structural complexity of the central nervous system. In fact, the evolution of the ' adjustor system,' whereby stimuli falling on the sense organs are translated into the right kind of action, is a very large part of the history of higher organisms at any rate up to man. In his case, however, there is in addition an internal mental realm of stimulating ideals and emotions built up in some sort of relationship eventually with that Ultimate Spiritual Environment in which he 'lives, and moves, and has his being,' and where something more than the mere working of an ' adjustor system' has to be taken into account.

Particularly in any purely objective examination of this ascending series of the forms of life, we note an increasing power, through associative memory, of modifying present behaviour in the light of past experience. The past is increasingly brought to bear on the present, and the future is more intelligently foreseen. There is growing independence of, and control over, the environment, and an increase in intensity of the psychical faculties. Evolution from monad to man reveals itself as a gradual winning of freedom. The disconnected moments of the life of the lower animal become a unified life-purpose of achievement in the case of man. In short, ' there has been a main direction in evolution,' [1] and advance in this direction has led at the same time to the production of greater intensity of certain qualities which are found to be valuable, and survival-determining. Further, it has proved to be perfectly consistent with failure to advance on the part of some forms, either by simply maintaining their position, or in other cases by actual degeneration ; that is to say, there is no inherent tendency to general progressiveness. Or, to employ once again the old figure first used by Lamarck : in the development of the tree of life some branches turn down, others maintain a horizontal position, while yet others grow upwards, all having issued alike from the trunk. Yet the tree is ever rising in its topmost branches, and this increase or intensifying of certain properties and capacities of living things both in the general average and particularly on the higher levels, *is* what we mean by progress. What may be seen in the forms of to-day

[1] Julian Huxley, *op. cit.* p. 27.

holds also of the geological series of the past, and the latter is in great part the cause of the former.

There is therefore nothing remarkable in the fact that biologists as a whole are inclined to some belief in progress, and it is one of the interesting paradoxes of history that Charles Darwin, in his seeming dethronement of man and linkage of him with the rest of the animal creation, thereby furnished the strongest basis for this higher belief. For it is surely a higher belief that considers man as part of a world process in which he plays his part best as he realises that it is purposive, and that he has not toiled thus far in slow ascent merely to be pushed over a precipice into the night. Darwin, indeed, was strangely optimistic in his outlook. ' As all the living forms of life are the lineal descendants of those which lived long before the Cambrian epoch, we may feel certain that the ordinary succession by generation has never once been broken, and that no cataclysm has desolated the whole world. Hence we may look with some confidence to a secure future of great length. And as natural selection works solely by and for the good of each being, all corporeal and mental endowments will tend to progress towards perfection.' [1] Herbert Spencer likewise had a strong belief in human perfectibility.[2]

Now, man being an element in that unity which is the animal kingdom—being in short a part of life—exhibits these characteristics of progress. Especially in his case, with his powers of memory, speech, and conceptual thought, does he bring his individual past to bear upon the present and definitely attempt to forecast the future, while that summed experience of the past, tradition, is made available for his use and assistance. The positive results and proof of this are manifest in the general advances in science : indeed, the idea of progress received

---

[1] *The Origin of Species*, p. 669.

[2] Cf. his article on ' Progress : its Law and Cause ' (composed ' at the pathetically slow rate of almost half a page per day ') in the *Westminster Review*, April 1857, and his *Social Statics*.

medicine, the circumstances become simply a challenge to action.[1] Never before has the vista of indefinite progress opened out so alluringly or so clearly : the basis for the belief in progress lies in the fact that man is the educable animal. Sound action consists not in shutting our eyes to the facts on the debit side, but in looking at them steadily, drawing the attention of the community to them, and studying them till the best manner of dealing with them discloses itself. All of them taken together can never show, as Julian Huxley rightly observes, ' that some sort of progress may not have occurred ' ; [2] rather do they indicate lines along which life yet remains to be made fuller and more worth living to still greater numbers of people. The ability to turn the edge of natural selection under certain conditions implies a corresponding responsibility on the part of man to counter and control the town-herding instinct, irresponsible multiplication from impaired or degenerate stocks, and the many other dangerous drags upon, and active hindrances to, human progress from militarism to communism.

It may, however, be objected that this increase of human perspective in time, arising from the ascertained results of geology and biology, and even this suggestion of a unity, whether purposive or not, that links the inorganic with the organic, does not necessarily remove us from the Greek cyclical conception. We know that the cycle is evidently very much longer than 72,000 solar years—apparently hundreds of millions of years— but do we still know that it is *not* a cycle ? And after all, what proof have we that human nature can be changed? Now, it may be that the Second Law of Thermodynamics, which states that the entropy [3] of the Universe tends to a maximum, holds throughout the Universe, although so to believe is a mere act of faith, and certainly at present we know of no method of cosmical rejuvenation.[4] Yet

---

[1] The proportions were supplied by a Senior Physician in Edinburgh Royal Infirmary.   [2] *Op. cit.* p. 57.

[3] *I.e.* the dissipation, and so unavailability, of energy.

[4] Cf. *antea*, p. 159.

the cycle, if cycle it be, is immensely long, so long that it resolves itself for us under little less than the guise of eternity, and in the midst of it we note the appearance of that—Life—which by its resistance to this Second Law prevents it from being absolutely true wherever and so long as life exists. Further, it becomes evident that the evolution of life in its advance towards higher forms, and towards man in particular, appears under the form of this long process just because that growing moralisation of the whole could not be achieved otherwise than by the agelong winning of freedom through effort and struggle. With a rapid process under such circumstances we could not have trusted the results. Evolution with its banishment of caprice and chance gives us a new sense of security in the issue. There is a definite movement, slow indeed, but over long stretches clear ; and it is just in these long stretches that the fluctuations come to mean less, giving less cause for momentary elevation or despair. It is eminently noteworthy how those who were in the grip of the cyclical conception of antiquity were pessimists to a man, and even within the period of the establishment of evolution, temperament in part has driven philosophers like Hartmann [1] into the depths of racial despair. On the contrary, we would maintain that under the teachings of science and of political history, and the vision that has come to men that out of all this welter of pain and debasement, of struggle and imperfection, progress towards perfection is being made, a calm confidence, deep-set, may take possession of us—a community of feeling with one who on the basis of some other kind of experience was able to say, ' He that believeth shall not make haste.' [2] To hold that events are nothing more than kaleidoscopic changes in the structure and arrangement of the wholly given, that nothing comes to pass within the movements of the process which may not be figured under some scheme comparable to the aggregation and dispersal of

[1] *Philosophy of the Unconscious.*   [2] Is. 28 [16].

the molecules that constitute a cloud, must ever generate an attitude to life with little stimulus to endeavour or encouragement to live in any way that is seriously worth while. To refuse to believe in progress is to refuse to believe in life.

A final consideration concerns itself with the question as to whether human nature can be changed, for in this would seem to be the ultimate criterion of progress, which really in the end consists in the growing creation of men actuated by goodwill towards the fellow-man and towards God. It is a commonplace of history to remark how civilisations have come into being, grown, reached their zenith, and then passed away, but the moral disease that in every case has been the root cause of this decline has not always received its due emphasis. Nobody could, however, have stated the facts more forcefully than did Sir Francis Galton in the case of Greece : ' We know, and may guess something more, of the reason why this marvellously-gifted race declined. Social morality grew exceedingly lax ; marriage became unfashionable, and was avoided ; many of the more ambitious and accomplished women were avowed courtesans, and consequently infertile, and the mothers of the incoming population were of a heterogeneous class. In a small sea-bordered country, where emigration and immigration are constantly going on, and where the manners are as dissolute as were those of Greece in the period of which I speak, the purity of a race would necessarily fail. It can be, therefore, no surprise to us, though it has been a severe misfortune to humanity, that the high Athenian breed decayed and disappeared ; for if it had maintained its excellence, and had multiplied and spread over large countries, displacing inferior populations (which it well might have done, for it was naturally very prolific), it would assuredly have accomplished results advantageous to human civilization, to a degree that transcends our powers of imagination.' [1]

[1] *Hereditary Genius: an Inquiry into its Laws and Consequences,* p. 331.

Reference has already been made to the importance of the ideal and the part played by this inspiration from the spiritual environment in the life of man. Helvétius, the eighteenth-century Encyclopædist, held that ultimately the natures and characters of men are moulded by their environment, and can be so moulded. Conduct depends on motives, and these in turn, in proportion as conduct is truly rational, upon the force of ideas. Therefore transform the ideas of men, and society will in consequence be transformed. Even more strongly has the same position been asserted in the name of modern science. 'Throughout the course of human history,' says a distinguished anthropologist, 'Man's attitude has been determined, not by the alteration of the structure of the mind, but by the intellectual and moral influences which have been impressed upon each individual's mind by the community in which he lived. Whatever the inborn mental and moral aptitudes of any individual, whatever his race and antecedents, it is safe to say that if he were born and brought up in a vicious society he would have learned, not merely to converse in the language distinctive to that particular group of people, but in all probability to practise vicious habits. The fact that his skull was long or broad, or his hair blond or dark, or the matter of his ancestry, whether he belonged to the Alpine, the Nordic, or the Mediterranean races, would count for little in this process in comparison with the potent moulding force of the atmosphere of the family and the society in which he grew up during the years of his mental plasticity.' [1] Individual and racial decay has always set in when man has lost sight of the ideal. 'Where there is no vision,' said the wise man, 'the people cast off restraint.' [2] By learning to understand the world, and the nature and purpose of the process of which he is a part, man will increasingly adapt himself to it so as to increase the sum of happiness in human life :

[1] Prof. G. Elliot Smith, *op. cit.* pp. 133, 134.
[2] Prov. 29 [18].

he is doing so to-day.   And in this process of true adaptation, which takes the form of losing himself to save
himself—as true of nations and churches as of the
individual—the spirit of man does undergo change.
As motive and inspiration to such activity, however, he
requires an ideal, and power to realise it—a situation
which could hardly be expressed better than in these
words taken from no treatise on philosophy or handbook
of religion, but from a textbook of science : ' Let us
elevate the standards of public opinion by every means
in our power, and then natural selection and sexual
selection, which are greatly influenced by public opinion,
will secure the evolution of the race.   The progress will
be slow, painfully slow, but it will be real.   This does
not mean that we shall cease trying to improve individuals.
Each individual, who is led to a more desirable attitude
toward life, will act as leaven in the community in which
he lives, raising somewhat the standards of the whole
community.   I believe that in the continued influence
of Jesus we find the greatest force tending to the improvement of the individual character and to the elevation of
public opinion, and so to the evolution of mankind in
desirable directions.' [1]   ' There is a new creation,' said
St. Paul, ' whenever a man comes to be in Christ ;
what is old is gone, the new has come.' [2]   To refuse to
believe in progress is to refuse to believe in God.

[1] Maynard M. Metcalf, *An Outline of the Theory of Organic Evolution*,
p. 179.
[2] 2 Cor. 5 [17] (Moffatt's trans.).

CHAPTER XII

JESUS' VIEW OF THE UNIVERSE

IT is related of Henry Drummond that as a little boy he used to wonder ' why God had not made everything scarlet, like the inside of a penny trumpet.' [1] To any one who has ever felt the commanding power in the shrill monotone of the penny trumpet of bygone days, or gazed wonderingly into its flaming funnel, this boyish fancy in creative artistry may not appear so utterly bizarre, yet as a matter of fact it would not have been the kind of world with which we are familiar. Newton's Law of Gravitation states that the attraction between two bodies is represented by a stress proportional in magnitude to the product of their masses, and inversely proportional to the square of the distance between them. Now, there is no reason that we know of why the stress might not have been inversely proportional to the cube of the distance between the attracting bodies, and the mathematics of such a universe could be worked out up to a certain point. Yet, as we know, our world is not of that character ; it is one where the attracting force varics as the square of the distance between the bodies. Indeed, examples might be multiplied indefinitely to show that ours is not any old kind of a world ; it is a particular kind of world. The business of science is to let us know this particular character on its physical side, and in proportion as we come to understand it better we shall adapt ourselves better to it. In proportion as we realise, through fuller understanding of the laws of their activity, that volcanoes, for example, are just as

[1] *Henry Drummond* (Famous Scots Series), p. 31.

normal a part of the terrestrial economy as glaciers, acting on the one hand as safety-valves, and on the other restoring to the atmosphere part of the carbon dioxide which is constantly being locked up by sedimentary rocks and plant life, and without which life would soon cease, we shall no longer ' charge God with foolishness ' [1] or worse, but rather ourselves, when misfortunes follow the building of cities near their slopes, or along seismic lines of fracture on the earth's surface.

The teaching of Jesus, as preserved for us in varying degrees of authentication, could be put into a brochure of a few pages, yet it is impossible to suppose that He did not have a View of the Universe and had not thought long and deeply about it. Study of that teaching from the scant hints we have of it discloses the fact that He maintained that in its spiritual and moral aspects the Universe in which man finds himself is likewise a particular kind of Universe, and that only by behaviour of a quite definite kind, individually and nationally, can he react to it in such a way as to secure his salvation, achieve full self-realisation, and promote civilisation and real progress. It is worth while attempting to outline this teaching from this especial angle, as also to represent the kind of life based by Him upon it, and then see how far the growth of knowledge and the course of history have lent confirmation. And this for two reasons. The appeal of Christianity has hitherto, almost wholly, been presented in the form of a call to loyalty to a Person. This central and vital aspect can never be forgone, and the individual who can say with St. Paul, ' I know Him whom I have believed, and I am persuaded that He is able to guard that which I have committed unto Him against that day,' [2] is speaking out of an experience of which no double-edged psychological theory of self-induced illusion can ever rob him. And for the late childhood of the race that was sufficient, but for its early adolescence, upon which we are now entering,

[1] Job I 22.   [2] 2 Tim. I 12

something more will be increasingly required. Nothing was more remarkable about the Great War than the degree in which, quite consciously in the minds of men, the driving force was loyalty to ideas and ideals rather than to individuals. Thus Germany entered the war not so much under any overpowering devotion to the Kaiser, as under the influence of certain conceptions relating to the Fatherland and its supposed rightful place in the world. The Allies took up arms true to certain undertakings on 'a scrap of paper,' and America followed suit 'to make the world safe for democracy.' Even in the case of Bolshevism, the loyalty has been primarily to communistic principles rather than to the individual Lenin. But, in the second place, if it can be shown that more than 1900 years ago One came amongst men, and taught specifically concerning man, the nature of the Universe and the method of true adaptation to it, and if it appears that history and the course of events are gradually demonstrating that His interpretation is supremely true, and in that measure is profoundest revelation, they may well turn again, and, asking, Who is this that told men so verifiably truly regarding God and the world, and the method of saving adjustment to them both ?, be concerned to learn of Him.

According to Jesus, the world in which we live is God's world—is, as we might say, a limited manifestation of Himself—and He is directly and actively present and interested in it. He makes His sun to rise on the evil and the good, and sends the rain with refreshing impartiality upon the just and the unjust.[1] He clothes the grass of the field ; [2] He also feeds the birds of heaven ; [3] He knows the corresponding needs of men and women,[4] and will provide for them. God's providence is over all His creation, yet in a peculiar degree attends His children. 'Are not two sparrows sold for a farthing ? And not one of them lights on the ground without your

[1] Matt. 5 45.   [2] Matt. 6 30 ; cf. Luke 12 28.
[3] Matt. 6 26 ; cf. Luke 12 24.   [4] Matt. 6 32.

R

Father ; but the very hairs on your head are all numbered.
Fear not, then, you are worth far more than many
sparrows.' [1]   The Universe is so entirely God's concern,
taking its colour and character from Him and regulated
by Him, that the really trusting soul, ' seeking first the
Kingdom of God and His righteousness,' [2] should not
' be anxious for the morrow.'   The relation is one of
complete dominion ;   God the Father is to Him ' Lord
of heaven and earth ' ; [3]   the heaven is ' the throne of
God,' the earth is ' the footstool of His feet.' [4]   God is
Spirit Who may be worshipped, and with Whom relationship may be entered into, at any time or place.[5]   Therefore
it is that when the disciples are thrown into a panic as
their fishing-boat seems likely to go down in the squall
on the Lake of Galilee, He is awaked only to wonder
at them—' Why are ye fearful, O ye of little faith ? ' [6]
If religion provides above all else a sense of security or
at-homeness in the Universe, no one ever showed this as
Jesus did.   He moved through the world as if He had
the key to it all, as it were, in His pocket, as if He knew
the whole secret of it, and were its Master.   And it
could all be pressed into His exposition of divine truth
just because, fundamentally, it was for Him a spiritual
thing.   To the mind of Jesus the Universe was a spiritual
reality through which God expressed His goodness to
the sons of men.   Jesus' thought of God is always practical ; it concerns and asserts His active relation to the
world and to man.   Such a trust as was His reveals
religion at its highest—as that which carries and bears

---

[1] Matt. 10 [29, 30] ; cf. Luke 12 [6, 7].   Indeed, the translation might
almost run, ' And not one of them hops down on to the ground without your Father.'   Prof. J. E. M'Fadyen informs me that if we assume
a Semitic original for this saying, the word in it which corresponded
to πεσεῖται, rendered ' shall fall ' in A.V. and R.V., probably carries
in such a context the meaning *lights (upon)*, exactly as in Gen. 24 [64],
where the Hebrew word for *fall* must mean to light or alight; Rebekah
' lighted ' (surely not fell !) ' off the camel.'

[2] Matt. 6 [33, 34]. [3] Matt. 11 [25] ; cf. Luke 10 [21].
[4] Matt. 5 [34, 35] ; cf. Luke 23 [22]. [5] John 4 [21-24] ; Matt. 18 [19-20].
[6] Matt. 8 [26].

man up, rather than something that is a load ' grievous
to be borne,' [1] and that weighs him down. ' Even to
old age I am He, and even to hoar hairs will I carry you :
I have made, and I will bear; yea, I will carry, and will
deliver ' ; [2] yet for many, the conception of religion is,
to borrow a practical analogy, that of a sinker, rather
than a float.

So far as Jesus' thought of *Nature* is revealed in the
Gospel records, there is no suggestion of her as charac-
teristically ' red in tooth and claw with ravine.' [3]   There
may be something to be said from this point of view,[4] but
apparently it is not fundamental truth.   No other religious
teacher of mankind speaks so lovingly of Nature.   Whether
He refers to her order—' Do men gather grapes of thorns,
or figs of thistles ? ',[5] her mystery—' The wind bloweth
where it listeth, and thou hearest the sound thereof,
but knowest not whence it cometh, and whither it
goeth ' ; [6] or her restfulness and freedom from care—
' Consider the lilies of the field, how they grow; they
toil not, neither do they spin ',[7]—He saw in all these
varying aspects a revelation of the goodness of God.
His teaching here is something far deeper than any mere
' parable from Nature,' for He saw right to the heart
of actual things.   Yet amidst many tender descriptive
touches that show how accurate was His observation of
Nature, there is never anything that might be called
sentimental in His treatment of her, just because He was
so directly related to, and so completely understood,
Nature.   Indeed, it is in a figure from Nature that He
discloses the inwardness of the climactic act of His life—
' Except a grain of wheat fall into the earth and die, it

[1] Matt. 23 [4].   [2] Is. 46 [4].   [3] *In Memoriam*, lvi.
[4] And Jesus does not ignore the facts : cf. Matt. 24 [28] ; John 10 [12].
Modern science may be said to give its support to this general point of
view : cf. Prof. J. Arthur Thomson, *Science and Religion*, pp. 184-195.
[5] Matt. 7 [16].
[6] John 3 [8] (A.V.) ; cf. Mark 4 [27].
[7] Matt. 6 [28] ; cf. Luke 12 [27].   ' The lilies,' says A. B. Bruce (*E.G.T.*,
in loco), ' are viewed individually as living beings, almost as friends,
and spoken of with affection '

abideth by itself alone ; but if it die, it beareth much fruit.' [1] One might almost say that from His convinced belief in the universal immediate activity of the Father, and of this world as His world, there followed this interesting result that Jesus does not seem to have thought of things as natural and supernatural, or of a contrast between the general providence of God and ' special ' providences.[2] To His deep, penetrating gaze such distinctions simply did not exist.

Once again, Jesus so loved Nature—seemed in her solitary presence to come so immediately into living communion with God—that continually He sought to be alone in such surroundings for rest and spiritual refreshment, particularly before the great crises in His life. So He was ' led by the Spirit in the wilderness during forty days, being tempted of the devil.' [3] When He heard of the execution of John the Baptist, He ' withdrew . . . in a boat, to a desert place apart.' [4] This action was not the outcome of momentary fear, or an endeavour to go into hiding ; the multitudes very quickly found out where He was, and followed Him by land. But the death of John was a profoundly moving and critical event to One who had testified of him that ' among them that are born of women there hath not arisen a greater than John the Baptist,' [5] and Jesus wished to be alone with God while adjusting Himself to this development. So, also, after sending the fed multitudes away, ' He went up into the mountain apart to pray,' and from that night of prayer walked down the mountain-side right on to the waters [6] to where the disciples were in a boat ' in the midst of the sea, distressed by the waves ; for the wind

---

[1] John 12 24.

[2] Indeed, in Matt. 26 53 Jesus admits the possibility, but rejects the idea as contrary to the divine method in things. Situations such as those described in Luke 11 20 and 12 24 alike betoken the immediate presence and providential activity of God.

[3] Luke 4 1 ; cf. Matt. 4 1.

[4] Matt. 14 13 ; cf. Mark 6 31.

[5] Matt. 11 11 ; cf. Luke 7 28.

[6] Cf. A. G. Hogg, *Redemption from this World*, pp. 92, 93.

was contrary.' [1] And when Peter's sinking faith was restored by the firm hold of Jesus' hand, and he made to wonder at himself by the half-chiding, half-soothing query, 'O thou of little faith, wherefore didst thou doubt?' there was only one possible verdict as the surgings of the disciples' fears fell with the wind, 'Of a truth thou art the Son of God.' [2] 'A high mountain apart' [3]—it might almost be called part of the formula of the secret life of Jesus, even as the Old Testament saint had exclaimed, 'Lead me to the rock that is higher than I.' [4]

Again and again there comes in this undertone of communion with God in prayer amidst the solitude of Nature, whether on mountain-side, in a desert place, or in a garden. 'And in the morning, a great while before day, He rose up and went out, and departed into a desert place, and there prayed.' [5] Even the wild village dogs never stirred as the Saviour of men passed firmly yet quietly down the street to pray for the sleeping world. Luke states very definitely that just before each of three great events in His life—the choosing of the twelve, the great confession, and the Transfiguration—Jesus was praying. Indeed, before the first of them 'He went out into the mountain to pray ; and He continued all night in prayer to God.' [6] The Transfiguration is definitely connected with prayer by St. Luke : 'as He was praying, the fashion of His countenance was altered.' [7] The repetition of the phrases almost looks like a formula, but such a

---

[1] Matt. 14 23-25 ; Mark 6 46-52.

[2] Matt. 14 31-33.

[3] Matt. 17 1 ; cf. Mark 9 2.

[4] Ps. 61 2. In an early address from this passage, Henry Drummond illustrated its fundamental truth by a reference to a distinguished teacher who had made a profound impression upon him, as having deliberately and successfully set himself to attain supreme eminence in his science, but 'who is the loneliest man I know.'

[5] Mark 1 35 ; cf. 6 46, Luke 5 16. As to Jesus' method in prayer, cf. Matt. 6 5-15, Luke 22 31, 32.

[6] Luke 6 12, 9 18, 9 29 ; cf. 21 37, and Matt. 6 6.

[7] Luke 9 29.

formula could only have issued from what was a rule of life. On any view of the Person of Jesus, the supreme and constant place that prayer had in His life is peculiarly noteworthy. And it is just here, in this recognition of the fundamental value of prayer as a means of correspondence and co-operation with the mind and will of God, and of setting man in new and determining relations to God, that it is possible to test the truth of Jesus' method.

With regard to *Man*, Jesus gave to the world a new conception of the value of the individual human life. ' How much then is a man of more value than a sheep ! ' [1] ' Fear not therefore : ye are of more value than many sparrows.' [2] But from these modest bases of comparison He develops such a wealth of positive potentiality and destiny in man that at last nothing can be found to equal it in value. ' What shall a man be profited, if he shall gain the whole world, and forfeit his life ? Or what shall a man give in exchange for his life ? ' [3] So valuable is each human life in itself, and so precious to God, that Jesus' fiercest denunciations are reserved for those who in any way would damage or influence for evil a young or guileless life, so that it should miss or be thwarted in its self-realisation. ' Whoso shall cause one of these little ones which believe on me to stumble, it is profitable for him that a great millstone should be hanged about his neck, and that he should be sunk in the depth of the sea. . . . It is not the will of your Father which is in heaven, that one of these little ones should perish.' [4] Jesus enjoyed watching the faces of little children, just as He loved to go a walk on the Sabbath,[5] or look out over the landscape.[6] And children came to Him because they instinctively realised that He liked their childish ways.

But this value of the human life does not inhere simply

[1] Matt. 12 12.   [2] Matt. 10 31.
[3] Matt. 16 26 ; cf. Luke 9 25.   [4] Matt. 18 6, 14 ; cf. Luke 17 2.
[5] Mark 2 23 ; Matt. 12 1 ; Luke 6 1.   [6] Based on Mark 13 3.

in itself : it comes from the fact that man is called to
co-operation with God in His purposes for the world.
Jesus believed that He was a co-operator with God in
His purposes for the world.   Jesus believed that He was
a co-operator with God in the work of overcoming
evil and bringing in the reign of God.   ' My Father
worketh hitherto, and I work.' [1]   He called on men
to become sympathetic fellow-workers with Him in His
redemptive mission, and any pretext for failure to do so
moved Him to the depths of His being.   ' He entered
again into the synagogue ; and there was a man there
which had his hand withered. . . . And He saith unto
the man . . . Stand forth.   And He saith unto them,
Is it lawful on the sabbath day to do good, or to do harm ?
to save a life, or to kill ?   But they held their peace.   *And
when He had looked round about on them with anger*, being
grieved at the hardening of their heart, He saith unto the
man, Stretch forth thy hand.   And he stretched it forth :
and his hand was restored.' [2]   Jesus turned from them
to ask the apparently impossible of this man, as He does
of all men, and the man's faith made it the really possible.

On the question of moral evil Jesus spoke often, warn-
ing men as to its nature, and enlightening them with
regard to its origin.[3]   As to the idea of a progressive overcoming of evil, it seems clear at any rate from the parable
of the tares and His explanation of it,[4] as also from the
parable of the fishing-net,[5] that He expected evil-doing
in some degree to be persistent to the end of the world,
i.e. the consummation of the age, when the wicked would
be separated by the angels and cast into a furnace of fire ;
throughout, some sort of a selective process is at work
Yet He had such a belief in the power of good not merely
to endure but to overcome, that He apparently contemplated with equanimity this prospect of the co-existence
of evil to the end.   Even when He was in closest grip

---

[1] John 5 [17].
[2] Mark 3 [1-6] ; cf. Luke 13 [16].
[3] Matt. 5 [28] ; Mark 7 [21-23].
[4] Matt. 13 [24-30, 36-43].
[5] Matt. 13 [47-50].

with the power of evil, this invincible faith in the ultimate triumph of good never left Him—' I beheld Satan fallen as lightning from heaven ' ; or once again, in terms familiar to His age, ' Henceforth ye shall see the Son of man sitting at the right hand of power, and coming on the clouds of heaven.' [1] His belief in the possibilities for good in man was infinite : ' Ye therefore shall be perfect, as your heavenly Father is perfect ' [2]—surely the boldest words that ever passed human lips. And this full develop-ment could be attained by active faith. ' Have faith in God,' He said to the disciples as they wondered at the withered fig-tree : ' All things whatsoever ye pray and ask for, believe that ye have received them, and ye shall have them.' [3] God can so fill a dedicated life with Himself, that in witness-bearing, even under hostile conditions, that man need have no fear—' Be not anxious how or what ye shall speak : for it shall be given you in that hour what ye shall speak. For it is not ye that speak, but the Spirit of your Father that speaketh in you.' [4] But above all, in His conception of the divine relation to man, God is to Jesus the God of the living, and not the God of the dead.[5] There is, therefore, no time or room for preoccupation with death. ' Follow me,' He said to a disciple who was gripped by the futile obsession for an imposing family burial, ' follow me ; and leave the dead to bury their own dead.' [6]

In regard to the relationships with the *fellow-man*, Jesus spoke often and much, directly and indirectly. ' Blessed,' He said, speaking out of His singular ex-perience, ' are the meek, the merciful, the peacemakers.' [7] In His heart there was continued blessedness, because He was meek and merciful, and the reconciler of men to God. Accompanying such purity of heart as was His, and the correlative of His uniquely intuitive comprehending

---

[1] Luke 10 [18] ; Matt. 26 [64].
[2] Matt. 5 [48].
[3] Mark 11 [22, 24] ; cf. also Luke 17 [6].
[4] Matt. 10 [19-20].
[5] Matt. 22 [32] ; cf. Luke 20 [38].
[6] Matt. 8 [21, 22] ; cf. Luke 9 [57, 60].
[7] Matt. 5 [5, 7, 9].

spirit, went an understanding of the Universe and a consequent conscious revelation of verifiable, saving truth by Him, that at some point or other in the circle of relatedness compels the recognition in Him of the immediately divine. ' Blessed are the pure in heart,' He said, again speaking out of His own experience, ' for they will see God,' [1] not so much with reference to some future state as here and now. It was a fact of present-day experience concerning the pure-hearted ; they can see the evidence of God's activity where other men are blind. So also He had said, ' Seek ye first His kingdom, and His righteousness ; and all these things will be added unto you ' ; it was not so much a promise as just His reading of life,[2] His interpretation of the kind of world in which the lot of mankind was cast. [3]

Or take, by way of further example, His remarkable teaching on non-resistance of evil.[4] It is very difficult in a post-war twentieth century to think it through, and it has never been deliberately tried on any great scale, largely owing to lack of faith in man and God. Yet apparently it has represented what was literally and fundamentally sound doctrine. Propounded by Jesus in an atmosphere surcharged with intense nationalistic feeling against the Roman domination,[5] this teaching—the outcome of inward struggle—with its inclusion of a positive element to which attention will be immediately directed, although rejected at the time, was later seen by many to have been the better way. Only very slowly can it win general acceptance, for it involves complete submission in all humility to the will of God. To the Jews of His day, whose conception of the Messiah,

---

[1] Matt. 5 [8].
[2] Matt. 6 [33]; cf. Luke 12 [31]. The persistent misuse by the N.T. translators of ' shall ' for ' will ' in the case of a simple future tense has obscured much of the real point of the teaching of Jesus.
[3] So also should be understood such a passage as Matt. 26 [52].
[4] Matt. 5 [39-40], [43-45].
[5] This is well brought out by V. G. Simkhovitch, *Toward the Understanding of Jesus*, chap. v.

purely objective and external, was of one who should deliver them out of the toils of their national enemies, ' and from the hand of all that hate us,'[1] such teaching was more than unacceptable ; it was abhorrent. It seemed to involve the surrender of all that had been humanly hoped for. Yet, as a matter of fact, Christianity subsequently offered no resistance to the Roman government, and in the end captured it. It is conceivable, accordingly, that a time will come when with the general advance in public and private morality the resistance of evil will only stimulate and increase it. The body politic will be in so healthy a state that ignoring of, and non-resistance to, evil will be the natural attitude to adopt, because it will be powerless to achieve any devastating harm. Meanwhile most men will probably agree with Admiral Mahan that ' the province of force in human affairs is to give moral ideas time to take root '—until, that is to say, ' the fulness of the times ' of moral development.[2] The world is very old, but man, even with half a million years behind him, is comparatively young.

The positive element in that teaching, to which reference has been made above, may be described as that something-moreness of Christianity which goes even yet so far beyond the ideas of His time and of ours—' except your righteousness shall exceed the righteousness of the scribes and Pharisees, ye shall *in no wise* enter into the kingdom of heaven.'[3] It is all so familiar as to mean very little or next to nothing to us, and until men win back some sense of the kind of world in which they are living, and wherein consist its real meaning and true adjustment to it, this teaching will continue to mean little, and moral progress will be delayed. This positive element, detailed in such a passage as Matthew 5 [21-37], reaches its climax

[1] Luke 1 [71].

[2] At the same time, it should be already clear that between men force gives no security which it cannot take away : stability and peace are alone assured by a co-operative and understanding consent.

[3] Matt. 5 [20].

in the command, 'Love your enemies, and pray for them that persecute you.' [1] Such a command, involving a complete change of mental attitude to the enemy, national or individual, and the spiritualising of the popular conception of the Messiah, was even more difficult for the average Jew of that day to accept than it is for the Gentile of the twentieth century. Yet such acceptance is of the essence of Christianity, involving that fundamental and eternal relationship of the individual to God which Jesus signified by His reference to the kingdom of heaven as 'within' men. [2] At the same time, it has carefully to be borne in mind that in speaking of 'love' in relation to the fellow-man, Jesus, so far as we can judge by the word employed ($\dot{a}\gamma a\pi\dot{a}\omega$), [3] did not primarily have in mind that emotional affection which we instinctively associate with the use of that term to-day, but rather a feeling of admiration or esteem—'that interest in and activity for others, which we find in a social order, as contrasted with self-interest and individual action.' [4] Forgiveness, said Jesus, is to be carried to the extremest length, for it is both the highest wisdom and of the very nature of God : no man is ever to say, 'I can never forgive him that.' 'Then came Peter, and said to him, Lord, how oft shall my brother' (*i.e.* not Andrew merely, but the man, for example, who ran up the jerry-built tower at Siloam [5]—'I can never forgive him,' said the widow of one of the eighteen, as she looked at her young family), 'how oft shall my brother sin against me, and I forgive him ? until seven times ? Jesus saith unto him, I say not unto thee Until seven times ; but, Until seventy times seven.' [6]

---

[1] Matt. 5 [44] ; cf. Luke 6 [27].
[2] Luke 17 [21]. As the result of His presence, and in the hearts of those who had accepted Him, it could also be said to be then 'amongst' men.
[3] Matt. 22 [39] ; Luke 10 [27] ; Mark 12 [30, 31].
[4] E. L. Heermance, *Chaos or Cosmos ?*, p. 133.
[5] Luke 13 [4].
[6] Matt. 18 [21, 22].

Forgiveness is a fundamental attitude, an elemental
law of living in this particular kind of world that can
never for a moment be abrogated by the individual
without disastrous consequences to himself.

Greatness is the reciprocal of service. Round the
frieze of the Director's room in the Mellon Institute of
Industrial Research at Pittsburgh run the words, ' *Et
quicunque voluerit inter vos primus esse, sit vester servus.*' [1]
This likewise was exemplified in His life—' Even as the
Son of man came not to be ministered unto, but to
minister, and to give His life a ransom for many.' [2]
The Programme of Christianity,[3] as Henry Drummond
called it, is a social and redemptive programme, in which
the discrete distinction of mankind into nations and
races plays no primary part. Jesus was the first to declare
authoritatively that the children of God are confined to
no particular nation or race.[4] His conception of the
rule of God is really that of a spiritual commonwealth
or republic. He never speaks of God directly, in relation
to men, as King, or in any term that suggests an absolute
monarchy, although He employs the old Jewish conception of the kingdom of God. His usual word for
God is ' Father,' and His thought is of a democracy,
knowing only an aristocracy of service. ' Be not ye
called Rabbi : for one is your teacher, and all ye are
brethren. And call no man your father on the earth :
for one is your Father, which is in heaven. Neither
be ye called masters : for one is your master, even the
Christ. But he that is greatest among you shall be your
servant. And whosoever shall exalt himself shall be
humbled ; and whosoever shall humble himself shall
be exalted.' [5] It is the ' gentle-men ' who shall inherit
the earth,[6] those, that is to say, who while alive and alert

---

[1] ' Whosoever would be great among you shall be your servant:
and whosoever would be first among you shall be your bond-servant.'
Matt. 20 [26-27], 23 [11] ; cf. Mark 10 [43-44].

[2] Matt. 20 [28].   [3] Luke 4 [17-21] ; cf. 7 [13-23].

[4] Matt. 15 [21-28], 25 [32] ; John 10 [16].

[5] Matt. 23 [8-12].   [6] Matt. 5 [5].

to take advantage of opportunities, are yet, even more, considerate of others' rights and interested in the welfare of the fellow-man. ' The unsocial man is excluded from God's family as abnormal ; in fact, he excludes himself.[1] The same doom is pronounced on the unsocial nation.[2] Service is the inexorable test, which spells destruction to those who fail to meet it.' [3]

Again, Jesus' view of the coming of the kingdom of God is essentially developmental : ' So is the kingdom of God, as if a man should cast the seed upon the earth ; and should sleep and wake during night and day, and the seed should sprout and grow, he knoweth not how. The earth beareth fruit of herself ($a\dot{v}\tau o\mu\acute{a}\tau\eta$) ; first the blade, then the ear, then the full corn in the ear.' [4] ' The kingdom of God cometh not with observation.' [5] ' He added and spake a parable . . . because they supposed that the kingdom of God was immediately to appear ' : [6] that is indeed a parable for to-day. Human progress or development consists in the gradual recognition of, and hearty co-operation with, the rule or kingdom of God. At the same time, to Jesus' eye this rule of God had actually begun,[7] and He was absolutely confident, as we have seen, of its final victory.[8] For One with such fixed conviction and certainty of mind upon this issue, asceticism was an impossible rule of life,[9] so far as it meant aloofness from human affairs and mere conformity to a bare formality of restriction. Yet the development of God's purpose for the world requires the co-operation of man with God, and this God expects of man.[10] In fact, it is the test of life,[11] the basis upon which that attainment and evaluation of individuality, which in the end means persistence, depend : because only in such co-operation can goodness of character be de-

[1] Matt. 22 [11-13], 18 [17], 25 [30, 46].   [2] Matt. 21 [33-43] ; Luke 13 [29, 30].
[3] Luke 20 [9-18] ; Matt. 7 [24-27].   The quotation is from E. L. Heermance, op. cit. p. 15.   [4] Mark 4 [26-28].
[5] Luke 17 [20].   [6] Luke 19 [11].   [7] Luke 17 [20-21] ; Matt. 12 [28].
[8] Mark 9 [1] ; cf. Luke 12 [32].   [9] Matt. 6 [16-18] ; 9 [14, 15].
[10] Matt. 25 [31-46] ; Luke 10 [25-37].   [11] Matt. 25 [31-46]

veloped. Life on any other basis tends to increasing selfishness, which in the end is death. Prayer is the practical recognition of this co-operation, the signifying of acceptance of this understanding on the part of the individual.

But further, Jesus teaches us that just because the world is a world of this particular kind, and because of the solidarity of the human race, profounder than any of its differences, true development and assured progress can only come by activities that are based on, and inspired by, a recognition of the Fatherhood of God and the brotherhood of man. It is, in short, good business and the condition of progress to be at once filial and brotherly. Hatred is damning ;[1] revenge is folly.[2] We must 'love our neighbour as ourselves,' and that means ' making his welfare a common concern.'[3] The real way to receive is not to grasp but to give, because human nature is such that it responds to generosity ; giving promotes an atmosphere of goodwill which begets further giving in return. ' Give, and it shall be given unto you ; good measure, pressed down, shaken together, running over, shall they give into your bosom. For with what measure ye mete it shall be measured to you again.'[4] In all this there is a very definite, challenging, and verifiable theory of the Universe, and of human relationships in it, about which it can be asked, To what extent do modern science and history bear it out ?

Our earlier consideration of the question of cosmogony,[5] with its revelation of an energetic, orderly universe, left us with something corresponding to Jesus' conception of a dynamic or spiritual universe, understanding by the term ' spiritual ' that which gives the impression of progressive activity towards an end. Science describes, the philosophy of science explains, and religion interprets ;

---

[1] Matt. 5 [22].   [2] Matt. 5 [23-26, 38-42].
[3] Luke 10 [25-37]. The phrase is from E. L. Heermance's admirable study, already quoted, p. 12.
[4] Luke 6 [38].   [5] Chap. III.

and description, explanation, and interpretation are alike elements in the process of man's mental and spiritual adjustment or adaptation to the Universe. Each is necessary, the one to the other, and must enter into any intelligent understanding of the world as a whole. Science leaves us with descriptions which philosophy explains in terms of a phenomenal dynamic Universe ; religion interprets the whole most satisfactorily, after an examination of all other interpretations, as the self-expression or unfolding of the activity of a creative God. Jesus, with perfect intuition, and conveying an unassailable impression of authority in what He said, interpreted the Universe ' as expressing the activity of a moral and altruistic God.' [1] The impression grows that He was right, and when men come more fully to realise this, their attitude both to the world itself and to Jesus will undergo a vital change. Men are directly in contact with God in His world all the time although they may not know it, and past their blunderings, short-sightednesses, and often wilful refusal to co-operate, His will is being slowly done.

Jesus then spoke of the world as energised by, or the activity of, a God who is spirit, and who can be worshipped in spirit and in truth at any time and place. To His mind this activity assumed the character of a progressive development which required in its later stages the loyal and understanding co-operation of men, just because of what is involved in man's growing attainment of freedom. Not merely is man, and the rule of God amongst men, the purpose of creation, but from a certain stage man is intended to become a joint agent and creator. Now it looks, at any rate, as if man were the intended climax of the evolutionary process. Organic evolution may be studied from many points of view, but it shows itself to be of the nature of ' energy traffic,' to use F. J. Allen's phrase,[2] of ever-increasing

[1] E. L. Heermance, *op. cit.* p. 32.
[2] Quoted in *The Evolution of the Earth and its Inhabitants*, edited by R. S. Lull, p. 85.

complexity of commerce on the part of living forms
with the environment. But that environment itself
has also been the arena of progressive changes not merely
in its inorganic aspect, but also so far as the organic
aspect, whether plant or animal, is considered in relation
to any particular species. The adaptability in the case
of any particular species—and that is, in the end, of
the individuals comprising it—may lie in the direction
of chemical readjustment enabling it to utilise new types
of food or develop greater disease-resistance, or some
new successful method in capturing prey, avoiding
enemies, or protecting the young. And this growing
adaptability, on an ever-widening and deeper scale, has
culminated in man, who is progressively subduing
Nature by the simple process of learning to understand
her, and co-operating with God in setting right the misuse
of growing freedom that has ever followed in the wake
of progress. The process has worked out, and is working
out, in this way. It is difficult to believe that it has all
been a chapter of accidents; and further, it is proving
itself to be in many particular respects the kind of a
world that Jesus stated it to be.

In briefest outline reference may be made to certain
empirical tests. Man himself shares or co-operates in
creation fundamentally in the perpetuation of the race.
This is an aspect in which his activity is still too often
merely impulsive, unintelligent, and with little or no
sense of responsibility, so eliciting, in a certain measure
justifiably, the strictures and call for State action by the
eugenists.[1] Now, Jesus spoke very solemnly upon the
sacredness of human marriage,[2] and St. Paul was not
less insistent.[3] Monogamy, parity of sexes, and chastity
are proving, in the racial experience, to be the lines of
progress. Departure from these ideals has consistently
meant the degradation of man and woman alike, loss

[1] Cf. *e.g.* Prof. E. M. East, *Mankind at the Cross Roads.*
[2] Matt. 5 [31, 32]; Luke 16 [18].
[3] 1 Cor. 6 [19].

of self-control and virility, a lowered birth-rate, and weakened, if not diseased, offspring. There is an adjustment or adaptation to this particular kind of Universe in this respect which literally means more abundant life, and a failure in adjustment which as literally means extinction.

There are many other directions in which Jesus' conception of man as called to be a conscious co-operator with God in the development of the world is gradually being recognised as that one which best produces those results that in the long run mean advance in civilisation. Could we but get the right angle, regarding all work as co-operation with God in the guidance and control of what are really divine forces in the development of the world, there is no work or calling that would not then be holy, and the place whereon the worker was standing holy ground. In the degree in which man subdues the earth and secures dominion over the creatures, grows his measure of responsibility to the inanimate and animate alike. There is a conduct towards the earth itself, not merely in relation to the fellow-man of to-day in our own and other lands, but to posterity, that is only less important than conduct towards the lower animate creation. Dominion here does not mean irresponsible ownership to do therewith as one likes, in all recklessness and wastefulness. The Lord God ' took the man, and put him into the garden of Eden to dress it and to keep it,' [1] not to tear it up so as to leave great mounds of ugly waste, like the slag-heaps that disfigure so many landscapes. Some day a public conscience will be developed upon these matters. This idea, indeed, lies in part at the basis of a work by a distinguished horticulturist, entitled *The Holy Earth*,[2] where not merely is the suggestion developed of the farmer as being daily in direct contact with the incessant activity of God Himself in Nature,

[1] Gen. 2 [15]. Cf. also Plato, *Rep*. iii. 401.
[2] By L. H. Bailey, for many years Director of the College of Agriculture at Cornell University U.S.A.

but as also beginning to recognise ' a range of responsible
and permanent morals ' [1] in this relationship, as he learns
that in order to succeed he must put back into the soil
as much as he takes out of it.   Dr. Bailey's interest is
how to secure a succession of efficient and contented
farmers, supported by a community that recognises
its obligations at once to the farming element and to
Holy Earth herself.   There are in his opinion important
yet secondary elements entering into the solution of the
problem, *e.g.* ownership as opposed to tenantry, technical
training, labour and labour-saving machinery, market
facilities, adequate financial returns, convenient means
of getting about.   But primary, and of superlative importance in this respect, are the elements of character
and inspiration and motive.   Technical education enables
the countryman ' to make use of the rain and the abound-
ing soil, and the varied wonder of plant and animal
amidst which he lives,' but how beyond ' the essential
physical mastery . . . shall he take them into himself,
how shall he make them to be of his spirit, how shall he
complete his dominion ?   How shall he become the man
that his natural position requires of him ? ' [2]   The
answer is found in the suggestion of the necessity of the
realisation by the farmer and by the rest of the community
alike that ' the backbone of the rural question is at the
bottom a moral problem,' [3] and that, while the farmer
may be legally the owner of his land, he is morally a
trustee.   As Dr. Bailey puts it, ' he is engaged in a
quasi-public business,' [4] the agent of society to understand and co-operate with the earth, and ' the divinity
that made it,' in increasing its productiveness.   A man
cannot be a good farmer unless he handles ' all his
materials, remembering man and remembering God.   A
man cannot be a good farmer unless he is a religious
man.' [5]   The Universe, of course, plays fair, and a
godless man who employs the most up-to-date methods

[1] *Op. cit.* p. 23.   [2] *Op. cit.* p. 28.   [3] *Op. cit.* p. 36.
[4] *Op. cit.* p. 32.   [5] *Op. cit.* p. 33.

will secure corresponding value, but he will lack that motive and inspiration under which the finest work is done.[1] The sense of co-operation with God for social ends, as He is revealed in the objective Universe, will dignify all labour, and prevent that other motive of economic necessity from continuing to be the brutal, selfish element that all too long, apart from isolated cases, it has proved to be. But with this goes inevitably some readjustment of the conditions of labour in the interests of the worker, so that he shall regain the sense of craftsmanship, of being a creator and not a cog.

Human co-operation in the unfolding and developing of the world may further be traced in the progressive character of man's organisation of his food supply, of his care of public health, prevention of avoidable disasters like conflagrations, and growing concern about housing conditions, infantile mortality, industrial, colonial, and international relations.[2] It becomes increasingly clear how he ought to act and what it would be possible to do; the measure of his failure is simply the degree in which he is unwilling to accept and act upon what are proving to be the lines of true adjustment to the Universe as declared by Jesus. Only ignorance or prejudice prevents us from wiping smallpox for ever off the face of mankind; and if men and women had reached the requisite degree of mutual self-respect, venereal disease could be stamped out in a generation just as yellow fever has been cleaned out of Central America. Jesus definitely spoke as if the Universe—that partial manifestation of the Ultimate Environment of men—were on the side of righteousness and altruism.[3] And it is possible to

---

[1] So also, at the commencement of the Great War, the Germans reaped the advantages of their preparedness and most modern methods, but a stage was ultimately reached when the question of motive and inspiration became the decisive factor.

[2] These and other issues have been suggestively studied by E. L. Heermance in his *Chaos or Cosmos ?*

[3] Matt. 5 [6, 7, 17-20], 6 [14, 15]; Luke 6 [36]; cf. A. G. Hogg, *Redemption from this World*, p. 131.

show, on a review of personal and business relations in the world to-day, that ' man is succeeding in proportion to his recognition of character and mutual service ' [1] and dependence. Such recognition has been found to provide the conditions under which the individual establishes or secures the most favourable reaction, and it can only be a question of time till humanity as a whole, under the working of the Spirit of God, comes to see this, and determines to make it the basis of conduct. As a matter of fact, leaders in certain industries and lines of business in the United States have drawn up codes of ethics for their particular businesses which are being accepted and followed by the firms of best repute ; on examination these private rubrics turn out to be profoundly Christian. Co-operation, *i.e.* social altruism, is proving increasingly to be a group, and even a national, good, and it is realised that sympathy and mutual aid, rather than selfish individualism, provide the atmosphere of progress. Jesus taught that consideration for others, in effect for all others, without distinction, is the method of the Universe—God's method, acting in and through it ; and in recognition of, and action on, that plan, man is finding his true happiness and progress to consist.

This rediscovery that Jesus, so far from being a dreamer, was a true revealer of the actual world-order, comes with all the greater surprise inasmuch as the first glance at the objective world process generally results in an impression unfavourable to His standpoint. Certainly some Jewish and Christian thinkers in the past were disturbed by the apparent success in many instances of the wicked and unscrupulous, and were accordingly tempted to dwell on a scheme of readjustment of rewards and corresponding retribution in some future state. This is, however, to surrender the moral character of the actual working Universe, and many seem imme-

---

[1] E. L. Heermance, *op. cit.* p. xx ; several chapters are devoted to illustration of this point. Cf. also Arthur Nash, *The Golden Rule in Business.*

diately willing to do so. But both the degree of understanding with which, and the time scale against which,
these earlier thinkers could view the world process were
limited compared with what is at our disposal to-day.
As a result, another kind of conclusion is gradually forcing
itself upon the minds of increasing numbers of men, to
the effect that self-control, honesty, and justice are very
slowly, yet very surely, proving to be community assets,[1]
and that Jesus was right in extending honour and goodwill
from narrower groups, like the family, to society as a
whole, as the basal principles of development in the order
of the world in which we find ourselves. Any individual
who by his activities develops an atmosphere of goodwill
finds that it pays, and that he moreover becomes more
social and more efficient. Christianity works because it is
supremely true, and therefore supremely livable, which
is very different from the pragmatic position that a theory
is true because it works. The selfish man is seen increasingly to be the unsocialised man, and in that measure
he proves less efficient. Peace was promised in the angel
song to men of goodwill,[2] and the discovery of the value
of goodwill, and the possibilities in it, lies ahead of rather
than behind us even to-day. True democracy really
consists in regarding social and economic questions from
the point of view of society as a whole, rather than from
that of any class, however powerful or however numerous.
It means recognition of the capacities of the brother-
man, and esteem for and trust in him wherever he
proves worthy of that esteem, and continued and even
deeper interest when he proves unworthy. Righteousness
is, then, apparently being justified by the cosmic process.
Man's chief business is to adjust himself to that process,
to co-operate with it and help to make it increasingly
perfect : such conscious adaptation is of the essence of

[1] Cf. in this connection *The New Society*, by Walter Rathman, the
German Foreign Minister, financier, and industrialist (who was assas-
sinated in 1922), where he pleads for the reconstruction of civilisation
upon a spiritual basis.

[2] Luke 2 [14].

religion. The openly selfish theory of adjustment is evidently not going to succeed in the long run ; it cannot, because it becomes increasingly clear that that is not the kind of world in which we are living. In consequence, human society is slowly feeling its way experimentally towards a more just solution of the problem of the equitable distribution of the rewards of honest production, a solution in which regard is being had to the provision of opportunities for the fullest development of personality, and to the establishment of the principles of co-operation and mutual interest even to the point of service and self-sacrifice ; and this is what Jesus taught. He had much to say about social solidarity, which has been rather overlooked in the attention given to His teaching about the individual. According to Him the true adjustment of man to the Universe can only follow on his recognition of such conceptions as spirit, human solidarity, morality, and goodwill, as being elemental in the tissue of it. As a matter of fact, survival value is growingly found to characterise these groups or associations of men, from corporations to nations, which recognise and deliberately act on principles of justice, goodwill, and mutual service. Indeed, the failure of militarism and the bankruptcy of the old diplomacy leave Christianity as the only practical politics. Of all the men who sat round the Paris Peace Conference Table of 1919 in any important capacity, history has already shown that none was more far-seeing than General Smuts, whose practical proposals objectively embodied the spirit of the principles under consideration. ' The Peace Treaty,' he is reported to have said at a later stage, ' will fade into merciful oblivion, and its provisions will be gradually obliterated by the great human tides sweeping over the world. But the Covenant will stand as sure as fate. It must succeed, because there is no other way for the future of civilisation.'[1]

---

[1] *New York Evening Post*, 3rd March 1921, quoted in *A History of the Peace Conference of Paris*, edited by H. W. V. Temperley, vi. 582.

In the long run progress in civilisation will be in proportion to the triumph of reason and common interest over force and naked selfishness, simply because these qualities reflect something of the very nature of God Himself, and their exercise is therefore the way of true adjustment to our ultimate Divine Environment. The development of the kingdom of God is a cosmic enterprise in which we may be co-operators with God, but to do so effectively we must learn His character and His laws, and as we co-operate we come to know Him better.

To sum up : there are physical and biological relationships in the structure of the Universe which we are gradually learning to understand, in the knowledge of and obedience to which lies the progressive adjustment of man to his environment. And there are also moral laws and relationships which are as really a part of the structure of the Universe as the physical and biological relationships, and which can as clearly be deduced from the study of action and reaction in the personal sphere. In knowledge of and obedience to these, even more than in the case of the others, lies the secret of the future advance of civilisation : upon them depends adjustment to the ultimate spiritual Environment. Jesus set forth and exemplified in the simplest and most direct manner the nature of these principles, and history is progressively justifying the truth of His statements.[1] In this way He is becoming to mankind more and more the Lord of Life, though He is not less the Master of Death, and the future becomes significant not by way of antithesis or contrast with the present, but as its continuation, development, and culmination. To realise what these principles mean in relation both to time and to eternity, as also what is accordingly implied in His life and work, is to discover in Him the Son of God. It is also to begin to appreciate that added interpretation

[1] 'At present there are probably more people who feel that Christ is the only hope of the world than there ever were in the lifetime of men now living' (George Bernard Shaw, *Yale Review*, January 1923).

of human life on the part of the one who best understood Him—' Beloved, *now* are we the sons of God, and it doth not yet appear what we shall be : but we know that, when He shall appear, we shall be like Him ; for we shall see Him as He is. And every man that hath this hope in him purifieth himself.' [1]

[1] 1 John 3 [1, 2].

EPILOGUE

THE world in which we find ourselves is, then, a particular kind of world in all its aspects, and man's salvation lies in part in his growing understanding of that world,— a knowledge, however, that can only ever be ' in part ' [1] on this terrestrial plane of things. For, in the poet's words :

> ' I dimly guess what Time in mists confounds;
> Yet ever and anon a trumpet sounds
> From the hid battlements of Eternity;
> Those shaken mists a space unsettle, then
> Round the half-glimpsèd turrets slowly wash again.' [2]

None the less, these successive glimpses reveal an ever-growing coherent and harmonious unity, which constitutes the most impressive fact in all consideration of the actual world-process. It is significant in itself, and needs no buttressing with subjective theories of values. In any case a doctrine of values [3] is surely the most pathetic of futilities except in so far as it is an expression of the recognition of a revelation of progressive worth in the world-process. As interpreted by modern science, and by Jesus, ' the pioneer and the perfection of faith,' [4] that process is found to be a realm of order and of law, of mystery indeed, yet of the progressive overcoming of evil, and apparently ' informed and sustained by an ideal

[1] I Cor. 13 [13].
[2] Francis Thompson, *The Hound of Heaven*.
[3] According to J. S. Mackenzie, ' to gain a clear understanding of what value really means . . . is not as easy as it might at first appear ' (*Ultimate Values*, p. 87).
[4] Heb. 12 [2] (Moffatt's trans.).

281

purpose.' [1] For it is of the essence of their teaching that ' what a man soweth, that shall he also reap,' [2] and it is of their faith that man can be a co-operator with God in His purpose for the world. The past may be taken as a pledge of the future even if ' it doth not yet appear what we shall be.' [3] The finality of Christianity lies in the experience resulting from the faith that ' God so loved the world, that He gave His only begotten Son, that whosoever believeth on Him should not perish, but have eternal life.' [4] But such a belief is belief in Jesus as the supreme expression of the spiritual energy at work in the world-process, and in His view of the Universe, with outcome in the conformity of the believer's life to His, through His re-creative power. And from this highest point of view—that of the intelligent securing of the individual's saving adaptation to the Ultimate Environment which is God—Science and Religion may be seen to be at one in character and in endeavour.

[1] W. G. de Burgh, *The Legacy of the Ancient World*, p. 434.
[2] Gal. 6 [7].
[3] 1 John 3 [2].
[4] John 3 [16]. According to Moulton and Milligan (*The Vocabulary of the Greek Testament*, Pt. v. 416), the word μονογενής means 'literally "one of a kind," "only," "unique" (*unicus*), not "only-begotten," which would be μονογεννητός (*unigenitus*), and is common in the LXX. in this sense.'

INDEX